The Rational Southerner

# The Rational Southerner

*Black Mobilization, Republican Growth,
and the Partisan Transformation of the
American South*

M.V. HOOD III, QUENTIN KIDD, AND
IRWIN L. MORRIS

OXFORD
UNIVERSITY PRESS

# OXFORD

UNIVERSITY PRESS

Oxford University Press, Inc., publishes works that further
Oxford University's objective of excellence
in research, scholarship, and education.

Oxford   New York
Auckland   Cape Town   Dar es Salaam   Hong Kong   Karachi
Kuala Lumpur   Madrid   Melbourne   Mexico City   Nairobi
New Delhi   Shanghai   Taipei   Toronto

With offices in
Argentina   Austria   Brazil   Chile   Czech Republic   France   Greece
Guatemala   Hungary   Italy   Japan   Poland   Portugal   Singapore
South Korea   Switzerland   Thailand   Turkey   Ukraine   Vietnam

Published by Oxford University Press, Inc.
198 Madison Avenue, New York, New York 10016

www.oup.com

Library of Congress Cataloging-in-Publication Data
Hood, M.V.
The rational southerner : black mobilization, republican growth, and the partisan transformation of the
American south / M.V. Hood III, Quentin Kidd, and Irwin L. Morris.
    p.   cm.
Includes bibliographical references and index.
ISBN 978-0-19-987382-1
1. Southern States—Politics and government. 2. Political culture—Southern States.
3. African Americans—Southern States—Politics and government. 4. Racism—Southern States.
5. Party affiliation—Southern States. 6. Republican Party (U.S. : 1854– ) 7. Democratic Party (U.S.)
8. Southern States—Race relations. I. Kidd, Quentin. II. Morris, Irwin L. (Irwin Lester), 1967– III. Title.
JK2683.H66   2012
306.20975—dc23     2011047152

9 8 7 6 5 4 3 2 1

Printed in the United States of America
on acid-free paper

*For our families*
*Ashley, Madison, McKinley, Maitland, Austin,*
*and Addie Grace*
*Holly and Brandon*
*Chris, Maddie, and Cameron*

CONTENTS

This book has its roots in a research agenda born out of a mutual interest in Southern politics that began over a decade ago. We have always been captivated by the question of political change, and the South is among the most fascinating places in American politics in which to study that phenomenon. Our initial work looked at the changing ideological orientation of Southern Democratic senators. In that early work (published in 1999 in the *American Journal of Political Science*), we identified the forces – black voters and the Republican Party – affecting the roll call voting behavior of Southern Democrats that subsequently came to play distinct roles in the *theory of relative advantage*.

We explored the relative influence of these two forces on the specific issue of roll call voting on civil rights in a follow-up study (published in 2001 in *Legislative Studies Quarterly*) and then proposed the theory of relative advantage in a study examining the rise of the Republican Party in the South between 1960 and 2000 (first published in 2003 in *American Politics Research* with a follow-up study published in the 5th edition of *Controversies in Voting Behavior*). To implement an even more rigorous test of our theory, we searched for a more robust methodology. We turned to Granger causality testing for panel data and implemented this approach to examine the transformation of the post-World War II party system in the South (published in 2008 in *Political Analysis*).

To date, we have produced various pieces to the puzzle of the dramatic and transformative political change in the American South. What was needed, however, was a concerted effort to put all these pieces together to form a single coherent and comprehensive explanation. This book, then, is intended to present a comprehensive description, explanation, and analysis of our theory of political change in the region over the last half-century. While Southern politics is our central focus, we also explain how the theory of relative advantage provides insight into partisan dynamics, racial/ethnic politics, and political transformations more generally.

The Rational Southerner

# Theory and Background

CHAPTER 1 | Introduction

SOME YEARS AGO, A friend of one of the authors took a job at a small state school in Oklahoma. Having spent little time in Oklahoma, the author asked the friend whether he thought Oklahoma was in the Midwest, the South, or the Southwest. The friend simply replied "Yes."

Obviously, some states have a regional identity that is far easier to determine (and agree upon). There is little question that New Hampshire is in New England or that Arizona is in the Southwest. But is Pennsylvania a Midwestern state? And where does Kentucky fit? And just how many regions does the United States include? The U.S. Census Bureau divides the fifty states into four regions—the Northeast, the South, the Midwest, and the West—and nine subregions. The Federal Reserve System is divided into a dozen regions. Some would argue that certain states fit into more than one region. Although Philadelphia clearly seems to be a Mid-Atlantic city, Pittsburgh is much more like Midwestern cities such as Chicago. Nacogdoches, Texas, is almost certainly a Southern town, but how could El Paso not be in the Southwest?

Despite all the arguments and discussion over the number of regions, the placement of states in the regions, and the substantive significance of both, there is one American region that has a very clear historical identity—the South, defined as the eleven states of the former Confederacy. For most of the century and a half following the Civil War, the uniqueness of Southern politics was taken for granted. The long Democratic domination of what was known as the "Solid South" simply had no analogue anywhere else in the United States.

From the late 1940s to the present day, the South has undergone the most dramatic political transformation of any region in the country. The most important structural change during this time period was the passage of the 1965 Voting Rights Act (VRA), and there is little doubt that the VRA made the subsequent mobilization of African Americans possible. With this mobilization came a unique partisan transformation as well. An area that was once solidly Democratic (i.e., with very few Republican officeholders of any type and no state-level GOP officials) is now largely dominated by the Republican Party. In a region where it was once all but impossible to win public office of any type—local to statewide—running as a Republican, the GOP now controls far more Senate seats, House seats, gubernatorial mansions, and state legislatures than the Democrats.[1]

One of the most interesting aspects of this transformation is the wide variation in the pace and extent of change across and within various geographic units. Some Southern states have held substantial numbers of Republican supporters since the publication of Key's seminal *Southern Politics in State and Nation* (1949). For example, Republicans were particularly prominent in the more mountainous areas of North Carolina, Tennessee, and Virginia—thus Key's apt descriptor "mountain Republicans." The absence of a long history of limited Republicanism did not, however, prevent a dramatic shift of partisan power among conservative whites once the GOP gained a toehold in other states (i.e., Mississippi and South Carolina). As we seek to understand the transformation of the Southern party system, we must remain cognizant of these significant variations. A compelling explanation must not only tell us why the South became more Republican, it must also explain why some Southern states (and areas within states) became more Republican at varying rates.

Scholars have suggested numerous explanations for the regionwide partisan shift. It is difficult to imagine the growth and development of the GOP in the South without the leftward shift of the national Democratic Party, particularly on the issue of civil rights, begun during the Roosevelt administration and extended during the Truman, Kennedy, and Johnson administrations. Roosevelt cultivated support among African Americans, and they comprised a significant segment of his electoral constituency. Truman integrated the U.S. military, created the Federal Employment Board to promote fair hiring practices in the federal government, and created the Committee on Government Contract Compliance to fight employment discrimination by private military contractors. Although Kennedy was not personally responsible for any significant civil rights legislation, his legacy of support for civil rights paved the way for the passage of the Civil Rights Act, the Voting Rights Act, and the Fair Housing Act during the Johnson administration.

The frustration of conservative Southern Democrats with increasing support for civil rights by the national Democratic Party was in evidence by 1948 when Strom Thurmond ran for the presidency on the Dixiecrat ticket, and this frustration clearly grew over the next two decades. But this "top-down" explanation—dissatisfaction with the national party leading first to the repudiation of national Democrats (presidential candidates) and then over time leading to the rejection of state and local Democrats, and then the party itself—obviously provides no rationale for the wide variation in Republican growth across the region. If national-level dynamics are the central cause of Southern Republican growth, why did the GOP grow so much more quickly in some states (e.g., Virginia) than it did in others (e.g., Mississippi)? And why have the lagging states now surpassed the early-growth states? National-level, top-down theories provide no answer.

To explain regional and subregional variations in Republican growth, we must find causal factors that also vary across these levels. Scholars searching for these causal factors have tended to focus on the demographic characteristics of the Southern population—particularly the white Southern population—during the time period of the partisan transformation.

In the recent literature on Southern politics, the role of *class* has attracted a great deal of attention. During the post-war era, the Southern economy underwent a dramatic transformation from a rural economy dominated by agriculture to a more industrialized economy driven increasingly by urban areas (Cobb 1999 and Sosna 1987). This economic transformation dramatically increased the standard of living of a large group of Southerners, particularly white Southerners. According to class-based explanations of Republican growth, as significant numbers of white Southerners moved from the working class to the middle class or from the middle class to the upper-middle or upper class, their policy preferences became more consistent with those of the national Republican Party.

More than half a century ago, Key (1949) suggested the possibility for this type of economic and political transformation when he discussed what he referred to as the *dilution* of the South's agriculturally dominated rural economy. For Key, an obvious implication of the shift away from an agricultural economy to an industrial economy would be an increased attachment to the Republican Party. A significant segment of the most recent research on the growth of the Republican Party in the South identifies economic development as the driving engine behind partisan change (see, for example, Lublin 2004 and Shafer and Johnston 2001, 2006). Although there is no question that both Southern Republicanism and the Southern economy have grown since the early 1950s, it has been difficult to demonstrate a relationship between the variation in economic growth across the states and counties of the South and the growth of the GOP in these same areas. For example, according to census data, the Southern states with the largest per capita income growth from 1960 to 1980 were (in order) Virginia, Florida, and Texas. The states with the largest GOP growth during the same time period were (in order) Mississippi, South Carolina, and Georgia. Ironically, Mississippi realized the smallest increase in per capita income during this time period. At the most basic level, there are obvious problems with a class-based explanation.

Another prominent explanation for Southern partisan change is *migration* patterns—both white in-migration and African American out-migration. A significant body of research suggests that the growth of Southern Republicanism is primarily a result of the influx of Republican-minded migrants from other regions of the country (Bass and De Vries 1976). This research contends that the bulk of Southern in-migrants during much of the past sixty years were white and middle class and that these migrants have become integral components of the Southern GOP (Scher 1997). We might reasonably infer that in-migration (specifically *white* in-migration) has had some impact on the relative strength of the two major political parties in the South, but the significance of this effect—and whether or not it remains a significant source of GOP growth—is controversial.

Some opponents argue that the impact of in-migration on Southern partisanship has waned recently, particularly since the mid-1980s, a time period in which the party loyalties of Southerners differed little (and were actually somewhat more Republican) than the party loyalties of Americans in other regions of the country (Stanley and Castle 1988). Others contend that cohort replacement and conversion of existing voters, as opposed to in-migration, explains the growing tendency among Southerners to identify as Republicans (Petrocik 1987). Note that the in-migration thesis is based on the presumption that in-migrants were more Republican than the native population. In the context of recent migratory trends—particularly the dramatic influx of Hispanics into the South—this presumption is questionable. The mechanism by which recent *white* in-migration—at a time during which such in-migrants were not necessarily more Republican than native white Southerners—may have led to Republican Party growth remains unexplained.[2]

Students of religion and politics propose an additional demographic explanation for the growth of Southern Republicanism among conservative whites. They note that evangelicalism has grown dramatically over the past fifty years, and white evangelical Protestants have become increasingly more likely to identify with, and vote for, the Republican Party (see Kellstedt 1989; Green et al. 1996; and Green et al. 1998). White evangelicals are more likely than those of other religious traditions to hold conservative views, especially in regard to social issues (Wilcox 2000). During the time period of Republican growth in the South, evangelicals have become increasingly drawn to a Republican Party identified as the standard-bearer for social conservatism. The increase in Republican support among evangelicals is striking. Although white evangelicals comprised only half (50 percent) of the combined vote for presidential contests in the 1990s (Green et al. 1998), nearly three-quarters of white evangelicals voted Republican during the 1994 Congressional elections. In the same year, white evangelicals comprised a plurality of the GOP, making up 30 percent of Republican Party identifiers nationwide (Green et al. 1996).

We cannot ignore the obvious attachment of white evangelicals to the Republican Party; however, Southern religious culture has always included a prominent strain of evangelicalism—think of the *Playboy* issue in which presidential candidate Jimmy Carter discussed his status as a "born again" Christian. Explaining just how evangelicalism among Southern whites has driven the surge in Southern Republicanism is difficult, and the empirical connection between evangelicalism and the growth of Republicanism, at either the regional level or the subregional level, remains unestablished. Although one can make a plausible case for the role of evangelical attachment in the growth of the Republican Party in the South, hard evidence of this relationship is surprisingly limited.

In the face of these varied explanations for the growth of Southern Republicanism, we argue that a complete understanding of Southern party politics requires a full appreciation for the role that race has played and continues to play in the region. Scholars have long contended that white conservatism was directly related to the size of the black population, arguing that as proximity to a large population of African Americans increased, the *racial threat* perceived by whites also increased. What Key (1949) referred to as the "black-belt hypothesis" resulted in greater support for conservative candidates in areas with proportionately more blacks. Subsequent research in this vein uncovered support for Key's hypothesis (see Aistrup 1996; Black 1976; Black 1978; Giles 1977; Giles and Buckner 1993, 1996; Giles and Evans 1986; Giles and Hertz 1994; Glaser 1994; Matthews and Prothro 1966; and Wright 1977). As the Republican Party was increasingly viewed as the party of conservatism— especially racial conservatism—it became an increasingly desirable alternative to the Democratic Party. Some limited evidence indicates that black context is directly related to growth in Republican partisanship (see, for example, Giles and Hertz 1994).

Support for Key's hypothesis (that black context is directly associated with white conservatism) and its extension to partisan politics (that black context is associated with Republicanism), while strong, is not unequivocal (see Coombs, Hibbing, and Welch 1984; Bullock 1985; Voss 1996; and Whitby 1985). From a theoretical standpoint, it is important to remember that Key's hypothesis of a black-context effect was not based solely on an *electoral* threat. At the time Key was writing (mid-to-late 1940s), African Americans were nearly two decades away from the *beginning* of effective enfranchisement in the South. Key's characterization of the relationship between black context and white conservatism during the time period about which he was writing—the late nineteenth and early twentieth centuries— depends, at least in part, on the presumption (by conservative whites) of a cultural or physical threat not fully captured by a potential *electoral* threat decades from materialization.

But in the six decades since Key wrote, the VRA (and subsequent judicial and legislative actions) led to the end of de jure disenfranchisement, and significantly curtailed de facto disenfranchisement, of Southern blacks. This mobilization of the African American electorate effectively transformed Southern political dynamics. In the new Southern polity, conservative whites might still view African Americans as a threat, but, as we argue below, that threat is far more likely to be viewed as one of an *electoral* nature than one of a *physical* nature. To the extent that this is the case, we err by maintaining our preoccupation with racial context in our efforts to explain increasing white support for the Republican Party.

Some practical issues make the attribution of Republican growth to black racial context problematic. Although conservative white voters may have changed their allegiances and shifted from the Democratic to the Republican Party, blacks are still overwhelmingly strong supporters of the Democratic Party. So, in those areas where white "flight" to the Republican Party is most likely, the potential black Democratic base will be most numerous. In areas with large black populations, there is both a nearly tangible ceiling placed on potential Republican support and a very real floor placed on the loss of Democratic support. Similarly, the recent period of dramatic Republican growth has come during a time when the size of the black population in the South has decreased. How is it possible to attribute substantial Republican growth to black context when the relative size of the black population has not grown at all, and in some areas has experienced a relative decline?

For us, the political significance of the slight decline in the relative size of the black population in the South pales in comparison to the dramatic increase in the size of the mobilized black electorate in the region. Though the relative size of the black population in the South has not grown over the past half-century, the African American portion of the electorate (i.e., registered voters) has grown dramatically. It is the concomitance of black mobilization and Republican growth that is so striking; yet the region-level focus of so much of the existing research on Southern politics has tended to obscure the interrelationship of these two trends and to preclude the examination of these phenomena. Just as studies of the growth of Southern Republicanism have ignored the potential influence of the political mobilization of the black population, more traditional explanations for black mobilization—for example, the decrease in formal and informal electoral discrimination and the rise of overt black political empowerment (as manifest in the increasing prevalence of black elected officials and viable black presidential candidates)—have yet to examine the potential effects of the political opportunities resulting from the exodus of conservative whites from the Democratic Party.

Our working assumption is that the character of specific political opportunities—local *strategic* dynamics—played a decisive (and unexplored) role in the development of the Southern Republican Party *and* the mobilization of the black electorate. We will argue that conservative Southern whites responded to black mobilization by moving into the Republican Party. As blacks moved into the electorate—and the Democratic Party—conservative whites faced increased challenges to their control of the party. As the GOP in the South gathered momentum—largely due to efforts of Republicans outside the region—local Republican Party organizations became increasingly viable mechanisms for exercising political influence and control. So, we argue, the attractiveness of the Republican Party for conservative whites—on the dual dimensions of *control* and *viability*—was enhanced during this time period. Thus, conservative white Southerners took advantage of these strategic opportunities by becoming Republicans.

Blacks also faced new political opportunities, particularly in the Deep South states where their relative size was greatest. As conservative whites migrated to the Republican Party, blacks found new opportunities within the Democratic Party. Although party viability was not a problem for the Democrats, blacks were now in a position to play a prominent role in party leadership. In the Deep South, blacks were in a position to be the controlling interest in the state Democratic Party. So, as conservative whites left the Democratic Party, the incentives for blacks to mobilize and join the Democratic Party increased, especially in those areas where the relative size of the black population could produce the greatest effects.

In this book, we describe the political transformation of the modern South and present our own perspective on this party system transformation. We begin by providing a broad overview of the transformation of the Southern political landscape—focusing specifically on the transformation of the

Democratic and Republican parties and the growth of the black electorate over the past sixty years. We then move beyond this qualitative and largely descriptive depiction of political transformation to the presentation of our own theoretical explanation for the primary dynamics of this partisan change—the theory of *relative advantage*.

The next chapter provides a detailed description of the Southern political transformation from the 1950s through the present day. We first look at the increasing success of the Republican Party in the region by tracking the success of GOP candidates at the national, state, and substate levels and by charting individual-level growth in identification with the Republican Party using longitudinal survey data. As has been noted by a number of existing studies, Southern whites were drawn to Republican Party candidates—particularly at the presidential level—before they viewed themselves (or identified) as Republicans.

We also describe the growth in black mobilization from the 1960s until the present. It is difficult to overestimate the enabling significance of the VRA for black electoral mobilization; however, post-1965 black mobilization followed a variety of trajectories within various geographies (i.e., states, counties, and parishes). In some areas, black mobilization rivaled or exceeded white mobilization quickly; in other areas, black mobilization continues to lag behind white mobilization to this day. Previous explanations for this growth (and somewhat less commonly, the variation in growth) have focused on factors relating to socioeconomic and demographic characteristics of blacks in the region, largely ignoring the political dynamics that have shaped these trends.

Finally, we combine individual-level survey data on race, party identification, and ideology with aggregate-level data on political party registration in the region to create an ideological profile of the Republican and Democratic Parties over time. We use these data to construct a series of graphical snapshots that reveal the racial composition, ideological position, and relative size of the parties in comparison to one another beginning in the late 1960s. Examination of these figures reveals an increasingly liberal and shrinking (in terms of total registrants) Democratic Party over time, contrasted with a starkly conservative and growing GOP. Over the last half-century, one can also note an increased reliance on black registrants to fill Democratic Party ranks in the South.

The political transformation of the modern South has been the focal point of a large and growing body of literature. What has been missing—and what has been needed for some time—is an examination of the strategic aspects of this transformation. Traditional explanations for Republican growth have focused on demographic change (in-migration or generational replacement) and/or the slow and apparently inexorable movement of conservative (and increasingly wealthy) white Southerners into the party they "should" have supported long ago.

In chapter 3, we argue that both GOP growth and black mobilization manifested significant strategic components that are largely ignored—or at the least, underemphasized—in the existing literature. We contend that GOP growth is a direct function of black mobilization, as conservative whites responded to a relative shift in the potential political benefits of Democratic Party versus Republican Party membership. From a political standpoint, the relative advantage of the Republican Party (compared to the Democratic Party) increased over this time period, but the extent of this relative advantage for the GOP varied considerably across, and within, the Southern states.

Although often spawned by the formation of societal cleavages, the idea of relative advantage encompasses more than the demographic fuel necessary for the fire. Some catalyst must also present itself, and such a spark often takes the form of policy orientations and/or ideological positions held by existing politicians and attributed to existing political orientations. Citizens identify with, and vote for, candidates of political parties for a variety of reasons. Among the factors that influence peoples' decisions to support one party or the other are (1) the relative competitiveness of the party in a wide variety of political arenas (viability) and (2) the relative consistency of each party's political objectives with a citizen's own objectives (control). Evidence of viability could come in numerous forms, from the increasing competitiveness of Republican candidates to the increasing frequency of party-switching on the part of prominent elected officials. The mobilization of the black population—an almost uniformly Democratic electorate—made it increasingly difficult for conservative whites to maintain control of the local Democratic Party machinery. As control of the local Democratic Party became tenuous, the party apparatus became less valuable to white conservatives.

This chapter also includes a discussion of the new strategic opportunities that African Americans enjoyed at this time. Viewed from the perspective of blacks in the region, the Democratic Party offered the best hope for exerting political influence. In the Deep South, which contained larger numbers of blacks, opportunities to exert leverage within the party were even greater than in the rest of the South. This result—that GOP growth spurs black mobilization in those states with relatively large black populations, but not in states with smaller numbers of blacks—is predicted by the theory of relative advantage.

Chapter 4 includes detailed case studies of the transformation of the party system in two Southern states, Georgia and Virginia, one representative of the Deep South and the other the Rim South. Using a variety of secondary sources (histories of the state and biographies of prominent state politicians and political leaders) and primary sources (newspapers, documents available from archives and libraries, and in-person interviews), we are able to show the theory of relative advantage "in action" and how it provides important insights into the political change in these two states from the pre-Civil Rights era to the present.

Following the case studies presented in chapter 4, we subject our explanation of Republican growth to a rigorous battery of quantitative tests in chapter 5. We begin by employing a panel Granger framework that indicates black mobilization causes GOP growth in a consistent manner across the eleven former states of the Confederacy. We expand upon this analysis by specifying a pooled-time series model covering the 1960–2008 period. In short, we find clear evidence that GOP substate party competition and black mobilization are positively related to state-level Republican growth.

In chapter 6, we examine the implications of the theory of relative advantage in the context of substate political dynamics. Using parishes in Louisiana and counties in North Carolina as the units of analysis, we analyze the relationship between partisanship (voter registration) and race (voter registration) in a pooled-time series framework from 1966 through 2008. Chapter 7 includes individual-level analyses designed to probe the effects of black mobilization at both the mass and elite levels. Using survey data of GOP party activists from 1991 and 2001, we examine the propensity of these individuals to have switched parties based on the degree of black mobilization at the county level. We then make use of the two longitudinal datasets (the American National Election Studies, 1972–2008 and the Southern Focus Polls, 1992–2001) to draw inferences about mass partisan identification in relation to black political mobilization. The prevalence of support for the theory of relative advantage at each of the three levels of analysis—the state, substate, and individual levels—is striking.

In chapter 8, we assess the extent to which the implications of relative advantage theory for black mobilization are supported by the empirical record. Again, using a panel Granger framework, we are able to demonstrate that Republican growth causes black mobilization in the five Southern states with the largest black populations, or those located in the Deep South. We incorporate this information into a pooled-time series model (1960–2008), where we find clear evidence that GOP growth is positively related to black mobilization in the Deep South (though not in the Rim South), even after taking into account a variety of other potential explanations. This chapter includes analysis similar to that undertaken in chapter 6 at the substate level. Again using parishes in Louisiana and counties in North Carolina, we analyze the relationship between partisanship (voter registration) and race (voter registration) in a pooled-time series framework from 1966 through 2008. Just as in the case of GOP growth, we find strong evidence in support of the implications of relative advantage theory for understanding the dynamics of black mobilization during the last half-century in the South.

We conclude with a discussion of the broader implications of the theory of relative advantage for the future of Southern Republicanism and the mobilization of Southern blacks. We re-emphasize the significance of race in Southern (and national) politics. We caution that those who ignore these racial dynamics do so at their own risk. We also offer some conjectures about the future role of Hispanics in Southern politics and discuss the role of these Southern political dynamics in the future of national politics.

| A Half-Century of Political Change in the South

IN ADDITION TO WINNING the state of Florida in the presidential election of 2008, Barack Obama also won the states of North Carolina and Virginia, something a Democratic presidential candidate had not done since 1964 (Virginia) and 1976 (North Carolina). It was a big deal, but it was also a reminder about how much the South has changed in the last half-century, from a solidly Democratic region to a region so solidly Republican that, when a Democratic candidate for president won these two Rim South states, it counted as a major electoral victory. In this chapter, we describe the Southern political transformation from the 1950s through the first decade of the twenty-first century. We first look at the increasing success of the Republican Party in the region by tracking the electoral victories of GOP candidates at the national, state, and substate levels. We also chart individual-level growth in identification with the Republican Party using longitudinal survey data. As has been noted by a number of existing studies, Southern whites were drawn to Republican Party candidates—particularly at the presidential level—even before they viewed themselves (or identified) as Republicans.

We also describe the growth in black mobilization from the 1960s until the present. While it is clear beyond question that the Voting Rights Act (VRA) significantly enabled black electoral mobilization, post-1965 black mobilization followed a variety of trajectories both between and within the Southern states. In some areas, black mobilization rivaled or exceeded white mobilization quickly; in other areas, black mobilization continues to lag behind white mobilization to this day. Explanations for this growth (and somewhat less commonly, the variation in growth) have focused on factors relating to socioeconomic and demographic characteristics of blacks in the region, largely ignoring the political dynamics that have shaped these trends.

Finally, we combine individual-level survey data on race, party identification, and ideology with aggregate-level data on political party registration in the region to create an across-time ideological profile of the Republican and Democratic Parties in North Carolina and Louisiana. We use this data to construct a series of graphical snapshots that reveal the racial composition, ideological position, and relative size of the parties in comparison to one another beginning in the late 1960s. Examination of these figures reveals an increasingly liberal and shrinking (in terms of total registrants) Democratic Party over time, contrasted with a starkly conservative and growing GOP. Over the last half-century, one can also note an increased reliance on black registrants to fill Democratic Party ranks in the South.

## A Half-Century of Growth in Southern Republicanism

In *Southern Politics in State and Nation*, Key describes one kind of Southern Republican—the presidential Republican—as a type of political schizophrenic: "He votes in Democratic primaries to have a voice in state and local matters, but when the presidential election rolls around he casts a ballot for the Republican presidential nominee. Locally he is a Democrat; nationally, a Republican" (1949, 278). What Key saw in 1949 as schizophrenic political behavior we might today see as perfectly rational political behavior.

The transformation of the South from an overwhelmingly Democratic region to a solidly Republican region has its roots in the political behavior of these presidential Republicans. Between 1900 and 1952, there were only two elections in which any Southern state gave a majority of their votes to a Republican presidential candidate: 1920 and 1928. In the presidential election of 1920, Warren G. Harding managed to win the Rim South state of Tennessee with 51 percent of the vote. Tennessee had a long history of Republicanism and again went for the Republican presidential candidate Herbert Hoover in 1928, along with four other Rim South states, Florida, North Carolina, Virginia, and Texas. Hoover's success in these Southern states in 1928 was likely the result of Democratic nominee Al Smith's New York Catholicism and his opposition to Prohibition (Key 1949, 318).

From 1928 to 1952, no Southern state went Republican in a presidential election. In fact, none even came close, although regional variations in support for the Republican Party were evident: In most of the Rim South states, Republicans managed to win a plurality of votes. A third of Tennessee voters consistently cast their ballots for Republicans between 1928 and 1948. In

1948, Virginia gave 41 percent of its votes to Thomas Dewey, the highest percentage of votes won by a Republican presidential candidate in any Southern state between 1928 and 1948.

The election of 1952 marked the return of Republican Party success at the presidential level in the South, a trend that within a generation would become regional domination. However, Republican presidential victories varied across the region, showing up first and most evidently in Southern states that were not part of the Deep South. In both 1952 and 1956, the contest was between the popular war hero General Dwight D. Eisenhower and Illinois Governor Adlai Stevenson. Eisenhower was personally popular in the South, having grown up in Texas and Kansas, and captured Virginia, Texas, Tennessee, and Florida in 1952. He came close to capturing South Carolina with 49 percent of the vote and Louisiana with 47 percent of the vote. In 1956, he again won Virginia, Texas, Tennessee, and Florida, but also added Louisiana to the Republican column.

The elections of 1960 through 1968 marked a period of political soul-searching and electoral calculus for Southern voters at the presidential level. In 1960, Southerners were not especially attracted to Richard Nixon, but they were also leery of the Boston Catholic John F. Kennedy. While three Rim South states—Virginia, Tennessee, and Florida—went Republican, two others, including one Deep South state nearly did so: Texas, North Carolina, and South Carolina. Kennedy beat Nixon in the South by just under 500,000 votes out of nearly ten million votes cast. In 1964, the regional variations switched: Five Deep South states, attracted to the states' rights message of Senator Barry Goldwater and weary of Lyndon Johnson's support for civil rights, went Republican. Although only the Deep South states went Republican, all Southern states except Texas gave over 40 percent of their votes to the Republican ticket. The 1968 presidential election was tumultuous. The Southern states divided their support largely between the Republican Party (Florida, North Carolina, Tennessee, and South Carolina) and George Wallace's populist American Independent Party (Alabama, Georgia, Louisiana, Mississippi, and Arkansas). Only Texas went Democratic.

What is clear about the 1960s is that Southern voters were consistent only in the inconsistency of their presidential party voting patterns. While there was steady growth in support for the Republican Party, there was significant subregional variation in terms of where that growth was taking place: Rim South states went for the Republican Party in 1960, Deep South states went for the Republican Party in 1964, and in 1968, Rim South states went mainly for the Republican Party while Deep South states went mainly for Wallace's American Independent Party. The 1970s, however, marked the arrival of the Republican

Party at the presidential level in the South. In the ten presidential elections from 1972 to 2008, the Republican Party captured all eleven Southern states five times. Four of the five elections in which the Republican ticket did not capture all eleven Southern states (1976, 1980, 1992, and 1996) were elections with a Southern Democrat on the ballot, helping the Democratic nominee capture three states in the region. The 2008 election saw a surge in African American turnout with Barack Obama on the ballot. At the presidential level, the Republican Party gained dominance in the early 1970s and that dominance has waned little since.

The rise of Southern Republicanism at the presidential level was followed a decade later at the senatorial level. Nearly ten years after Eisenhower won the first Southern state for a Republican presidential candidate in decades, John Tower won a special election in Texas in 1961 to replace Lyndon Johnson in the U.S. Senate. Tower's victory with 50.6 percent of the vote marked the first time a Republican had won a U.S. Senate seat in a Southern state in the twentieth century.

Tower spent two years as the lone Southern Republican Senator before Strom Thurmond switched parties in 1964 and joined him. Howard Baker became the second Republican Senator elected from the South in the twentieth century, winning the 1966 Tennessee election against former Governor Frank Clement with nearly 56 percent of the vote. Within a decade of Tower's win, Republicans held a quarter of all Southern Senate seats and within two decades, the GOP had captured half of them. By the mid-1970s, support for Republican senatorial candidates in the South had reached levels where Republicans were considered to be approaching a competitive status, and by the mid-1980s, they had reached competitive parity with Democrats (Black and Black 1987). In 2005, Republicans held a three-to-one advantage over Democrats.

Republican Party success at the senatorial level, like its success at the presidential level, varied across the region. The Rim South states of Texas, Tennessee, Florida, Virginia, and North Carolina were where Republicans won initially.[1] Mississippi was the first state in the Deep South to elect a Republican when Thad Cochran won a three-way race in 1978 with 45 percent of the vote. Most Republican Party successes in the Deep South came in the mid-1980s and mid-1990s.

Republican successes at the congressional level lagged behind presidential and senatorial Republicanism by several decades. As Figure 2.1 shows, Republican presidential candidates won handily in the South from 1972 on, and if not for George Wallace running on the American Independent ticket in 1968, Republican wins in the South would date to that year. The only exceptions to this trend were 1976, when the Watergate scandal and a Southern Democrat on the ticket helped the Democrats, and 1992 and 1996, when two Southern Democrats were again on the ticket. Yet, as Lamis (2005) notes, even though Bill Clinton thoroughly understood his party's presidential weakness in the South, the Clinton-Gore ticket was able to capture only four Southern states each time.

As Figure 2.2 shows, Republican senatorial victories surged in the mid-1980s, retreated in the late 1980s and early 1990s, and then surged again in the mid-1990s. This second surge in the mid-1990s was accompanied by remarkable gains in the region at the congressional level. In the 1996 election, Republicans won nearly 60 percent of the South's U.S. House seats. But these gains were not uniform across the region.

Figure 2.3 shows the congressional balance of power in each of the eleven Southern states included in our study from 1951 to 2009. Negative numbers indicate a balance in favor of the Democratic Party, and positive numbers indicate a balance in favor of the Republican Party. In all eleven states except Texas, Florida, and Georgia, a noticeable shift in the Republican direction happened in the 1966 and 1968 elections. The most dramatic shift occurred in Virginia, where the congressional delegation favored the Democratic Party by six seats in 1964, was evenly split in 1968, and by 1972 favored the

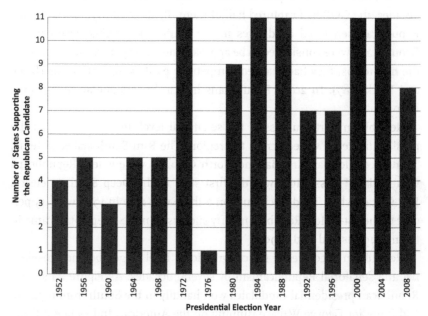

FIGURE 2.1 Support for Republican Presidential Candidates in Southern States, 1952–2008

Republican Party by four seats. Republicans in Virginia grew their majority to as high as plus-seven over the Democrats throughout the 1970s and into the early 1980s before giving Democrats back a majority throughout the 1990s, and then taking it back again at the turn of the century.

Arkansas has been the most difficult Southern state for congressional Republicans, where they have done no better than to split the delegation with Democrats. During most of the period between 1966 and 2008, however, Republicans have held only one of the state's four congressional seats.[2] In Florida and Georgia, Democrats held a relatively stable advantage over Republicans until the mid-1980s, when Republicans took a majority of congressional seats and have since held an advantage. In Texas, Republicans made steady gains on Democrats over time, finally taking a majority in 2004.

The remaining states, Alabama, Mississippi, North Carolina, South Carolina, and Tennessee, follow a similar pattern: Republican gains in the 1960s and 1970s were followed by retreats in the 1980s and early 1990s, and then gains again from the mid-1990s to the present. This pattern varied, with Republicans gaining decisive majorities in the congressional balance in the mid-1990s in Alabama and South Carolina, but gaining less decisive control in Mississippi and actually retreating in North Carolina and Tennessee. Regardless of the regional variation in growth, Republicans dominated the Southern congressional delegation by 2008.

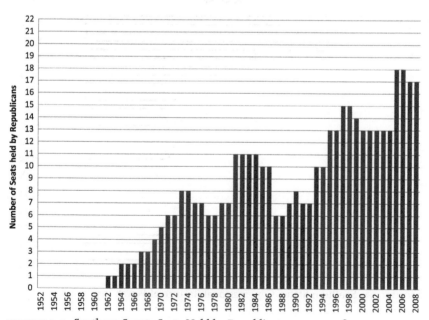

FIGURE 2.2  Southern Senate Seats Held by Republicans, 1952–2008

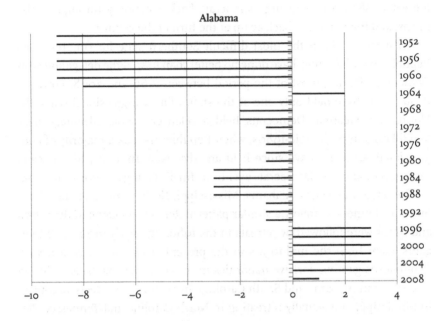

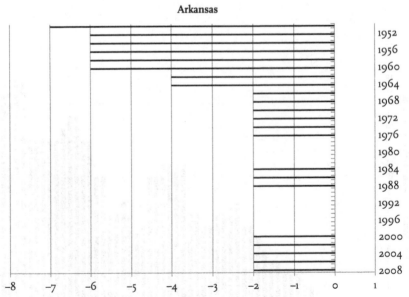

FIGURE 2.3 Southern States' Congressional Balance of Power, 1951–2008

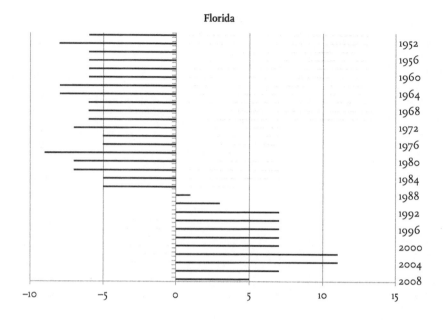

Florida

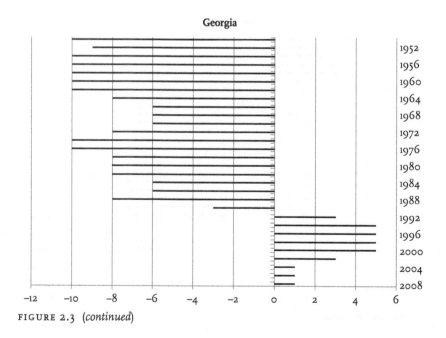

Georgia

FIGURE 2.3 (*continued*)

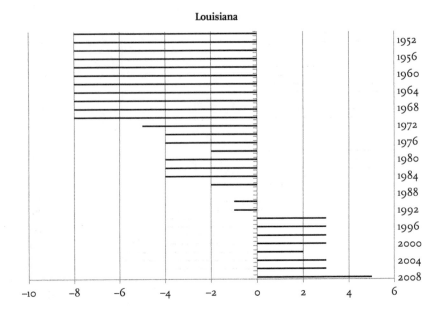

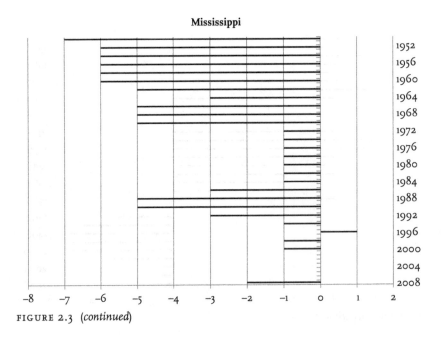

FIGURE 2.3 (continued)

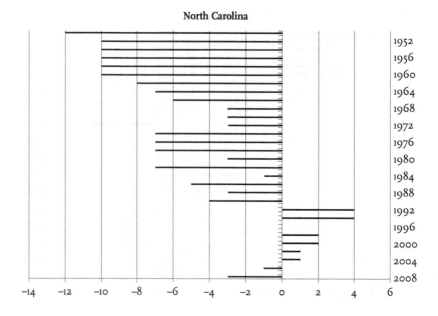

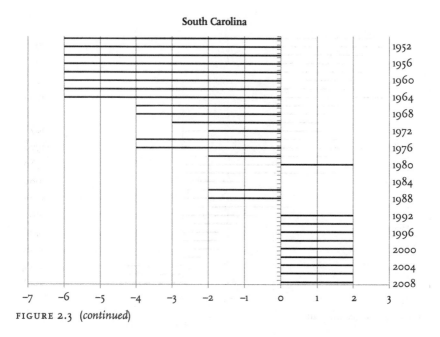

FIGURE 2.3 *(continued)*

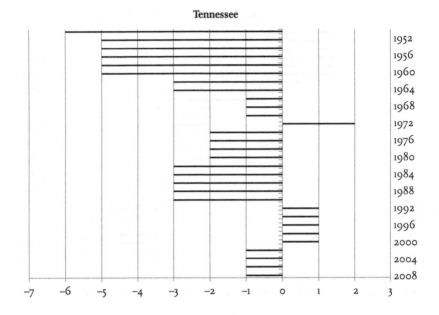

Tennessee

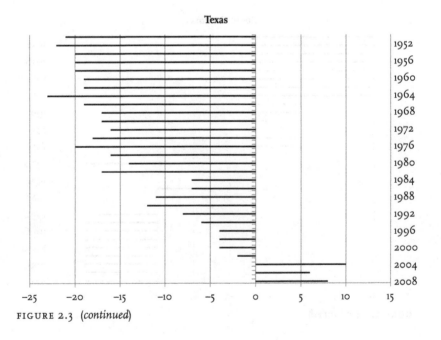

Texas

FIGURE 2.3 (*continued*)

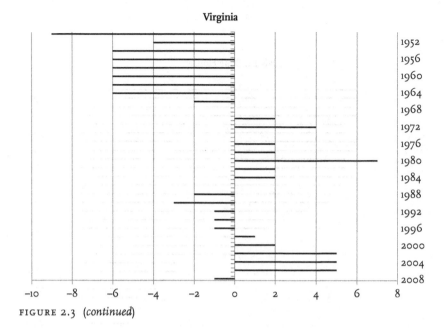

FIGURE 2.3 *(continued)*

Growth in Southern Republicanism at the state legislative level has been much slower than at any other level. Although Republican candidates for federal offices could increasingly attract a majority (or winning plurality) of votes, at the legislative level, they continued to struggle. As Maggiotto and Wekkin (2000) note, part of the reason for this slow rate of penetration at the subregional level was due to the lack of viable local Republican organizations. Republican successes at the national and state levels, however, enlivened interest at the local level, and as local organizations matured, they cultivated strong Republican candidates for local office (Scher 1997). This process inevitably happened at different rates across the South and thus resulted in non-uniform substate Republican growth.

We can see this subregional variation in state legislative Republican growth in Figures 2.4 and 2.5. As with Figure 2.3, Figures 2.4 and 2.5 represent the balances of power between Republicans and Democrats at the legislative level, in this case at the state house and senate levels from 1954 to 2008. Negative numbers indicate a balance of power in favor of Democrats, and positive numbers indicate a balance of power in favor of Republicans.[3] Several observations can be made about the growth of Southern Republicanism represented in these data. Although the growth has not been uniform across the South, in all Southern states, Republicans have made substantial electoral progress in the last half-century at the state legislative level. This progress was much slower in the Deep South states of Alabama,

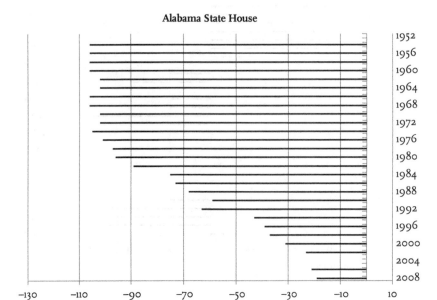

Alabama State House

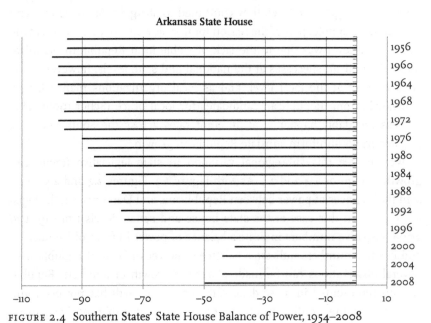

Arkansas State House

FIGURE 2.4 Southern States' State House Balance of Power, 1954–2008

# Florida State House

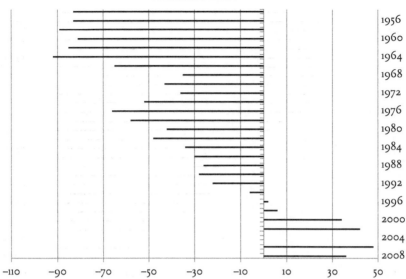

# Georgia State House

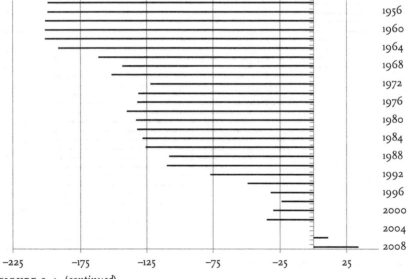

FIGURE 2.4 *(continued)*

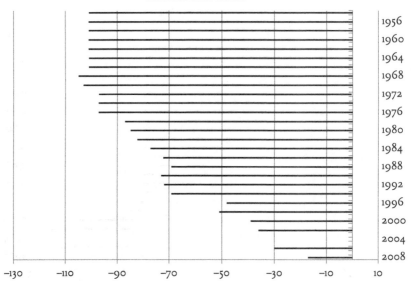

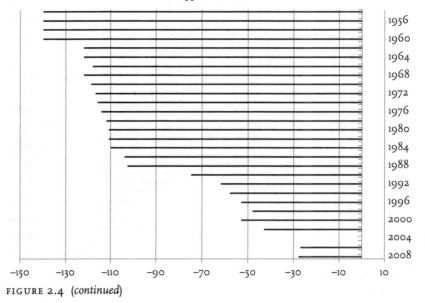

FIGURE 2.4 (*continued*)

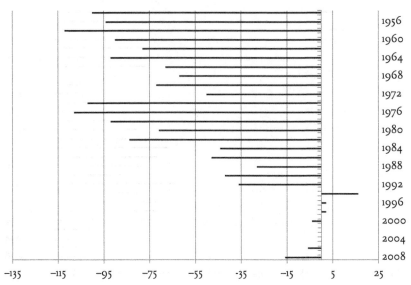

North Carolina State House

| | |
|---|---|
| | 1956 |
| | 1960 |
| | 1964 |
| | 1968 |
| | 1972 |
| | 1976 |
| | 1980 |
| | 1984 |
| | 1988 |
| | 1992 |
| | 1996 |
| | 2000 |
| | 2004 |
| | 2008 |

−135  −115  −95  −75  −55  −35  −15  5  25

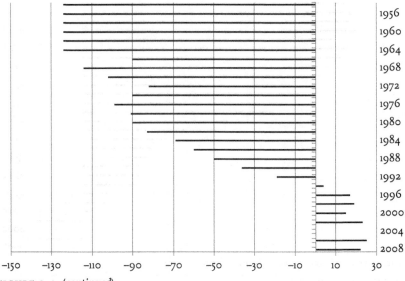

South Carolina State House

| | |
|---|---|
| | 1956 |
| | 1960 |
| | 1964 |
| | 1968 |
| | 1972 |
| | 1976 |
| | 1980 |
| | 1984 |
| | 1988 |
| | 1992 |
| | 1996 |
| | 2000 |
| | 2004 |
| | 2008 |

−150  −130  −110  −90  −70  −50  −30  −10  10  30

FIGURE 2.4 (continued)

### Tennessee State House

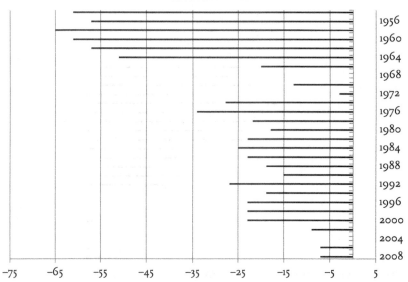

| | |
|---|---|
| | 1956 |
| | 1960 |
| | 1964 |
| | 1968 |
| | 1972 |
| | 1976 |
| | 1980 |
| | 1984 |
| | 1988 |
| | 1992 |
| | 1996 |
| | 2000 |
| | 2004 |
| | 2008 |

-75 -65 -55 -45 -35 -25 -15 -5 5

### Texas State House

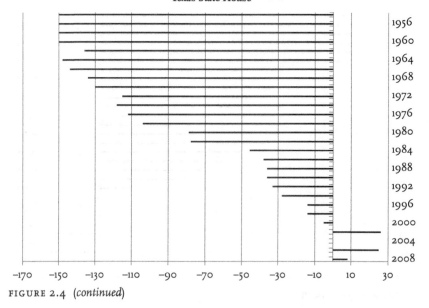

| | |
|---|---|
| | 1956 |
| | 1960 |
| | 1964 |
| | 1968 |
| | 1972 |
| | 1976 |
| | 1980 |
| | 1984 |
| | 1988 |
| | 1992 |
| | 1996 |
| | 2000 |
| | 2004 |
| | 2008 |

-170 -150 -130 -110 -90 -70 -50 -30 -10 10 30

FIGURE 2.4 (*continued*)

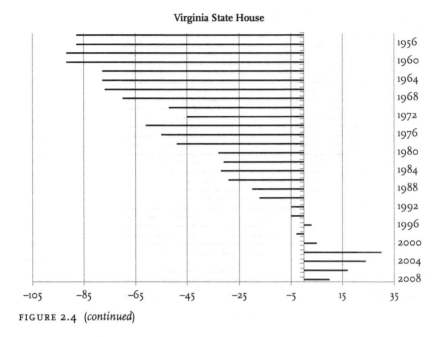

**Virginia State House**

| | |
|---|---|
| | 1956 |
| | 1960 |
| | 1964 |
| | 1968 |
| | 1972 |
| | 1976 |
| | 1980 |
| | 1984 |
| | 1988 |
| | 1992 |
| | 1996 |
| | 2000 |
| | 2004 |
| | 2008 |

−105    −85    −65    −45    −25    −5    15    35

FIGURE 2.4 *(continued)*

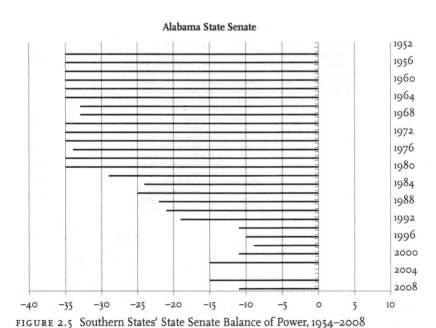

**Alabama State Senate**

| | |
|---|---|
| | 1952 |
| | 1956 |
| | 1960 |
| | 1964 |
| | 1968 |
| | 1972 |
| | 1976 |
| | 1980 |
| | 1984 |
| | 1988 |
| | 1992 |
| | 1996 |
| | 2000 |
| | 2004 |
| | 2008 |

−40    −35    −30    −25    −20    −15    −10    −5    0    5    10

FIGURE 2.5 Southern States' State Senate Balance of Power, 1954–2008

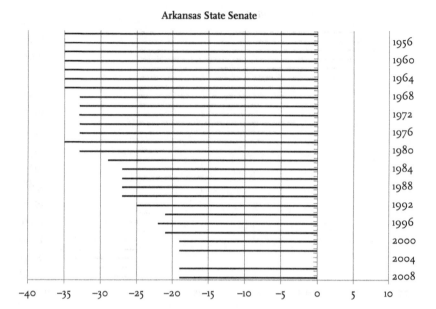

Arkansas State Senate

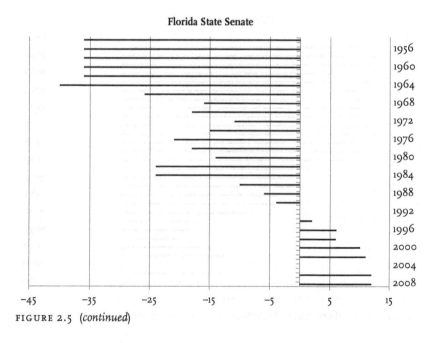

Florida State Senate

FIGURE 2.5 *(continued)*

## Georgia State Senate

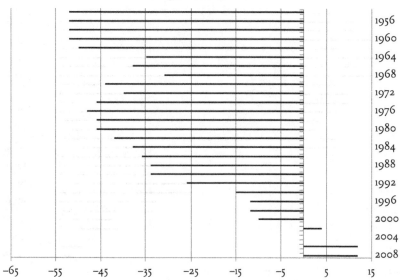

## Louisiana State Senate

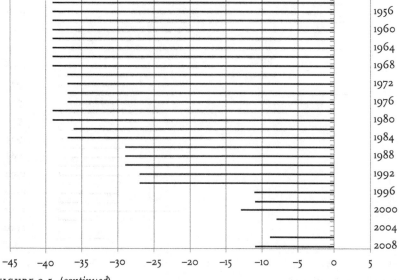

FIGURE 2.5 (*continued*)

**Mississippi State Senate**

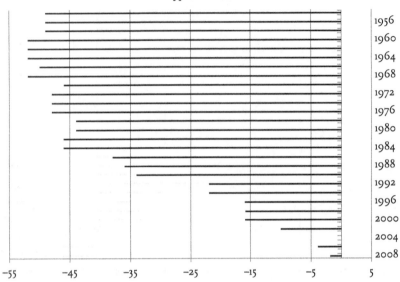

**North Carolina State Senate**

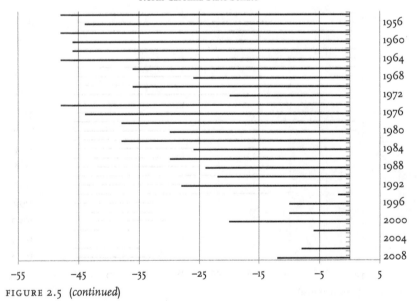

FIGURE 2.5 *(continued)*

### South Carolina State Senate

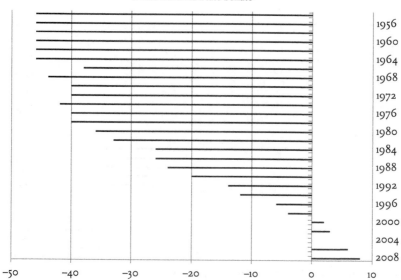

### Tennessee State Senate

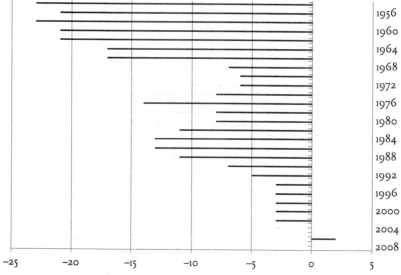

FIGURE 2.5 *(continued)*

**Texas State Senate**

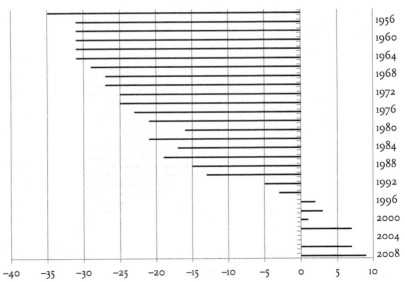

1956
1960
1964
1968
1972
1976
1980
1984
1988
1992
1996
2000
2004
2008

−40   −35   −30   −25   −20   −15   −10   −5   0   5   10

**Virginia State Senate**

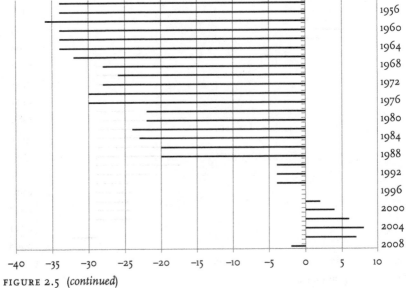

1956
1960
1964
1968
1972
1976
1980
1984
1988
1992
1996
2000
2004
2008

−40   −35   −30   −25   −20   −15   −10   −5   0   5   10

FIGURE 2.5 (*continued*)

Louisiana, Mississippi, and the Rim South state of Arkansas than it was in the other states. In Florida, Texas, Virginia, and South Carolina, Republicans gained majorities in both the state house and senate chambers in the 1990s.[4]

North Carolina and Virginia have emerged as the most competitive states in the region. Republicans in North Carolina took control of the House in 1996, gave it back to Democrats in 2000, and then took it back again in 2006. A similar pattern exists for Republicans in the Virginia Senate, where after achieving parity with Democrats in 1995 and holding the chamber for a decade, they gave control back to Democrats in 2007. Republicans gained control of the Texas Senate in the mid-1990s and the House at the turn of the century and, while giving up seats in both chambers to Democrats in subsequent elections, have managed to hold their losses to at least parity with Democrats.

In most Deep South states, Republicans have lagged behind their Rim South colleagues. In Alabama, Louisiana, and Mississippi, Republicans have narrowed the Democratic majorities in both the state House and Senate, but have been unable to secure majorities of their own. However, Republicans have found the going no more difficult than in the Rim South state of Arkansas. After substantial losses to Republicans throughout the 1980s and 1990s, Democrats still hold a sizeable majority in both the state House and Senate.

These data on Republican electoral growth at the national, state, and substate level chart the increased success of the Republican Party since the 1950s in the South, but they also demonstrate the extent to which Republican growth varied not only regionally, but also subregionally and across the different offices.

One last point to make about Southern Republicanism since the 1950s can be seen in Figure 2.6. Drawing on data from the American National Election Studies and the 2006 Cooperative Congressional Election Studies, we are able to track self-identification with the Republican and Democratic parties (and Independents) by white Southerners longitudinally from 1952 to 2008.[5]

As white Southerners moved away from identifying with the Democratic Party, they had two alternatives: identify with the Republican Party or take some third (Independent) route. Over time, it was clear that white Southerners came to identify more and more as Republicans, but this shift did not happen quickly. To be sure, many white Southerners tried on Independent clothing, such as in 1968 with George Wallace's American Independent Party. But, finding the Independent route to lack political viability, they turned to the more politically viable (and increasingly electorally successful) Republican Party. By the early 1990s, after a couple decades of Republican

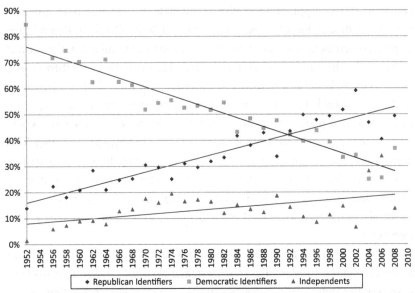

FIGURE 2.6 Party Identification of White Southerners, 1952–2008

presidential success in the South and increasing GOP success at the U.S. Senate and U.S. House level, more white Southerners self-identified as Republicans than as Democrats.

## A Half-Century of Growth in Black Mobilization

Being registered to vote is a gateway to other forms of political activity and, as a result, group voter registration rates are a strong indicator of the real and potential electoral and political strength of any group. Measurements of black voter registration rates in the South place African Americans into the context of the existing regional and state rates. This is a much more precise method of estimating the potential mobilizing influence of blacks as an electoral presence than alternative methods (for instance, using the size of the black voting age population as a proxy). Figure 2.7 charts black registration rates for the South as a region and for each individual state from 1950 to 2008. Information on black voter registration was collected from the *VEP News* and census publications, specifically the *Statistical Abstracts of the U.S.* and *Current Population Reports: P-20 Series on Voting and Registration.*[6]

There are several points to be made about these data. First, there is considerable variation in registration rates at the beginning and end of the period under analysis. The regional average in 1950 was just under 18 percent, but it varied from a low of 2.8 percent in Mississippi to a high of 31.5 percent in Florida. Generally speaking, Deep South states had lower African American voter registration rates in the early 1950s than did Rim South states. Among the lowest were Alabama, Mississippi, and Louisiana. Among the highest were Florida, Texas, and Tennessee. The 2008 regional average was just below 70 percent (68.4), but the level of variation was much smaller, with most states recording registration rates in the 70 percent range and only two (Arkansas and Florida) recording rates in the 50 percent range. Regionally and across the individual states, black mobilization as measured by voter registration rates has increased dramatically over the nearly sixty years under study.

Due to variations in state laws, the rate of growth for black voter registration from 1950 to 1960, and then from 1960 to 1970 and beyond varied considerably, even after many legal barriers to disenfranchisement were removed through federal action. Several states, such as Louisiana, North Carolina, and Tennessee, saw considerable growth in black mobilization early on. Tennessee's black registration rates jumped from 26 percent in 1950 to 58.9 percent in 1960 and then remained relatively level, with an upward spike in 1971 and then another in 1984. Louisiana had a registration rate of 12.8 percent in 1950 and 30.9 percent by 1960, but Louisiana's rate continued to climb on a relatively linear slope until the early 1990s when it dropped off, having reached a peak of 82.3 percent in 1992. Black registration rates in North Carolina in 1950 were 16.4 percent and reached 38.2 percent by 1960, ultimately reaching a high of 70 percent in 1971 before dropping down to around 50 percent

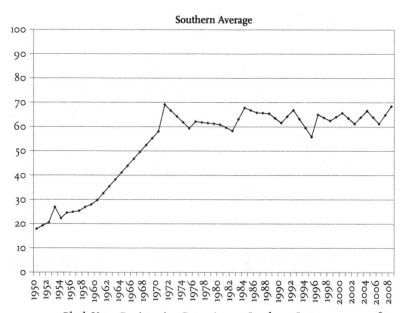

FIGURE 2.7  Black Voter Registration Rates Across Southern States, 1950–2008

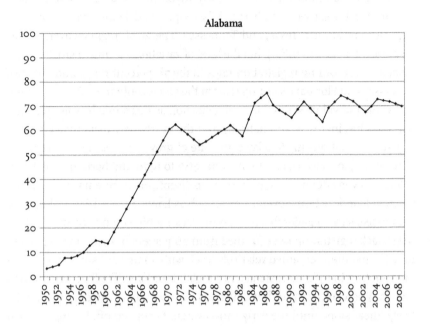

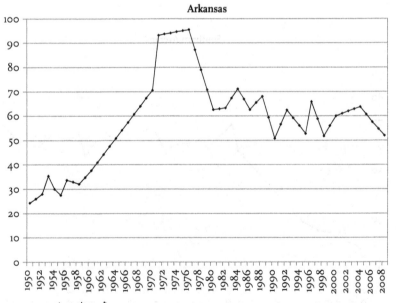

FIGURE 2.7 (*continued*)

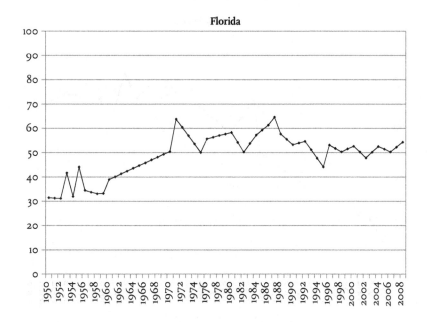

Florida

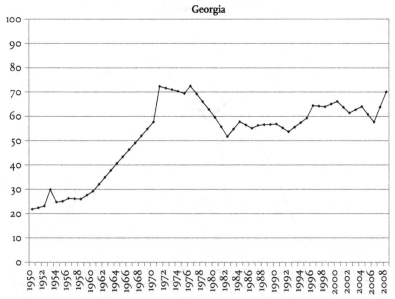

Georgia

FIGURE 2.7 *(continued)*

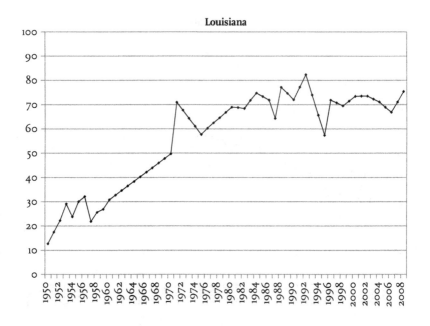

**Louisiana**

**Mississippi**

FIGURE 2.7 (*continued*)

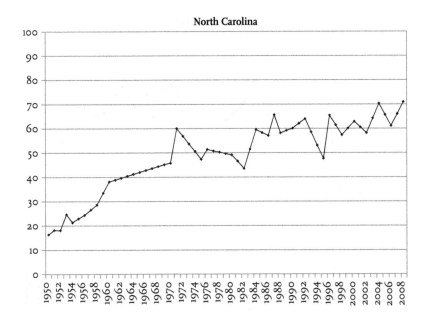

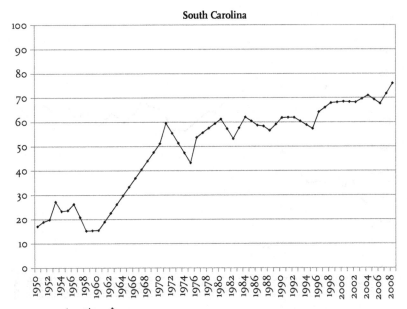

FIGURE 2.7 (*continued*)

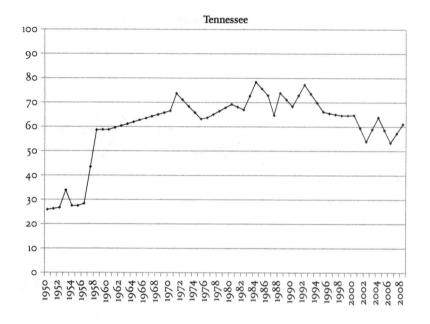

**Tennessee**

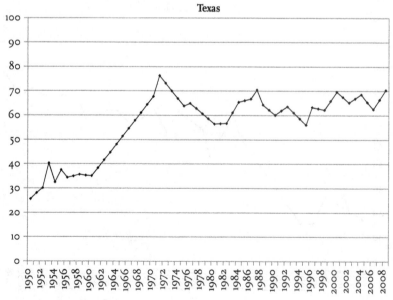

**Texas**

FIGURE 2.7 (*continued*)

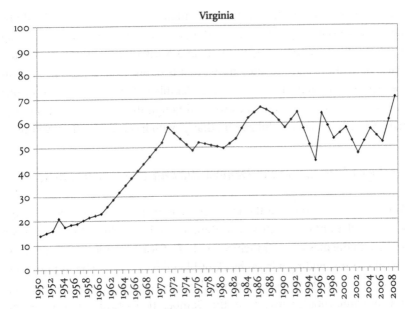

**Virginia**

FIGURE 2.7 *(continued)*

during the 1970s and then fluctuating between the 60 percent and 70 percent range from the mid-1980s to 2008. Most other states saw minimal growth between 1950 and 1960, but saw considerable growth during the decade of the 1960s.

The level of mobilization varied considerably across the region as well. The highest level of mobilization recorded in the fifty-eight-year period under analysis is 95.4 percent in Arkansas in 1976. Black registration rates in Arkansas for the first half of the 1970s hovered in the mid-90 percent range before dropping and fluctuating between the 50 percent and 70 percent range. Several states, including Alabama, Florida, Louisiana, Mississippi, and Tennessee, saw spikes in levels of mobilization in the mid-to-late 1980s, probably resulting from the presidential campaigns of Jesse L. Jackson in 1984 and 1988 (Walters 2005). Additionally, several states, including Georgia, Louisiana, Mississippi, North Carolina, South Carolina, and Virginia, saw spikes (or all-time highs for North Carolina, South Carolina, and Virginia) in 2008, most likely the result of the Obama candidacy of 2008. Several states also saw considerable drops in levels of mobilization in the 1970s. For instance, between 1975 and 1980, Arkansas saw a drop of 32.4 percent in black registration rates. Georgia saw a drop of 20.8 percent between 1976 and 1982. Texas black voter registration rates dropped 19.8 percent between 1971 and 1980, while South Carolina's dropped 16.3 percent between 1971 and 1975.

In sum, black mobilization rates have increased dramatically in Southern states over the last fifty-eight years, but this growth displays some interesting characteristics. For one, registration rates varied considerably across the states, both at the starting and ending points of our data collection. In addition, levels of mobilization varied considerably over the time period of our analysis and across the region as well. Although there has clearly been dramatic growth in black mobilization, that growth has been far from uniform.

## Ideological Profiles of the Democratic and Republican Parties

The leftward movement of the Democratic Party in the South is a staple observation of Southern politics. The Democratic Party's liberal shift has been credited to the mass re-enfranchisement of African Americans beginning in the mid-1960s, adding a large block of liberal party adherents to the Southern Democratic Party rolls. Additionally, scholars have noted the mass exodus of white conservatives from the Democratic Party and movement into the Republican Party, leading to a secular realignment toward Republicanism (Black and Black 1987). Hood's (2004) study of the racial and ideological transformation of the Democratic Party in Louisiana showed that, contemporarily, whites are actually more ideologically liberal than blacks, a sure indication that conservative whites and a large share of white moderates have shed their Democratic affiliation.

We are able to examine the nature and extent of the ideological change of both the Democratic and Republican Parties thanks to the availability of individual ideological self-identification data from the American National Election Studies (ANES) and the Comparative State Elections Project (CSEP). The ANES have collected this data biennially since 1972, but we can extend our analysis back in time with the CSEP data collected in 1968. We thus have ideological self-identification data for a sizeable sample of Southern residents from 1968 to 2008, allowing us to trace the transformation of both the Democratic and Republican Parties in the South over a forty-year period. Combining this individual-level survey data with aggregate-level registration data from Louisiana and North Carolina, we can also create specific ideological profiles of the Democratic and Republican Parties in these two Southern states over time.[7]

Table 2.1 displays a set of mean ideological scores for Southern Democrats (also separated by race) and Southern Republicans over seven successive time periods. Using the traditional seven-point ideological self-placement scale with a value of one representing respondents classifying themselves as *extremely liberal* and seven representing respondents classifying themselves as *extremely conservative*, we are able to derive an ideological distribution of respondents by party (and race for Democrats).

Several important points can be drawn from these data. First, they clearly show that Southern Democrats have become increasingly liberal over time and Southern Republicans even more conservative over time. The mean Southern Democratic score in 1968 was 5.64 and had dropped to 3.89 by the 2002–2008 time frame, representing a net change in the liberal direction of three-quarters of a point. The mean Southern Republican score in 1968 was 4.79, dropped to 2.36 in the 1972–1977 period, and then steadily moved in the conservative direction, ending at 5.81 in the 2002–2008 period. This represents a net increase of one (1.02) point more conservative than in 1968.

TABLE 2.1 Southern Democrats and Republicans—Mean Ideological Scores and Skewness

| TIME PERIOD | DEMOCRATS | | | REPUBLICANS |
| --- | --- | --- | --- | --- |
| | ALL | WHITE | BLACK | |
| 1968 | 4.64 | 4.82 | 4.06 | 4.79 |
| | .02 | .03 | −1.55 | −.34 |
| | (1,425) | (1,077) | (348) | (1,433) |
| 1972–1977 | 4.07 | 4.30 | 3.26 | 2.36 |
| | 1.32 | 1.31 | .70 | .30 |
| | (663) | (514) | (148) | (321) |
| 1978–1983 | 3.94 | 3.92 | 3.83 | 3.11 |
| | 1.60 | 1.54 | 1.86 | .36 |
| | (485) | (382) | (94) | (302) |
| 1984–1989 | 4.05 | 4.08 | 4.01 | 3.86 |
| | 1.68 | 1.70 | 1.55 | .51 |
| | (552) | (368) | (184) | (407) |
| 1990–1995 | 3.90 | 3.89 | 3.91 | 4.31 |
| | 1.67 | 1.33 | 2.10 | .73 |
| | (509) | (327) | (182) | (432) |
| 1996–2001 | 4.02 | 3.96 | 4.19 | 4.55 |
| | .50 | −.34 | 2.27 | .59 |
| | (393) | (274) | (119) | (349) |
| 2002–2008 | 3.89 | 3.92 | 3.82 | 5.81 |
| | 1.13 | .50 | 2.24 | 1.64 |
| | (505) | (371) | (134) | (569) |
| Net increase/ decrease | −.75 | −.90 | −.24 | 1.02 |

NOTES: Scores calculated based on the standard 7-point ideological self-placement scale (1 = extremely liberal; 7 = extremely conservative). Mean scores in bold; skewness in italics; number of responses in parentheses.

When we decompose the Democratic changes by race, we see that white Democrats have become more liberal over time than black Democrats. The mean score in 1968 for white Democrats was 4.82 and by the 2002–2008 period had dropped to 3.92, a movement in the liberal direction of almost one point (.90). The mean score in 1968 for black Democrats was 4.06 and by the 2002–2008 period had dropped to 3.82, a movement in the liberal direction of about a quarter of a point. White Democrats in this latter time period then were actually were more liberal than black Democrats by about a tenth of a point.

Knowing something about the ideological distribution of Southern Democrats and Republicans, as well as something about the partisan registration of voters in Louisiana and North Carolina (and racial divisions in Louisiana), we can combine these data to create a series of illustrations designed to depict the ideological transformation of the Democratic and Republican Parties in Louisiana and North Carolina during the preceding forty years. The first step in this process is to normalize the ideological distributions derived from the individual-level survey data to conform to the parameters of the Democratic and Republican Parties of Louisiana and North Carolina. This stage entails multiplying the actual number of party adherents (both white and black for Louisiana Democrats) in the states by the percentage derived from the ideological frequency distributions for Democratic (both white and black) and Republican Southerners. Once the party registration totals have been weighted to fit the accompanying ideological patterns, it is then possible to alter these distributions to account for the percentage of identifiers that each group contributed to each state's totals. This is accomplished by simply dividing the weighted distributions for Democratic (white and black in the case of Louisiana) and Republican registrants in each state for a given year.[8]

Figures 2.8 and 2.9 show seven panels, each representing the years 1968, 1975, 1980, 1986, 1992, 1999, and 2005, respectively. For Figure 2.8, the striped distribution represents the ideological distribution of blacks in the Louisiana Democratic Party, while the darker shaded distribution represents the ideological distribution of whites. The gray shaded distribution represents the ideological distribution of the Republican Party. In Figure 2.9, the darker shaded distribution represents the ideological distribution of the North Carolina Democratic Party and the lighter shaded distribution represents the ideological distribution of the North Carolina Republican Party. All panels depict the same scale for easy comparison across time periods. The horizontal axis represents the same seven-point ideological scale, with the far left representing the percentage of *extremely liberal* (EL) and the far right

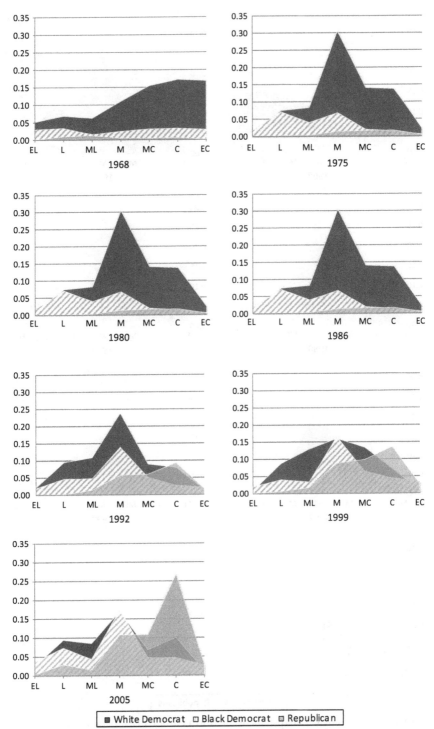

FIGURE 2.8 Ideological Snapshots of the Louisiana Democratic and Republican Parties

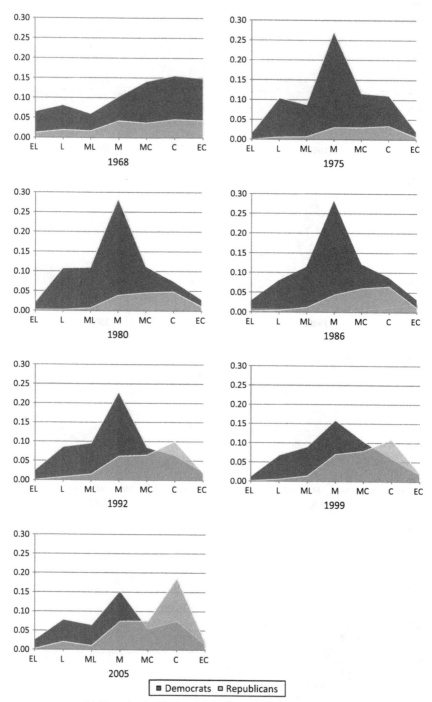

FIGURE 2.9 Ideological Snapshots of the North Carolina Democratic and Republican Parties

the percentage of *extremely conservative* (EC) in each party. The vertical axis on the left indicates the percentage that each point on the distribution contributes to the overall makeup of the party. For example, in the 1975 panel for North Carolina (in Figure 2.9), Democratic moderates (high peak on Democratic distribution) constituted 27.1 percentage of the total Democratic Party identifiers for North Carolina.[9]

Describing Figure 2.8 first, the size of each distribution relative to one another depicts over time that blacks in Louisiana comprise an increasingly greater number of Democratic Party identifiers than do whites and that Republicans comprise an increasingly larger proportion of the total Louisiana electorate relative to Democrats. In terms of ideological transformation, black Louisiana Democrats begin with a pattern of equal distribution across categories in the 1968 panel with a slight skew left, becoming even more positively skewed in the next time frame. This trend is interrupted in the 1980 and 1986 panels, which are characterized by a pattern of moderation and finally a skew slightly to the right during the final two periods. The distribution for white Louisiana Democrats is characterized by an extreme right skew in the 1968 panel. A period of moderation then follows over the next three periods with a decided shift to the left in 1992, a return to moderation in 1999, and then a tilt to the left in 2005. The distribution for Louisiana Republicans begins with a pattern of equal distribution across categories in the 1968 panel with a slight skew right. This pattern is reversed in 1975 with a slight skew left. A period of growth in size and conservative skew begins in 1980 and continues through 2008. In 1968, white conservative Democrats dominated Louisiana's electoral landscape. By 2008, conservative Republicans dominated Louisiana's party landscape, with white and black Democrats occupying similar places on the ideological scale.

For North Carolina, as seen in Figure 2.9, the size of each distribution relative to one another depicts over time that Republicans comprise an equally sizeable proportion of the electorate to Democrats and become an increasingly more conservative party than the Democratic Party. In terms of ideological transformation, North Carolina Democrats begin with a strong skew right and then move into a period characterized by a normal distribution (even if also a smaller portion of the electorate relative to North Carolina Republicans) with a slight skew to the right in 1975 and 1980. By 1986, the right skew is nearly gone, and from 1992 through 2008, the distribution appears normal and the size of the Democratic electorate drops considerably. Thus, the ideological distribution of North Carolina Democrats is one characterized by normality, and the size is considerably smaller in 2008 compared to 1968 relative to North Carolina Republicans.

The ideological transformation of North Carolina Republicans begins with a pattern of somewhat equal distribution across categories with a slight skew right and then becomes even more positively (conservatively) skewed in all subsequent periods, ending in 2008 with a very pronounced right skew. The size of the North Carolina Republican electorate appears to grow independently of the North Carolina Democratic electorate during the 1975, 1980, and 1986 periods (Democratic size does not appear to shrink as Republican size grows), but by 1992 Republican growth appears to coincide with Democratic shrinkage. This pattern continues into 1999 and 2008. The ideological transformation of the North Carolina Republican Party from 1968 to 2008 is one characterized by a sharp rightward skew and considerable growth.

Two important observations can be made from our discussion of ideological transformation. First, the Democratic Party in the South has become decidedly more liberal over time. In the current time period, white Democrats are actually more liberal than black Democrats, one sign that white conservatives and some segment of white moderates now call the Republican Party home. Although it may appear that blacks are a moderating force on the contemporary Democratic Party in the South, it should be emphasized that the movement of blacks en masse into the Democratic Party precipitated a concomitant exit of whites, first conservatives and later moderates. Second, and perhaps most important for our purposes, the examination of the North Carolina and Louisiana electorates demonstrates the uneven nature of the ideological transformation both across time and across parties.

## Conclusion

We demonstrated in this chapter the dramatic political transformation that occurred over the last half-century in the South. Republican Party candidates have become increasingly successful, first at the national level, then the state level, and more recently at the substate level. We then revealed how individual-level identification with the Republican Party has grown over time, although at different rates across the region. In addition, we described the growth in black mobilization from the 1960s until the present, demonstrating how this mobilization varied across the region. Finally, we combined individual-level survey data on race, party identification, and ideology with aggregate-level data on political party registration in the region to create an ideological profile of the Republican and Democratic parties in North Carolina and Louisiana over time. A series of graphical snapshots were presented that revealed the racial composition, ideological position, and relative size of the parties in comparison to one another beginning in the late 1960s, showing an increasingly liberal and shrinking (in terms of total registrants) Democratic Party over time, contrasted with a starkly conservative and growing GOP. We turn now to an examination of the strategic aspects and political implications of this transformation.

| The Strategic Dynamics of Southern Political Change

A REGION ONCE CHARACTERIZED as the "Solid South" because of its consistent and overwhelming support for Democrats at all levels of government has now become the epicenter of twenty-first-century Republicanism. As a unique laboratory for the examination of representation and electoral dynamics in twenty-first-century America, no region has undergone a more dramatic political transformation than the South. The single-party politics in the Democratic "Solid South" has been replaced by an intensely competitive two-party system. Republicans have become increasingly dominant in a region once ruled by Democrats, but this increasing dominance did not prevent Barack Obama from winning three Southern states in a region where blacks were denied the ballot not all that long ago.

The roots of this political transformation extend far deeper than the 1965 passage of the Voting Rights Act (VRA), but this legislation did signal the end of an era in Southern politics. As Black and Black argue, the VRA "was the grand turning point in modern times for the reentry of blacks into Southern politics" (1987, 136). One of the most important suffrage documents in American history, the VRA provided the opportunity for disenfranchised black Southerners to return to the political fold from which they were banished at the end of Reconstruction. Similarly, the VRA was a milestone in the development of the Republican Party in the South. Prior to the passage of the VRA, the South had one post-Reconstruction Republican Senator (John Tower–TX). As is clear from the data presented in the previous chapter, Republicans now hold a majority of Southern Senate seats, House seats, and Governors' mansions. Even at the mass level, the enormous Democratic advantage of sixty years ago—according to the American National Election Studies, Southern Democrats outnumbered their Republican counterparts by a margin of six to one in 1952—has all but disappeared.

As we saw in the previous chapter, growth in white support for the Republican Party did not occur in a vacuum. The region has also witnessed a dramatic and concomitant growth in black political mobilization. What caused the dramatic growth in Southern Republicanism? Why did growth rates for black mobilization vary so substantially across the region? Although these political dynamics share a regional context, the extant literature addressing these questions is distinctive and independent.

## Explaining GOP Growth: Various Variables, Distinct Theories

What caused the dramatic growth in Southern Republicanism? The literature identifies a long list of possibilities. Unfortunately, there is little agreement on the relative importance of the various causal factors or the ways in which the effects of these factors might have interacted. In this regard, Stanley and Castle's assessment of the literature more than two decades ago, is still apt:

> . . . one hallmark of scientific research, cumulative knowledge, has not characterized the study of Southern partisan change. Indeed, scholars disagree not only about the overall trends but also about the impact of the . . . processes capable of producing shifts in Southern partisanship (1988, 240).

Southern Republicanism has grown dramatically over the past sixty years, but this growth was not uniform over time. Early Republican strength was located in the mountain areas (see Key 1949), where support for Republican presidential candidates predates the civil rights era. Other areas in the region did not see significant GOP development until the Reagan years (as we showed in chapter 2). This subregional variation is significant for our purposes, because theories focused on the rise of Southern Republicanism must address not only regionwide growth but also state-level variation in growth and, ideally, substate variation as well.

We do not dispute the contention that transformation of the Democratic Party at the national level—begun during Franklin Roosevelt's administration and culminating during the Johnson administration—played an important role in the drift of conservative white southerners to the Republican Party. The leadership role of conservative Southerners in the national Democratic Party waned during this period, and the demographics of the core Democratic constituency changed as well. The ideological transformation of the national-level Democratic Party does not explain, however, the dramatic variation in Republican growth across the South. If national-level effects are the primary determinant of Republican growth, why did the GOP grow so much more quickly in some states (Tennessee and Virginia) than it did in others (Alabama and Mississippi)? And why did these lagging states catch up (and surpass) the early-growth states by the end of the twentieth century? National-level explanations provide no leverage here.

The difficulty in explaining wide variation in the subregional (and substate) growth in Republicanism poses a significant dilemma for proponents of the national politics or "top-down" explanation of GOP development. One organizationally oriented alternative to the "top-down" perspective is the relatively newer "bottom-up" characterization of Republican growth (see Aldrich 2000). Those who contend that southern Republicanism grew from the bottom point to evidence that suggests *consistent* support for Republican candidates at the state and substate levels actually preceded consistent support for national-level Republicans. Although the evidence that proponents of the bottom-up perspective present is compelling, it is in itself no *explanation* for the dynamic it represents. Even if we are willing to accept that Republican support did grow first from the state and substate levels rather than the national level, we still don't know why it did so. Later in this chapter, we provide an explanation for Republican growth, which, at least in part, rests on a bottom-up dynamic.

Explanations for both regionwide growth and subregional variation in growth in the existing literature have tended to focus on the demographic characteristics of white Southerners from the post-World War II era to the early twenty-first century. In most (but not all) cases, there is a significant demographic shift that favors the modern Republican Party. Still, whether these demographic shifts are of sufficient magnitude (and in the appropriate location) to explain both regional and subregional Republican growth remains an open question.

The demographic dynamic with the most straightforward theoretical impact on Southern Republicanism is white *in-migration* and black *out-migration*. Several studies have suggested that a driving force in the growth of the Republican Party in the South has been the influx of Republican-minded migrants from other regions of the country and the exit of Southern blacks— a consistently Democratic constituency (see Bass and De Vries 1976). The out-migration of blacks—particularly during the decades of the 1950s, 1960s, and 1970s—prevented the relative growth of the Southern black population and, thus, the growth of this component of the Democratic Party in the region. To the extent that this out-migration enabled Republican growth, it will be captured by the variables tapping black context and black mobilization. However, the in-migration of whites from other regions—and most in-migrants have been white (see Scher 1997 and Stanley and Castle 1988)—requires further elaboration.

An increasingly large body of research indicates that the bulk of Southern in-migrants during the past fifty years were white and middle class and, further, these migrants have become integral components of the Southern GOP. Although it is difficult to argue with the contention that in-migration has had some impact on the relative strength of the two major political parties in the South, the magnitude and extent of this effect remains unclear. For example, some suggest that the impact of in-migration on Southern partisanship has ebbed in the last two decades, a period in which the party loyalties of Southerners differed little (and were actually somewhat more Republican) than the party loyalties of Americans in other regions of the country (Stanley 1988). Still others argue that cohort replacement and conversion of existing voters, as opposed to in-migration, explains the growing tendency among Southerners to identify as Republicans (Petrocik 1987). Note that critics of the in-migration thesis were prevalent even during a time when it was still possible to imagine that in-migrants were more Republican than the native population. In the context of current demographic trends—especially the dramatic in-migration of Hispanics—this presumption is difficult, if not impossible, to justify. More specifically, how the in-migration of whites in recent years played a role in increasing GOP identifiers remains unexplained. It is one thing to point to the in-migration of whites as a source of Republican growth during the days of the solidly Democratic South; it is quite another to suggest that a similar dynamic has played out during the last two decades—a period during which the South has been as Republican (if not more so) than the regions from which in-migrants have moved.

Other scholars point to alterations in the region's economy when explaining the increasing popularity of the Republican Party. Historians have long pointed to the transformation of the South's economy beginning in World War II as a watershed event for the region (see Cobb 1999 and Sosna 1987 for a discussion of this event). Highlighting the potential political consequences of this economic transformation, proponents of this class-based explanation of Republican growth argue that it is (1) the growth in Southern wealth (particularly among whites) and (2) the opposition to social welfare programs among middle-class and working-class whites that have made the Republican Party increasingly attractive (Shaffer and Johnston 2006).

The potential for this type of transformation and its associated effect on party politics was noted by Key (1949). Key mentioned the possible political ramifications associated with what he termed as the *dilution* of the region's agricultural economy. Key stated that a natural outgrowth of this economic transformation would include "industrial and financial interests that have a fellow feeling with northern Republicanism" (1949, 674), thus creating a stronger, and in some ways, more natural linkage between Southerners and the GOP. More recently, Shafer and Johnston (2001, 2006) credit economic development as the driving engine behind partisan change in the Southern legislative delegations and among white southerners more generally. Proponents of the economic school argue:

> Accordingly, if the white South still represents by far the larger share of Southern voters, as it does, and if it represents the entire population of those shifting to the Republican Party, given the monolithic partisan character of black Southerners, then it must be *economic development and class politics* that claim the lead role in transforming the political order of the South (Shafer and Johnston 2006, 178, emphasis added).

There is little question that both support for the Republican Party in the region and major economic changes have occurred simultaneously over the past fifty years. The presence of these regionwide dynamics, however, obscures state-level patterns that are very difficult to reconcile with class-based explanations of two-party growth. Figure 3.1 is a scatterplot of the positions of each of the eleven Southern states based on (1) economic growth (in terms of per capita income) from 1960 to 2008 and (2) growth in support for the Republican Party over the same period. Income is a crucial indicator of economic conditions for proponents of class-based explanations of Republican growth. According to Figure 3.1, there does not appear to be any evidence of a positive relationship between income and Republican growth during the time when such growth was the most prevalent. If anything, Republican growth was actually somewhat stronger in those states where income actually grew *at a slower pace*. Although one cannot with certainty rule out this causal linkage, it is apparently not a straightforward task to empirically demonstrate the relationship between economic factors and Republican strength.

Scholars studying the intersection of religion and politics provide an additional demographic explanation for the growth of southern Republicanism among conservative whites. They note that evangelicalism has grown dramatically over the past fifty years, and white evangelical Protestants have become increasingly more likely to identify with, and vote for, the GOP (see Kellstedt 1989; Green et al. 1996; and Green et al. 1998). Individual-level survey data indicate that white evangelicals are more likely than those of other religious traditions to hold conservative views, especially in regard to

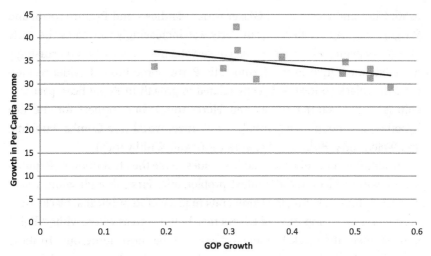

FIGURE 3.1 Income Change and GOP Growth

social issues (Wilcox 2000). Over the last several decades, evangelicals have become increasingly drawn to the Republican Party, identified as the standard-bearer for social conservatism. Specific evidence of this trend is plentiful. For example, white evangelicals comprised half (50 percent) of the combined Republican vote for Presidential contests in the 1990s (Green et al. 1998). In the pivotal 1994 congressional elections, three-quarters of this group (75 percent) voted Republican. In the same year, white evangelicals comprised a plurality of the GOP, making up 30 percent of Republican Party identifiers nationwide (Green et al. 1996).

The attachment of white evangelicals to the Republican Party, especially in the South, is difficult to ignore. However, the empirical connection between evangelicalism and the growth of Republicanism, at either the regional level or the subregional level, remains unclear. There is a plausible case for the role of evangelical attachment in the growth of the Republican Party in the South, but actual evidence of this relationship is, at best, quite limited.

Finally, a full understanding of party politics in the South depends upon an appreciation for the role that race has played and continues to play in the region. For many years, white conservatism was directly related to the size of the black population. As proximity to blacks increased, the racial threat perceived by whites increased. This dynamic, what Key (1949) called the "black-belt hypothesis," resulted in greater support for conservative candidates in areas with proportionately more blacks. A number of subsequent analyses uncovered evidence that supports this hypothesis (see Aistrup 1996; Black 1976; Black 1978; Giles 1977; Giles and Buckner 1993, 1996; Giles and Evans

1986; Giles and Hertz 1994; Glaser 1994; Matthews and Prothro 1966; and Wright 1977). As the Republican Party was increasingly viewed as the party of conservatism—especially racial conservatism—it became an increasingly desirable alternative to the Democratic Party. Some limited evidence indicates that black context is directly related to growth in Republican partisanship (see, for example, Giles and Hertz 1994), but support for the Key hypothesis, although substantial, is not unequivocal (see Combs, Hibbing, and Welch 1984; Bullock 1985; Voss 1996; and Whitby 1985).

In addition, a number of practical issues make the attribution of Republican growth to black racial context problematic. First, though white voters may have stopped voting for Democrats in place of Republicans, blacks were overwhelmingly supportive of Democrats. In those areas where white "flight" is most likely, the black Democratic base will be most numerous. In these same areas then, there is both a very real ceiling placed on potential Republican support and a very real floor placed on the loss of Democratic support. It should be noted as well that GOP growth has come during a time when the size of the Southern black population has fallen. How is it possible then to attribute substantial Republican growth to black context when the relative size of the black population has not increased and in some areas has experienced a relative decline? We return to these issues later in the chapter.

## Understanding Black Mobilization

The South provides a unique laboratory for the examination of participation in early twenty-first-century democracy. A crucial component of the transformation of Southern politics is the mobilization of African Americans, a population long excluded from participation in electoral politics. In a place where they could not even vote little more than a generation ago, African Americans are becoming the cornerstone of Democratic electoral victories. Ironically, the party that for so many years prevented African Americans from playing any role in Southern politics now depends on African American votes for its success.

In 1868, the ratification of the Fifteenth Amendment enfranchised African American males. During the Reconstruction years (which lasted less than decade), African Americans played an integral role in Southern House and Senate elections. In fact, the very first African American representatives and senators were elected from Southern states during this time period, and these legislators were Republicans. But the end of Reconstruction, which followed the Hayes-Tilden election of 1876, devastated African American political ambitions. Following Reconstruction, the Southern states quickly erected barriers to political mobilization—poll taxes, literacy and understanding tests, white primaries, and outright terrorism—and effectively disenfranchised much of the African American population until the passage of the VRA.[1]

The 1965 passage of the VRA clearly marked the end of an era in Southern politics. The VRA was one of the most important suffrage documents in American history because it provided the opportunity for disenfranchised African American Southerners to return to the political fold from which they were banished at the end of Reconstruction. As Black and Black argue, "[t]he Voting Rights Act was the grand turning point in modern times for the reentry of blacks into Southern politics" (1987, 136).

We do not discount the impact of the passage of the VRA on African American registration rates, but it is obvious from the briefest examination of the raw data that the rates at which registration rolls grew varied greatly from state to state. One reason we see such distinctive growth patterns is that individual states have very different rules for determining who can register to vote, where they can register, and what they must do to register. Even after the elimination of regionwide obstacles to registration, such as poll taxes and literacy tests, some states have significantly more restrictive registration requirements than others. Important structural differences include residency requirements, the number of days prior to an election that an individual must register to vote, purging requirements, the number of official registration sites, and felony disenfranchisement, to name a few. These types of structural factors influence the registration rates of the general population (see Knack 1995), and we expect to find similar types of influence for African American registration in the South.[2]

Although some evidence suggests that the growth trend in African American registration began prior to 1965 (see Timpone 1995), there is no doubt that the African American electorate in the South has grown exponentially since the passage of the VRA. However, both (1) the rate of growth and (2) the level of mobilization vary markedly among the Southern states. In a few Southern states—such as Virginia and North Carolina—a significant number of African Americans were registered to vote prior to the passage of the VRA. In others, the percentage of African Americans registered to vote was less than 20 percent. Today, African Americans in some Southern states have the highest registration rates of any racial/ethnic group. In other states, African American registration rates lag far behind.[3]

We know that registering to vote is one of the least costly forms of formal political activity and, not surprisingly, it is also one of the most common. To the extent that voter registration is an entrée to more costly forms of political activity, data on registration rates give us a reasonable indication of the upper bounds of the politically mobilized population within a state. Because poorly or inadequately mobilized populations are less likely to achieve their political goals than effectively mobilized populations, differences in political mobilization have important political implications (particularly for traditionally underrepresented populations), so it is important to understand what factors influence mobilization rates.

Individual-level models of political participation tend to focus on "resource-based" approaches to explaining registration and voting. Demographic factors such as age, education, income, and occupation—socioeconomic status (SES) variables—often correlate highly with registration and voting (see Verba and Nie 1972; Bennett and Bennett 1986; Conway 2000; and Wolfinger and Rosenstone 1980). The relationship between SES and voting also holds for African Americans (Tate 1991).[4] It is important to note that there is some disagreement about the specific causal relationship between SES and voting. Some argue that a direct relationship between SES and participation exists, whereas others contend that SES influences participation only indirectly, by influencing the extent to which citizens have "civic skills" (see Brady, Verba, and Schlozman 1995 and Verba, Schlozman, and Brady 1995 for a description of this debate). Nevertheless, no one seriously argues that SES does not play a role in the individual-level choice process regarding political participation.

Although standard mobilization models based on education, income, and political knowledge provide some leverage for explaining black mobilization, other group-oriented factors are equally, if not more, important (see, in particular, Leighley 2001 and Harris, Sinclair-Chapman, and McKenzie 2005). More specifically, there is evidence that African American turnout is influenced by *black political empowerment* and *social isolation*.[5]

Proponents of the empowerment thesis argue that demonstrable evidence of African American political influence will result in increased black mobilization (see Bobo and Gilliam 1990 and Browning, Marshall, and Tabb 1984). The standard indicator of African American political influence is the election of black officials, and there is evidence that the number of elected black officials is positively related to the level of political action in the African American community (Bobo and Gilliam 1990; Harris, Sinclair-Chapman, and McKenzie 2005; Leighley 2001; and Tate 1991).

Social isolation, on the other hand, tends to inhibit black political mobilization. Rather than focusing solely on individual circumstances (such as personal income or unemployment), social isolation theorists argue that negative economic and social circumstances within the African American community more broadly inhibit black political activity. Factors such as rising income inequality in the black populace, rates of unemployment, and the extent to which the African American community is victimized by crime (in the aggregate) constrain black mobilization even after controlling for individual-level circumstances. As in the case of the empowerment hypothesis, there is also empirical support for the effect of social isolation on black mobilization (Cohen and Dawson 1993; Dawson 1994; Harris 1999; and Harris, Sinclair-Chapman, and McKenzie 2005).

Recent work by Harris, Sinclair-Chapman, and McKenzie (2005) suggests that both political empowerment and social isolation influence black mobilization, but they also note that the dynamics that drive black mobilization (and broader political participation) vary considerably across regions. In particular, the dynamics driving black mobilization in the South are distinct from those driving black mobilization in the rest of the country. While political empowerment tends to matter far more in the South, social isolation has a far larger impact in the remaining states (Harris, Sinclair-Chapman, and McKenzie 2005). The distinctiveness of these results leads us to wonder if the model of black mobilization in the South is incomplete.

We must also wonder about the extent to which empowerment, in particular, is a useful explanation for one of the (if not *the*) foundational components of political mobilization—voter registration. Growth in the number of African American elected officials might reasonably lead to an increase in African American voter registration, turnout, and a variety of more demanding political activities. If the electoral manifestations of empowerment (in the form of black elected officials) produce an increased sense of efficacy, then greater political mobilization may well follow.

But then what explains the black mobilization that provided the constituency for the African American elected officials in the first place? Especially in the Southern context, the election of African Americans has depended upon the mobilization of African American voters. From that perspective, black voter registration must be viewed as a *cause* of the increase in the number of African American elected officials (and empowerment) rather than a by-product of this electoral success. Below, we consider the possibility that the dramatic growth in southern Republicanism and black mobilization are not independent phenomena.

## *The Theory of* Relative Advantage

Existing research fails to address a number of substantive questions. In particular, there is an incomplete understanding of the extent to which the *mobilization* of Southern blacks (as Democrats)—and not just the presence of large concentrations of blacks in the "black-belt" region (see Giles and Hertz 1994)—fostered an increase in Republican voting behavior. African American mobilization influenced roll-call voting patterns of both House and Senate members from the region (Hood and Morris 1998 and Hood, Kidd, and Morris 1999); did this mobilization also (albeit indirectly) bolster Republican ranks? What is lacking is a theory that provides an integrated, politically meaningful explanation of the two most dramatic and important changes in the Southern political landscape over the past half-century:

1. The growth of Southern Republicanism, and
2. The mobilization of the African American electorate.

Crucially, neither of these growth dynamics has occurred uniformly across the South; not only has there been considerable state-level variation in the growth of each of these populations, but there has also been considerable variation in the substate growth. A useful theory should explain not only the growth in these populations—it should also explain the variation in growth across the South. In the following section, we propose a theory that provides an explanation for the concomitant growth of each of these politically crucial factors. We begin by focusing on a novel explanation for Republican growth.

## The Growth of Southern Republicanism

There is good reason to accept the contention that the increasingly liberal orientation of the national Democratic Party on the issue of civil rights clearly engendered the dissatisfaction of conservative white Southern Democrats within their own party. But while national party dynamics may have provided the initial impetus for the regionwide growth of Republican voting behavior (see Black and Black 1987, 2002 and Carmines and Stimson 1989), it is also obvious that the rate of growth varied considerably among the states, and such variance cannot be explained by national party politics alone.

To explain subregional differences in Republican growth, previous work focused on a variety of disparate demographic and economic factors, such as in-migration, economic growth and transformation, the waning significance of agriculture, religious conservatism, and racial context among others.[6] Although it is often necessary in social science research to employ demographic variables as proxies for political phenomena, we would argue that a greater effort needs to be undertaken in Southern politics to incorporate more precise measures of theoretically salient political correlates. Continuing along this train of thought, we develop a set of models to directly test the supposition that the variation in Republican growth in the South is fundamentally a by-product of political change.

We argue that the engines of Southern Republican growth over the last sixty years were (1) the waning usefulness of the Democratic Party for the procurement of political and economic resources and the expression of white racial conservatism, and (2) the increasing electoral viability of GOP candidates in the South. In essence, Southern Republicanism grew because the differential change in the benefits of voting and identification with the Republican Party for whites, in comparison to Democratic affiliation, increased.[7] So, from a political standpoint, the *relative advantage* of the Republican Party with respect to the Democratic Party increased over this time period.

The reader might reasonably suggest that this contention is nothing more than a tautology; of course the Republican Party grew because membership in that party was increasingly more valuable than membership in the Democratic Party. This would be an accurate criticism if we were unable to explain the shift in the relative attractiveness of the parties, but these explanations are, of course, key aspects of our theory. In their work *Party Systems and Voter Alignments*, Lipset and Rokkan (1967) provide a useful framework for discussing social cleavages and a possible association with relative advantage theory. Especially relevant for the present study is the idea that various cleavage structures can lead to certain advantages for a specific party, relative to another party or parties (see, for example, Sundquist 1983). Although not all cleavages may relate to the concept of relative advantage, the racial dichotomy in the South certainly produced a context in which a defunct Republican Party once again became a viable alternative in the wake of the political disturbance brought about by the enfranchisement of blacks in the region (Katz 2001).

The idea of relative advantage encompasses more than the notion of transformative partisan cleavages. Transformation also requires a catalyst, and this catalyst often takes the form of policy orientations and/or ideological positions related to existing political structures. Citizens identify with and vote for candidates of political parties for a variety of reasons. Among the factors that influence peoples' decisions to support one party or the other are (1) the relative competitiveness of the party in a wide variety of political arenas, and (2) the relative consistency of each party's political objectives with a citizen's own political objectives. In the Southern context, Republican

Party support (relative to Democratic Party support) became more valuable because

1. Republicans were fielding increasing numbers of candidates for political office at all levels, causing the traditional Democratic Party monopoly over party nominations to dissipate; and
2. The mobilization of the black population—what quickly became an almost uniformly Democratic electorate—made it increasingly difficult for Southern conservative whites to maintain control of the local Democratic Party machinery. As the local Democratic Party became more difficult to control, the party apparatus became less valuable.

A viable Republican Party is a relatively new aspect of Southern politics. One of Key's (1949) primary criticisms of the Southern party system of his time was the absence of active and significant two-party competition in the region. Key hypothesized that it was this decided lack of interparty competition that, in turn, stunted the development of viable party organizations in the region.[8] During the last four decades, however, the Southern GOP has become an organizational equal of, and sometimes superior to, the Democratic Party in the region (see, for example, Maggioto and Wekkin 2000). During Key's time, the absence of party competition led to an elite-dominated political system, and Key is clear about the economic implications of this elite-dominated, one-party system: It favored the "haves" (Key 1949). So, for southern elites (especially the most conservative ones), the Democratic Party was not just the only game in town (or, more formally, the only viable political vehicle), it was also an efficient mechanism for translating political control into a stream of substantial economic resources.

From our perspective, the increasing viability of the Republican Party during the 1960s and early 1970s hastened the demise of Democratic dominance for two reasons: First, it provided an alternative political outlet. Second, two-party competition cut into the economic advantages enjoyed by Democratic elites during the era of one-party politics. The initial viability of Republican Party candidates alone is not likely to be a sufficient rationale for a wholesale shift away from the Democratic Party if white conservatives could maintain control of the Democratic Party. White conservatives could not, however, maintain control of the Democratic Party because of the strongly Democratic orientation of a large and newly mobilized population: African Americans.

We argue that white voters reacted not to black context, as during the pre-civil rights era, but instead to black mobilization. Since the passage of the

VRA, the mobilization of Southern African Americans has been extensive (Grofman, Griffin, and Glazer 1992), and there is evidence that this mobilization has had systemic political implications (Hood, Kidd, and Morris 1999). Initially, Southern conservatives opposed the development of the Republican Party. However, once disenfranchised black voters returned to the political arena, Southern conservatives shifted strategies and began to build a local Republican Party that would serve as an organized political alternative to the Democratic Party, which was increasingly the party of choice for African Americans (see Aistrup 1996; Aldrich and Griffin 2000; Maggioto and Wekkin 2000; and Rhodes 2000). As blacks moved into the Democratic Party in significant numbers, conservative white Southerners were forced to seek another vehicle for their political ambitions and objectives.

Some may view this hypothesized role of African American mobilization in Republican growth as a modern variant of Key's black-belt hypothesis. There are, however, important conceptual differences between Key's group-threat perspective and our relative advantage orientation. First, even if we accept the "threat" perspective, the nature of the threat is dramatically different. Key was writing during a time when blacks were structurally excluded from participating in electoral politics, so he was not referring to an electoral threat. Key's black-belt hypothesis depended on the fear of violence and/or the loss of the existing social order (Jim Crow). Key also focused on a latent threat; to the extent the mobilized black population was viewed as a threat, it was active. The black-belt hypothesis also provided no explanation for the hypothesized relationship between the viability of the Republican Party and the subsequent growth of the Republican Party. Our relative advantage perspective then is clearly different from Key's black-belt hypothesis.

Scholars have been preoccupied with the pattern of two-party emergence in the South for at least forty years. One prominent theory posits that two-party competition in the region began as a product of support for Republican presidential candidates (see Lamis 1988 or Aistrup 1996 for support of this theory of party change). Success at the presidential level then *filtered down* to statewide offices (i.e., governor, U.S. senator), which, in turn, led to increased levels of voting for GOP congressional candidates. Finally, this *top-down* process culminated in GOP viability at the substate level (i.e., state legislative seats). In *The Rise of Southern Republicans*, Black and Black (2002) highlight the importance of presidential campaigns, especially Reagan's, in producing a realignment at the congressional level in the region. Likewise, other research has uncovered a link between GOP state party election strategies and recruiting candidates to run in legislative districts with a tendency to vote for Republican presidential candidates (Bullock and Shafer 1997).

Recently, however, Aldrich (2000) and Aldrich and Griffin (2000) have challenged the *top-down* theory of party change in the region. Using a series of Granger causality tests, these studies demonstrated that GOP electoral successes at the national level are a direct product of, or are caused by, prior victories at the state level. Likewise, success in state legislative races was a precursor to winning U.S. House elections, so there is evidence that state GOP party-building efforts were the result of a highly complex process operating at multiple levels.

As theorized, state-level Republican Party strength relative to that of the Democratic Party is in part associated with the ability of the GOP to offer an alternative platform for the nomination and election of candidates to pursue policy objectives. The mechanisms of interparty competition are paramount for explaining the rise of the GOP in the South. Given the prior emphasis on, and disagreement about, Republican Party formation in the postwar South, it is imperative that we properly model this political dynamic at work. The theory of relative advantage leads us to expect a strong positive relationship between GOP organizational strength in the South and *subsequent* GOP growth. In subsequent chapters, we test this hypothesis.

## Black Political Mobilization

We can also extend our relative advantage perspective to the rise of black mobilization. Today, African American support for the Democratic Party, particularly in the South, is so overwhelming that we can provide little new insight into the choice between parties. However, as the conservatism of the traditional southern Democratic Party wanes, the value of mobilization in support of the Democratic Party increases. Let us assume, as we did for conservative whites, that the goals of African Americans are (1) maximizing the stream of economic benefits associated with party membership and (2) the achievement of public policy goals. Given these goals, we expect mobilization in support of the Democratic Party to vary by the likelihood that African Americans will play a significant leadership role in the party. The extent to which African Americans are in a position to lead or control a state or local party is primarily a function of the relative size of (1) the actual black segment of the Democratic Party and (2) the potential black component of the Democratic Party. If this is the case, then future African American mobilization should be a function of the following factors:

1. The relative size of the current black mobilized population,
2. The relative size of the black population, and
3. Recent Republican growth.

Note that the effect of Republican growth should vary across states and subregions in the South. More specifically, Republican growth will have the greatest impact on black mobilization in those areas in which black concentrations are highest. The obvious question is "Why?" The relative advantage perspective suggests an answer. If black mobilization is a function of the potential political (and economic) benefits associated with group mobilization, then we would naturally expect black mobilization to be a function of black context.

All else being equal, African Americans are more likely to mobilize in states where they make up a third of the population (such as Mississippi) than in states where they make up less than 15 percent of the population (Tennessee). In the first case, a mobilized and cohesive African American voting bloc is in a position to control/dominate the Democratic Party once a sufficient number of conservative whites leave for the Republican Party. In the latter case, the relatively small size of the African American population makes it difficult to imagine a scenario in which a *competitive* Democratic Party would be dominated by an African American voting coalition. There is little reason in such a scenario then to expect a relationship between GOP growth and black mobilization. In the former case, one would clearly expect GOP growth to boost black mobilization. As conservative whites exit the Democratic Party, African Americans come ever closer to solidifying control of it. Given this dynamic, relative advantage theory leads us to expect to find the following:

1. A significant, positive relationship between GOP growth and black mobilization in those states (and substate areas) in which the size of the black population is relatively large, and
2. No relationship between GOP growth and black mobilization in those states (and substate areas) in which the size of the black population is relatively small.

The key issue is, of course, the conceptualization and operationalization of *large* and *small*. Focusing solely on black/white context for the moment, if we assume a 70/30 split (70 percent Republicans/30 percent Democrats) for whites, a cohesive African American voting bloc that is 23 percent or more of the mobilized population would be sufficiently large to control the Democratic Party. If the split leans more toward the Republican Party, the percentage of African American voters required to dominate the Democratic Party declines. Note, however, if the white partisan split is too favorable to the Republican Party, the Democratic Party is no longer able to provide competition. Given a cut-point in the low 20 percent range, this suggests that we should expect to see GOP growth affect black mobilization in a certain group of Southern states—the Deep South—and we should expect to see no state-level GOP effect on black mobilization in the Rim South (see Hood, Kidd, and Morris 2008 for a more detailed discussion of this derivation). Using this operationalization, we can test both these hypotheses, and we do so in chapter 8.

## Conclusion

As we have seen in earlier research of the late twentieth-century South, political factors begat political change well into the twenty-first century (Hood, Kidd, and Morris 2004). Although there is no doubt that regional in-migration and economic transformation were ongoing phenomena during the period of time under study, these factors—along with other demographic variables such as black context and evangelicalism—do not appear to have a consistent effect on the growth of Southern Republicanism over the analyzed time period. We find no reason to believe then that economic or demographic change alone, however profound, would have broken the long-held constant in Southern politics of one-party Democratic dominance, absent political changes. We have also provided a new explanation for the two most significant components of the modern transformation of Southern politics: (1) the growth of the GOP and (2) the political mobilization of African Americans. Without empirical verification, our theory remains just that. To what extent do the data support the theory of relative advantage as a means for providing an explanation for political changes in the South? Before answering this question, we undertake a detailed historical examination of the Virginia and Georgia Republican Parties during the pivotal period of the mid-twentieth century.

CHAPTER 4 | ## Relative Advantage in Action
*Case Studies in the Evolution of Republican
State Parties in the South*

THIS CHAPTER PROVIDES TWO detailed case studies that examine the evolution of the Republican Party in Virginia and Georgia during the pivotal period leading up to, and during, the civil rights era. The focus of these case studies is on the search for historical evidence of the theory of *relative advantage* as it relates to the transformation of party politics in these two states.

To date, there has been little scholarly research that has sought to chronicle the history of Republican state parties in a detailed and systematic fashion. We hope to bridge this gap by taking an in-depth look at various aspects of the development of these two state parties that includes leadership, issue positions and platforms, congruity with the national party, and the specific coalitions that comprise party membership over time. By performing a chronological examination of state political parties, we should be able to unearth specific trends or transformational events, and from these create a logical narrative of political change.

In order to gain some insight into the political transformation of the party systems in these two states, we relied on a number of primary source materials. Chief among these were state papers of record. For the Virginia case study, we principally utilized the *Richmond Times-Dispatch* and for Georgia, the *Atlanta Journal*, along with other newspapers from both these states. Newspapers provide an excellent historical record of the 1950s and 1960s as events were painstakingly covered by print journalists. Hundreds of articles were examined in order to develop a general picture or bird's eye view of party politics in these two states. Quotations or documentation of specific historical events drawn from these news accounts are cited in the endnotes section for this chapter.

Other primary source documents pertaining to the state parties or electoral politics were also collected from the Richard B. Russell Library for Political Research and Studies at the University of Georgia, the Robert W. Woodruff Archives Library in Atlanta, and the Library of Virginia. *The Virginia News Letter*, currently housed at the Weldon Cooper Center for Public Service at the University of Virginia, was another primary source for the Virginia case study.

In addition to newspapers and archival sources, we also relied on other primary source data when possible, including in-person interviews with two early operatives of the Republican Party. Former Republican governor Linwood Holton was interviewed for the Virginia case study, and former U.S. congressman and Georgia gubernatorial candidate Howard "Bo" Callaway was interviewed for the Georgia case study. Finally, secondary sources, primarily books, were also used in an attempt to create the most complete picture possible of this period of history.

## *The Development of the Republican Party in the* Old Dominion

In his classic study of Southern politics, Key (1949) notes that besides the presidential Republicans, there was another breed of Republican called the mountain Republicans. Mountain Republicans existed in concentrated numbers large enough in three states, Virginia being one of them, to have the foundations of a viable competing political party.[1] Virginia's southwestern congressional district was regularly the scene of competitive elections between Republicans and Democrats, and when Republican presidential candidates won landslide elections, their coattails were occasionally long enough to help Republicans down ticket in the Shenandoah Valley and Tidewater regions of the state.

However, Key notes that outside of Virginia's southwestern congressional district where they were considered by Democrats to be "fighters" (hence the term the "fighting ninth"), Republicans were more often than not thought of as a mere faction of the Byrd organization, frequently entering the Democratic primaries to vote for the Byrd organization's anointed candidates. Republicans were philosophically different enough from Democrats that they did not want to become Democrats, but ideologically concerned enough that they often voted in the Democratic primaries for the more conservative candidate. This distinction is important to understanding the development of the Republican Party in Virginia. Indeed, one could not adequately understand the development of the Republican Party in Virginia during the 1950s and 1960s without having at least a cursory understanding of Virginia's Democratic Party between the 1930s and 1960s, and in particular the Byrd organization led by Harry F. Byrd, Sr.

Key described the Byrd organization (or machine) as a political oligarchy rooted in Virginia's rich history of political organizations with several minor regional factions thrown into the mix. The machine had two well-defined ideological factions that functioned almost like a two-party system within a single party. The dominant faction—called the "organization"—ruled the party with something akin to a soft fist, requiring political aspirants to travel a well-marked path with multiple opportunities to express fealty to Senator Byrd, the leader. The organization's ideological tilt was toward the conservative—on fiscal issues, race, and in relation to the federal government.

The opposition within the Byrd organization was relatively weak and often unable to win in primary races against organization candidates. The "anti-organization," as they were known, was often more progressive on fiscal issues (willing to support tax increases especially to fund public services), critical of the poll tax as a limit on democracy, and more open to support from and interaction with the federal government. When an anti-organization candidate did manage to successfully challenge the organization, such as with James H. Price's election as governor in 1937, the organization's strong hold on the General Assembly ensured that the result would not alter the status quo too much (Dabney 1971).

Into this political and ideological landscape the Republican Party had to fit and eventually grow. But the path was not easy, and there were many setbacks along the way. The division between the organization and the anti-organization within the Democratic Party ultimately provided a strategic opportunity for the Republicans. However, the going was not always easy. Unable to effectively challenge the Byrd organization at the best of times, Virginia Republicans often found themselves in internal strife—sometimes more intense and other times less so—that made matters worse. Conflict often centered on the choice for party chairman, but the internal strife was not solely about parochial control of the party leadership. By the early 1950s, new blood and a new generation of Republicans were beginning to challenge the old guard. A debate about the direction of the party began in earnest in the 1950s and ultimately played an important role in the direction the party took relative to black voters after 1964 (Vogt 1978 and Atkinson 1992).

The nomination battle between Ohio Senator Howard Taft and General Dwight Eisenhower in 1951 and 1952 exposed the rift between the old guard and the new blood in a dramatic way. The old guard was staunchly conservative and supported Taft, and they controlled the nominating apparatus of the party. For the most part, they were also resigned to the Republican Party's role in Virginia as little more than a toothless alternative to the Democratic Party at best and simply an adjunct of the Byrd organization at worst

(Atkinson 1992). The new blood, on the other hand, wanted a Republican Party that could stand as a credible alternative to the Democrats, and they saw the Eisenhower candidacy as a way to do that by attracting both new participants to the political process and Democratic converts.

The Taft-Eisenhower contest was fought both openly and by proxy across the state in mass meetings as the old guard faced challenges for city and district chairmanships from the young blood and at the state level for party chair. It resulted in a split delegation going to Chicago for the Republican convention in 1952, but with the majority of votes going to Eisenhower. This was by far the most active GOP nominating process in Virginia history up to that point, and out of it came a new level of interest in, and enthusiasm for, the Republican Party. Out of it also came a new leader—one of the young bloods—named Ted Dalton. Dalton clearly had his mind set on growing the party, and he had an idea about how to do it. In describing what he and his followers wanted for the Virginia Republican Party, Dalton said, "We also want to bring harmony to and unify the party, to build good will, and to attract new members. We will seek to bring in independents and former Democrats" (quoted in Vogt 1978, 263).

Dalton carried the momentum generated during the 1952 presidential race into a run for governor in 1953. He assembled a geographically balanced ticket of like-minded new-blood Republicans who aimed to offer a progressive alternative to the Byrd organization. The Dalton-led ticket got respect. An editorial in the *Richmond Times-Dispatch* offered almost heretofore unheard-of praise for a Republican statewide ticket:

> . . . the GOP has nominated three absolutely first-rate men . . . from the top ranks of Virginia citizenship. In ability, personality, and character they can match the three Democrats who are opposing them. . . . It bids fair to be the most important interparty contest for statewide office held in Virginia during this century.[2]

The Republicans offered an aggressive and progressive alternative to the Byrd organization ticket of Democrats, calling for general electoral reform including repeal of the poll tax, improvements to public education with the creation of a community college system, and many other initiatives focused on improving or expanding public services to Virginians. Indeed, it was this very progressivism on public services that cost Republicans the election. Among Dalton's many proposals was a bond package for highway construction. To many, this proposal sounded like risky financing by debt, and it represented a departure from the pay-as-you-go approach to highways that was the hallmark of the Byrd organization (Heinemann 1996).

Although Dalton and his ticket lost in 1953, they had a much stronger run than any Republican ticket in memory, and their progressive Republicanism represented a stark contrast to the old-guard Republican politics. Four years later in 1957, however, Dalton's second effort at the governor's mansion proved more difficult, and the progressive message played to a much less receptive audience. The reason for this was the Byrd organization's response to the 1954 *Brown v. Board* decision, a response known as "massive resistance."

When the 1954 decision was handed down by the U.S. Supreme Court, the response from the Byrd organization was initially mild disapproval, but over two years, that mild response turned into legislation in 1956 that resulted in school closings across the Commonwealth in 1958. It was a calculated move on the part of the Byrd organization that had a wide degree of support across Virginia, but most especially in Southside and rural Virginia (Heinemann 1996). As Wilkinson notes, it was Virginia's issue of the century; however, it also marked the last grasps at total control of the Commonwealth by the Byrd organization and ultimately ushered in a new political direction for the state (1968). With Dalton having run such a strong campaign for governor in 1953, Republicans were eager to have him run again in 1957. He hesitated, though, unsure how to handle the massive resistance issue. Ultimately, however, he did run, and he ran hard against massive resistance. Republican disunity on how to handle the issue of desegregation and the emotionally powerful anti-integration campaign run by Democrats resulted in a huge Democratic win.

Within two years of their huge win, having ridden the wave of anti-integration, Democrats backed down. Governor J. Lindsay Almond Jr., Dalton's opponent in 1957, announced in a January 1959 speech before the General Assembly that he was abandoning massive resistance. Seeing the inevitable coming, Dalton claimed the moral high ground for Republicans: "Virginia's Republicans have faced the facts. We told the truth when it hurt, but in the long run the people will remember we stood for right at all times regardless of the political costs."[3] Despite the turn of events, by 1959 Republicans seemed to be in no better shape than they had been a decade earlier. They felt the political consequences of massive resistance acutely, having borne the brunt of the Dalton and Eisenhower "liberal" position on desegregation. As a result, conservatives had little reason to gravitate toward the Republican Party, and the party itself seemed in disarray. Yet, the ultimate demise of massive resistance also produced a new reality for Democrats and the Byrd organization, one that would prove impossible to control (Atkinson 1992).

Having nowhere to go but up, Republicans began thinking strategically as they entered the 1961 gubernatorial campaign season. The opposition within the Democratic Party had put forward a whole slate of candidates to run against the Byrd organization's candidates. Democrats were clearly dealing with some discord, and Republican leaders wanted to await the outcome of the Democratic intraparty contest before completing their ticket. The thinking among Republicans was that, if the anti-organization slate won the Democratic primary, Republicans would have a chance of picking up Byrd conservatives by nominating conservative Republicans. In the end, however, the Byrd organization-backed slate won, and Republican plans for offering conservative Democrats an alternative choice were dashed. Nevertheless, the idea of picking off conservative Democrats by offering them a more conservative Republican ticket had taken root (Atkinson 1992).

A new crop of conservative Republicans began to push the party to the right in the early 1960s. Spurred on by new leaders like Richard D. Obenshain, the Republican Party began to extend a welcoming hand to conservative Democrats, a welcoming hand that represented a strategic move. Republican prospects, an increasingly large number of people believed, were better housed in conservatism consistent with that of the national Republican Party than in the progressivism represented by Dalton's two gubernatorial runs (Atkinson 1992). Obenshain articulated this view and the relative advantage for conservative Democrats in a 1963 letter to the editor of *The Richmond News Leader*. Arguing that the right home for conservatives was the Republican Party, Obenshain then went on to address the question of the role of Democrats:

> The News Leader recently suggested that this union of Southern conservatives might be prevented because we Republicans would be unwilling to surrender positions of party leadership to 'apostate Democrats.' Such a reluctance would have been true even in the recent past, but the leadership of the Republican party in the South is passing to the younger men, most of them motivated by an intense concern for the ultimate conservative victory. Instead of rebuffing Democrats, we have consistently welcomed all new Republicans—if anything, we accord higher honor to those who have the courage to break with the Democratic label and thus lead the transformation to a Republican South.[4]

In short, seeing the direction in which both the Democratic and Republican parties in Virginia and across the South were going, Obenshain was arguing to Democrats that there was a relative advantage to their crossing over and joining the Republicans: the opportunity to lead a transformation in Southern politics.

However, the leadership of the Republican Party that Obenshain referenced was not in complete agreement as to the direction the party should take. Nationally in 1963 and 1964, Republicans were debating their course via the candidacies of conservative Senator Barry Goldwater of Arizona and moderate-liberal Governor of New York Nelson Rockefeller. In Virginia, the debate was similar: Would Virginia Republicans do better by working toward a realignment in the form of a conservative coalition with Byrd Democrats or by adhering to their historical roots as a progressive and nonsegregationist party? By 1964, and with Lyndon Johnson's landslide victory serving as the backdrop, the strategic fork in the road was becoming clearer to Virginia Republicans. But Virginia's black voters also had a strategic choice to make at this time.

For Republicans, there were two viable options. The first option was to tack to the right and go after the conservative Democrats associated with the Byrd organization and the growing suburban populations. The key architect of this option, Richard D. Obenshain, had plenty of support within the party, including Virginia's only Republican members of Congress, Richard Poff who had represented the Sixth District in southwest Virginia since 1952 and Joel Broyhill who had represented the Eleventh District in northern Virginia since 1953. Poff and Broyhill were also the only Republicans to have signed the Southern Manifesto in 1956 opposing racial integration in public places. Both were representative of a new breed of conservative Southern Republicans elected in the 1950s and interested in smaller government, lower taxes, and, by extension, continued segregation.

The rationale for the conservative approach had two primary lines of argument. The first was that the moderate progressive politics practiced by Republicans in the past had not worked, such as calling for an end to the poll tax, advocating the expansion of health and education services, and opposing massive resistance. The Republican Party was often referred to as the "liberal" party in Virginia, and to make matters worse, when Republican leaders protested the label, they often offered up only the term "progressive" as an alternative in its place (Wilkinson 1968). Indeed, in the 1953 gubernatorial race. Ted Dalton's platform was considered so progressive that some anti-organization Democrats supported it as more Democratic than the Democratic candidate's platform (Latimer 1961, 61).

The second line of argument was less a criticism of past approaches than a strategic attempt to capture a group of voters that would inevitably be in play: conservative Democrats. As the conservative and segregation-based politics of the Byrd-controlled Democratic Party gave way to the reality of desegregation, suburbanization, and a growing state population, and as the

Democratic Party shifted left, Republicans guessed that conservative Democrats would increasingly find themselves uncomfortable and looking for a
new home. Wilkinson described Republican thinking in this way:

[Republicans] could eventually get the 'redneck' vote, if only because the red-
necks would have no place else to go. The time would come when the major
parties in Virginia could no longer afford to take an openly segregationist
stand, and rural segregationist would eventually have to join the more conservative of the two major parties. Republicans, benefiting from a conservative
national image, felt they could attract conservative Democrats who would for-
sake party before philosophy (1968, 232–233).

Strategically, the way Republicans would go forward with the conservative
approach was relatively simple: openly courting conservative Democrats,
which they did. For instance, in 1964 Richard Obenshain pointed out Democratic Governor Mills Godwin's support for Lyndon Johnson in a less-than-
veiled nod to unhappy conservative Democrats. He suggested that
Republicans should nominate a conservative ticket so that conservatives of
*both* parties would have a place to turn to in the next election.[5] Another
prominent Republican suggested the party convert a prominent conservative
Democrat to run as the Republican candidate for governor during the next
election (Atkinson 1992).

The second viable option for Republicans, advocated by the heirs of Ted
Dalton, was to tack a moderate course on civil rights and forge a coalition
between moderates, suburbanites, urbanites, and black voters. Looking back
through several decades of history, this option seems fanciful at best today,
but at the time it seemed as viable as any other option available to Virginia
Republicans. The key architects of this option were party leaders like Linwood Holton and Clyde Pearson. Pearson had served as a Republican in the
House of Delegates from Roanoke since the early 1950s when there were
only five Republicans in the entire chamber. He went on to run for governor
in 1961, laying out an early version of the type of campaign Linwood Holton
would run in 1965 and 1969, one that advocated a progressive Republican
Party on public services and race relations.[6] Holton, for his part, advocated
growing a Republican Party organically and did not support simply welcoming conservative Democrats into it.[7]

The rationale for the moderate approach had two primary lines of argument. The first was that the Virginia Republican Party historically was a
progressive party and should remain as such. This was as much an ideological and philosophical argument as anything else, but supporters also argued

that, at the state level, the increasingly suburbanized Virginia voter was interested in progressive approaches to problem-solving and not racially tinged politics. The progressive coalition that advocates of this approach envisioned included longstanding Republicans, black voters, labor union members, moderate suburban voters turned off by massive resistance and the Goldwater campaign, and nonpartisan voters who wanted Virginia to have two competitive political parties (Holton 2008, 57).

The second line of argument for the moderate approach was that it was the only approach that had actually shown any signs of success for Republican candidates. Since the early 1950s, Republican candidates had gained increasing support running on moderate-to-progressive platforms. Ted Dalton's 44.3 percent performance in the gubernatorial campaign of 1953 was a high mark for a Republican gubernatorial candidate, and Senator Byrd himself acknowledged that Dalton's campaign had given the Byrd organization the closest call it had ever had (Latimer 1961, 60). Even in the face of a worse showing in the 1957 gubernatorial campaign between Dalton and Lindsay Almond, where Almond ran on massive resistance and Dalton ran against it, advocates of a moderate approach could still see a silver lining in the substantial black vote received.[8] In fact, Republicans claimed that black support for Republican candidates was substantial in both the 1957 and 1961 gubernatorial races, and in some local races (Wilkinson 1968, 210).

Strategically, the way Republicans would go forward with the moderate approach was less straightforward than with the conservative approach. It would require assembling a winning coalition among groups that might disagree as much as they agreed. The points of agreement would need to be more important than the points of contention, and the points of agreement needed to revolve around a set of progressive policies. All of this would require a disciplined party speaking with one voice and nearly uniform campaign execution. Interestingly enough, if it worked, the moderate approach would leave many conservative Byrd Democrats without a political home—if the conservative Republicans who wanted to court them were right in their assessment that conservative Byrd Democrats would soon no longer find the Democratic Party to their liking. The result would ultimately place the Republican Party in the middle, between an increasingly liberal Democratic Party on their left and the conservative Byrd Democrats on their right (Eisenberg 1972).

In many ways, the Virginia Republican Party's search for an identity and a philosophical rooting was in the hands of African American voters, who also had two options. African American voters, unrestricted in their ability to vote after the repeal of the poll tax and passage of the 1965 VRA, could either join and support a moderate Virginia Republican Party and do what many conservative Byrd Democrats had done for years, which was to cross party lines and vote differently at the presidential level (in this case, for the Democratic presidential candidate), or they could join and support a historically conservative Virginia Democratic party that was responsible for Jim Crow and many of the other political, social, and economic restrictions blacks had faced for many decades.[9]

African American voting strength had increased substantially in Virginia between 1960 and 1968, by as much as two-and-a-half times (Eisenberg 1972). Additionally, black voter cohesion was the strongest of any group of voters in Virginia, with as much as 95 percent voting for the candidates endorsed by the Crusade for Voters. African American leaders clearly understood their potential electoral power and their choices, and intended to act in the most strategically advantageous way possible. Indeed, there was no better example of this rational behavior on the part of African American leaders than in the 1965 gubernatorial race between Democrat Mills Godwin who had supported massive resistance and Republican Linwood Holton who had opposed it. The Crusade for Voters, an organization created after massive resistance to increase black voter registration rates, endorsed Godwin. In explaining their decision, the leader of the Crusade for Voters, Dr. William Thornton, said that they hoped Godwin "would realize we'd help him to win and therefore do something for us" (Peirce 1975, 58).

Although the choices were real, historical and national forces made the decision less surprising perhaps than it might seem. As far back as the 1940s, even when the Byrd organization's electoral restrictions made voting difficult, African American voters in Virginia tended to ally themselves with the anti-organization side of the Democratic Party (Atkinson 1992, 17). This made some sense because, at that point, the only political party in the parts of the state with large black populations was the Democratic Party, and given its two clear factions, there was actually a choice for black voters to make. The Republican Party, which at the time existed largely in the mountainous western parts of the state that had very small African American populations, simply could not reach enough black voters to have an impact. Additionally, African American voters' support for Lyndon Johnson and dislike of Barry Goldwater after 1964 resulted in further black voter loyalty to Democrats.

In order to demonstrate the increasing importance of black Virginians to the Democratic Party, we collected over-time data on voting for this group. The top section of Figure 4.1 shows African American voting behavior in Norfolk, Richmond, and Roanoke during presidential elections. We have data for Norfolk from 1952 through 1968 and Richmond and Roanoke from 1948 to 1968.[10]

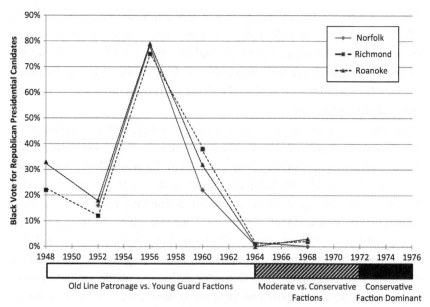

FIGURE 4.1 Black Voting Patterns and Factional Control of GOP in Virginia, 1948–1976

The pattern of black voting behavior is similar in all three cities, suggesting a very high degree of voter cohesion across the state. There are three behavioral trends of importance demonstrated by these data. First, the dramatic increase in Republican presidential voting between 1952 and 1956 is the result of the positions that President Eisenhower took on integration and civil rights. In his first run for president, Eisenhower garnered about 15 percent of the black vote (16 percent in Norfolk, 12 percent in Richmond, and 18 percent in Roanoke). Four years later, however, he was able to capture nearly 80 percent (78 percent in Norfolk, 75 percent in Richmond, and 79 percent in Roanoke) of the African American vote on his way to winning a second term in office. In the intervening four years, the Eisenhower administration had moved to support civil rights, and in Virginia the Byrd organization was moving closer to what would become known as massive resistance.

If 1956 marked the high point for African American Republican voting, between 1956 and 1964, black support for Republican presidential candidates dropped precipitously. In 1960, Richard Nixon's performance among black voters in Virginia was best in Richmond where he gained 35 percent of the vote, but in Norfolk he was able to capture only 22 percent. Nixon and the Republicans' softening support for civil rights and John F. Kennedy and the Democrats' increased attention to this issue were reflected in these numbers, as was Goldwater's anti-civil rights campaign in 1964, when

African American Republican voting dropped to near zero. Bloc voting by African American voters in 1964 was considered "vital" to the success of Democrats in Virginia, and political analyst Ralph Eisenberg could see the importance of the black vote, predicting at the time that African American support for Democrats would make them an important factor in the outcome of close elections.[11]

Between 1964 and 1968, black Republican voting patterns settled in the way Eisenberg predicted they would and remained at that low rate into the 1970s. In the 1968 presidential election, Nixon did best in Roanoke, gaining 3 percent of the black vote, but gained nearly none of it in Norfolk. Richmond African Americans gave Nixon 2 percent, a dramatic drop from his 1960 numbers. An indication of the strategic way in which African American leaders and organizations acted can be found in the 1969 gubernatorial election, in which the Crusade for Voters endorsed Republican gubernatorial candidate Linwood Holton over Democrat William C. Battle. In that election, black voting for the Republican attorney general and lieutenant governor candidates was similar to black voting for Nixon in 1968 at nearly zero, but black voting for Holton was nearly 40 percent.[12]

Holton's 1969 victory proved to be the high-water mark for the proponents of the moderate approach within the Republican Party. As Eisenberg observed after the 1964 election, African American voters were going to be a critical voting bloc in Virginia going forward, and as they increasingly voted as a bloc for Democratic candidates, a critical element of the moderate Republican platform went missing. With the black vote, as Holton demonstrated in 1969, the moderate approach had a chance; without it, moderate Republicans could not hope to construct a winning coalition.

The rational choice of African American voters was not the only problem for the moderate Republicans. Conservative Byrd Democrats were becoming unhappy with the increasingly liberal Democratic Party and were leaving it in large numbers. Rather than making the Republican Party uncomfortable for them, as Holton and his fellow moderates were attempting to do, conservative Republicans continued to invite them in. Oddly enough, the Holton governorship marked the period when the two factions of the Republican Party openly clashed over the fate of the Byrd Democrats, and Holton and his moderate tribesmen lost rather decisively.

Dick Obenshain, who had struggled to move the Republican Party to the right for a decade and found himself frustrated that Holton was unwilling to welcome the Byrd Democrats, became the Republican Party chair in 1972 and quickly set about putting out the welcome mat. Republicans had a string of electoral victories in the next several years, capturing their first U.S. Senate seat in nearly a century, a majority of the state's congressional seats, and dozens of House of Delegates and state Senate seats. Plans were made with the White House to have President Nixon help make a big push to convert a large number of prominent Democrats and flip Virginia, but the Watergate scandal got in the way. Instead, there emerged in the mid-1970s a group of former Byrd Democrats who aligned themselves with neither party. They came to be known as the "coalition," but even though they would not publicly join the Republican Party, they very often supported conservative Republican candidates (Atkinson 1992).

The transformation of Virginia from a one-party Democratic state to a two-party competitive state with a weighty group of independents who refused to align with either party was a long time in the making. There was no one critical juncture in the transformation. Instead, it is clear that the strategic decisions made by several groups—conservative Democrats and African Americans in particular—shaped the slow realignment over the course of several decades.

## *The Development of the Republican Party in the* Peach State

Perhaps it is telling that Key's account of pre-civil rights era Georgia does not include a discussion of the Republican Party in the state. Key's exclusion was understandable, given the fact that there was no functioning Republican Party in existence at the time—at least in terms of how political scientists characterize political parties. Party politics in Georgia, as in the rest of the South, was characterized by one party, that party being the Democratic Party.[13]

As with other one-party states, competition often revolved around fighting between various factions. Key described the Georgia system as bifactional, comprised of the more dominate and cohesive *Talmadge* faction and a second faction known as the *anti-Talmadge* forces.[14] The Talmadge faction represented the conservative element of the Democratic Party, supporting maintenance of the racial status quo (segregation and black disenfranchisement) and business interests, while strongly opposing labor and Roosevelt's New Deal. Geographically, the Talmadge forces were concentrated in rural sections of the state, primarily below the *fall line*. As in most bifactional systems where the dominant faction is organized around a demagogic figure, the *anti* forces were generally less cohesive (Key 1949).

As to the existence of the Republican Party in Georgia during this time, the answer is that there was one, at least on paper. It consisted of a small number of individuals who were solely interested in controlling and distributing patronage during Republican presidential administrations and in sending delegates to presidential nominating conventions. We might term such individuals *post office Republicans*, the name derived from the federal patronage jobs often associated with the postal service.[15] In Georgia, these Republicans were Taftites, supporters of Senator Robert A. Taft of Ohio, a conservative and Republican presidential candidate.[16] We should also note that the Georgia GOP was not *lily-white*, as there was active participation on the part of blacks within the party structure.[17]

The party was in no way involved in the type of activities typically associated with political parties, such as organization and voter mobilization or candidate recruitment and finance. These partisans did not even actively campaign for GOP presidential contenders within the state. Again, all electoral politics below the office of the presidency proceeded during this time within the confines of the Democratic Party primary. What was the Republican Party in Georgia during this time offered absolutely no opposition to the Democratic machinery.

In 1952, a major sea change occurred when what would become known as the Eisenhower faction assumed effective control over the Republican Party in Georgia after being seated as the legitimate state delegation at the national GOP convention that year.[18] The Taft faction, also known as *Old-Line Republicans*, accused these GOP newcomers of being former Democrats and, therefore, not the genuine article. The Eisenhower faction retorted that the Taftites were only interested in controlling patronage and delegate selection to the national convention and not in cultivating real two-party competition.[19] Both groups were right to an extent, although some in the Eisenhower faction were already Republican identifiers who had migrated from outside the region. In 1954, William B. Shartzer of the Eisenhower camp was elected party chair.[20] Despite subsequent efforts on the part of the Taft faction to regain power, the Eisenhower faction would remain firmly in control of the state GOP until they, themselves, were unseated by Goldwater forces.

Although some in the Eisenhower faction were certainly attracted to the GOP ranks by the Eisenhower presidential run, it is important to note that this group's affiliation with the GOP was in no way founded solely on presidential politics. Based largely in the growing Atlanta metro-area counties of Fulton and DeKalb, these Republicans were also interested in grassroots party-building activities.[21] These initial efforts involved some of the first attempts to legally organize the Republican Party in the state and holding county and district conventions in 1956.[22] An interesting *Atlanta Constitution* editorial from 1954 supported the development of a true two-party system in Georgia; however, the article tellingly concludes that "*the real trouble has been that the Republican Party has failed to sustain any effort to make itself attractive to the South."*[23] As will become evident, ten years later, the state GOP attempted to make itself attractive by shifting to the hard right on the issue of race.

Compared to 1952, the Georgia GOP was quite united in 1956, electing an uncontested delegation for Eisenhower to the national convention.[24] Although the Georgia Republican Party could certainly be described as economically conservative, they were in no manner more conservative than the state Democratic Party on the race question. This was especially evident at the 1956 Republican National Convention, where the Georgia delegation along with other Southern states pushed for, and won, a moderate civil rights platform plank. Georgia delegate Margaret Twiggs served on the civil rights committee and was instrumental in this effort.[25] The platform plank on civil rights accepted the Supreme Court position on desegregation and recommended compliance at the local level, but it did not advocate *force or coercive legislation* to achieve this goal.[26] As will be seen, the state party's position on race was one that cut a middle path while the Eisenhower faction remained in control. More conservative than Republicans outside the region and increasingly to the right of the national Democratic position, it was decidedly to the left of positions maintained by Georgia Democrats.

The reaction to the Eisenhower Administration's use of federal troops to desegregate Little Rock High School in Arkansas was viewed as a setback for the state GOP.[27] Officially, state party leaders refused to issue a censure of Eisenhower, taking again a very moderate approach while calling the incident *extremely regrettable*. One official remarked, "[T]his is not a political issue and the Republicans and Democrats alike in the South must not encourage extremists who are promoting violence and the destruction of our public school system."[28] But the issue of school desegregation in the South, of course, was a political one. Democratic leaders like Senators Russell and Talmadge and Lieutenant Governor Vandiver cried foul over the federal intervention in Little Rock. While the stance of the Georgia Republican Party would appear a very reasonable one today, in pre-civil rights Georgia, it was nothing short of left-wing. At the time, the Georgia GOP was most likely to the right of the position of the national party on the race issue. Even so, an editorial on the *Atlanta Journal* opined that Eisenhower's actions may have set the Georgia Republican Party back twenty years.[29]

This middle-of-the road stance continued at the 1960 state convention, where a plank to keep public schools in the state open in the wake of ongoing federal desegregation efforts was adopted. There was also much talk of the civil rights plank in the national platform. Chairman Shartzer indicated that the GOP plank would not extend beyond the one adopted at the 1956 convention, but there were fears that the plank was more liberal than that of the Democrats, and efforts were launched by New York Governor Nelson Rockefeller and his followers to adopt such a position.[30] In the end, a compromise plank was adopted that could be described as more moderate than the national Democratic position, but stronger than what Southern GOP delegates would have wanted.[31]

At the beginning of 1961, Shartzer was replaced by James Dorsey as state party chair.[32] Dorsey, an Eisenhower Republican, continued to guide the state GOP on a moderate course of action throughout his tenure in office. Dorsey had previously been part of H.O.P.E. (Help Our Public Education), which was a grassroots organization based in Atlanta that advocated keeping public schools open through limited and controlled desegregation, a middle-of-the-road position in the struggle for school integration (Kruse 2005 and Lassiter 2006).

An interesting set of articles devoted to the Georgia Republican Party summarized the state of party affairs at the end of 1961 in this manner:

> So far, the Republicans have absolutely nothing to offer along that line [actually winning political office] in state politics. . . . Then there is the race question. . . . Every Republican you talk to has a different idea about how the GOP candidate ought to handle the racial issue. . . . Republican ideas of strategy range from ignoring the whole thing to arguing that the Democrats already have proved that the governor can't do anything to preserve segregation anyway. It is certain that the Republicans won't advocate instant integration. A stand for moderation seems the most likely posture.[33]

The state GOP was in a sense caught between a rock and a hard place. If they tacked to the right on the race issue, they lost black support; if they moved to the left, they forfeited white voters who were economic conservatives but moderate on the race question. Instead, the party continued to chart a middle ground, which to those outside the region might have appeared to be even right-of-center. In terms of political maneuvering, it seemed virtually impossible, however, for the Republican Party to move to the right of state Democrats, as outlined in the following quote:

> The dilemma of Southern Republicans is this: The Southern Democratic leadership traditionally and consistently has occupied the conservative field in which the GOP has been working in its efforts to create that second party which the South so badly needs. It is simply not possible to get to the political right of the Deep South Democrats. It is folly for the Republicans to believe

they can be more conservative than the Southern Democratic leadership which has filibustered every civil rights proposal offered in the Congress, which opposes federal aid to education, and which has established a record of unrelenting conservatism since about midway of the New Deal.[34]

In 1962, the state GOP decided to run a candidate for governor for the first time since Reconstruction. A. E. Smith was nominated by the Republican Party to stand for election. Smith, an Eisenhower Republican, said the GOP should exploit a middle-of-the-road position and should appeal to all voters, including blacks. The state party platform that year mirrored this line of thinking, again offering a moderate position on the race issue by not specifically advocating desegregation. More precisely, the plank stated: "Satisfactory relationship between the races is essential to the progress of our great state. We must apply goodwill, tolerance, and common sense to race relations, and, most important, we must keep race relations out of politics."[35] The GOP's stance on race was never put to the test with voters in the gubernatorial race, as Smith was tragically killed in an automobile accident prior to the election.[36]

The transformation of the Georgia Republican Party leading up to the 1964 election cycle can only be aptly described as a complete paradigm shift. Even as the winds of change were beginning to blow in 1963, the GOP State Executive Committee chose not to actively oppose JFK's civil rights bill, but instead simply reaffirmed the party's position on civil rights as outlined in the 1960 and 1962 platforms.[37] None of the 1960 Georgia delegates to the national convention indicated they were supporting Goldwater and, as other Deep South states rallied behind the banner of the Arizona senator, the Georgia GOP appeared hesitant.

In 1964, a grassroots movement beginning at the county level signaled the takeover of the Georgia Republican Party by a conservative element pledged to back Goldwater. In the Atlanta metro area, the Fulton, DeKalb, and Cobb County Republican Parties all passed resolutions that instructed delegates to the national convention to vote for Goldwater. Chatham County (Savannah) delegates also followed suit.[38] Likewise, nine of ten congressional district conventions that preceded the state convention voted to pledge support for Goldwater.[39] At the state convention, the Goldwater forces completely subsumed the moderate Eisenhower faction. Republican State Senator Joseph Tribble, the Georgia chair of the Draft Goldwater Movement, defeated Alex Bealer, a Dorsey protégé, to become the GOP state party chair by a vote of 396 to 217.[40] The other top state party position, national committeeman, went to Goldwater supporter Roscoe Pickett. None other than Barry Goldwater himself capped off the state convention by giving the keynote address.[41]

Following the convention, a number of moderate GOP leaders in Atlanta publicly rejected both the leadership and the change in direction they had instituted for the state party. One of the changes involved strategies associated with black Georgians. At the convention, blacks were excluded from leadership positions within the party or as delegates to the national convention. Party Chair Tribble also candidly admitted that blacks will not support Goldwater, but the GOP *"can make up the difference with an increase in white voters."*[42] An individual identified simply as a prominent Republican remarked to the *Atlanta Journal* that *"what has been done here is to read Negroes out of the Republican Party in Georgia."*[43] Another *AJ* article described the Georgia Republican Party as being in an *"all-out battle for the Southern conservative vote."*[44]

Whether Tribble should have been so forthright is another question; however, he seems to have had a grasp on reality. Post-election analysis from the *Atlanta Constitution* indicated that blacks voted overwhelmingly Democratic (see Figure 4.2) and that one obstacle facing the GOP in future elections would be trying to reconcile *"its newfound strength in segregationist circles with any hope of recapturing its Negro support."*[45]

At the Republican National Convention, moderate elements led by Pennsylvania Governor William Scranton called for a stronger civil rights plank along with a repudiation of right-wing extremist groups. These efforts were blocked, with the Georgia delegation voting solidly against any proposal to strengthen the national party's position on civil rights. In the end, a diluted plank was approved that failed to openly stipulate that the 1964 Civil Rights Bill was constitutional.[46] By this point in time, the Republican plank on civil rights was far to the right of the Democratic platform position.

Georgia Republicans enjoyed some modicum of success in the 1964 election cycle. Goldwater, easily defeated by LBJ, won the electoral votes from the Peach State by polling 54 percent of the popular vote.[47] Goldwater's candidacy marked the first time Georgia had voted for a Republican presidential candidate. Georgia Republicans also picked up their first congressional seat since Reconstruction, along with an eleven-seat pickup in the General Assembly.[48] In 1965, a special election was held following a court-ordered reapportionment of the state House that saw the election of nineteen Republicans, bringing the total number in the House to twenty-one.[49] The GOP appeared to have some momentum going into the 1966 state election cycle. Indeed, one newspaper article noted in 1965 that the Georgia Republican Party was in better shape than the Democrats, organizationally speaking.[50] In 1965, Paul Jones of the Goldwater faction was elected state party chair, a sure indication that conservative elements were still firmly in control of the party.[51]

Although the change in issue positions on the race question was very evi-dent in 1964, we analyzed the events of the 1966 election cycle to provide a bookend for this case study. The 1966 election cycle looked to be a golden opportunity for the state GOP to build upon the gains made in 1964. The centerpiece of this effort involved putting a gubernatorial candidate on the ballot. The GOP did, in fact, nominate a candidate, 3rd District Republican Congressman Howard "Bo" Callaway. The party also contested eight of Geor-gia's ten congressional districts in 1966.[52]

Callaway was a key player in the noted shift that occurred within the Geor-gia Republican Party. He was from a wealthy middle-Georgia family with business interests related primarily to the textile industry.[53] Previously, Calla-way was linked politically to the Talmadge faction of the state Democratic Party and, as late as 1962, he had supported segregationist gubernatorial candidate Marvin Griffin in the Democratic primary (Bartley 1970).

Callaway reported that he was drawn into politics when he was asked to participate in the effort to draft Barry Goldwater to run for president. As part of this involvement, Callaway was elected as a delegate to both the district and state GOP convention, where he participated in the takeover effort pre-viously chronicled. From there, he was elected as a delegate to the Republi-can National Convention. Callaway indicated that he was very concerned about the ideological direction of the country, especially related to the policy positions of the Kennedy Administration. When Johnson was nominated after Kennedy's assassination, Callaway's calculus was in no way altered, as he viewed LBJ's claims of being a Southern conservative to be completely unfounded.[54]

Following the convention, Callaway reported that Goldwater asked him to run for Congress. He did and faced segregationist and former Democratic Lieutenant Governor Garland Byrd in the 3rd congressional district race. One would be hard-pressed to say which of the two was the most conserva-tive. As told to one of the authors by Callaway himself, he was able to paint Byrd as the more *liberal* candidate when he continuously asked the Democrat at a public debate who he was going to vote for in the presidential election, after announcing his unflinching support for Goldwater. Byrd refused to answer the repeated question and, as a consequence, his support for the ra-cially conservative candidate in the presidential race was left in doubt.[55]

When he arrived in Washington, D.C., Callaway was every bit the conser-vative he portrayed himself to be during the campaign. Following the elec-tion, he made it well known that he was dedicated to the repeal of the Civil Rights Act and wanted to curb the power of the Supreme Court.[56] In 1965, Callaway publicly opposed and voted against the 1965 VRA.[57] The next year, he offered an amendment (which passed) to civil rights legislation to curb the ability of federal agencies to impose pupil guidelines to achieve desegregation.[58] While in Congress, Callaway's ADA (Americans for Democratic Action) scores for both 1965 and 1966 were zero.[59]

As he entered the 1966 gubernatorial race, Callaway remarked that by that time "*[He] was very clearly a Republican*," as opposed to his characterization of himself in 1964 as simply being active for the Goldwater cause.[60] As such, we can use Callaway and his candidacy as a proxy for the state party's positions post-Goldwater. The gubernatorial race pitted Callaway against arch-segregationist and Democrat Lester Maddox. Although Callaway's issue positions on race and other matters were clearly defined by that time, perhaps only George Wallace could have credibly run to the right of Maddox on racial issues.[61] For example, Maddox was known for his stubborn and armed defiance of efforts to desegregate his restaurant, the *Pickrick*, following passage of the 1964 Civil Rights Act (Bartley 1970 and Kruse 2005).

Callaway was labeled by news sources as a segregationist, although when he was asked the question directly, he would decline to confirm or deny whether, in fact, he was a segregationist.[62] He would then typically respond in a nuanced fashion saying such things as *there is no quick answer* to such a question, that *he was not sure what people mean by such labels*, or that the term is vague and *means different things to different people*. He would quickly follow by expressing a racially conservative policy position such as declaring his support for freedom-of-choice plans for schools, attacking federal school desegregation guidelines, or decrying outside interference from the federal government in state affairs in general.[63]

Faced with the choice of a staunch and openly segregationist Democrat or a racially conservative Republican, moderate and liberal forces organized a write-in campaign behind former progressive governor and member of the *anti-Talmadge* forces Ellis Arnall, who had been defeated by Maddox in the Democratic primary.[64] In a flyer for *Write In Georgia*, the organization behind the campaign, the case was clearly made that there was little real difference between Maddox or Callaway, stating: "If you think there is a vast difference between Maddox and Callaway, the only difference is in appearances: it is a difference of imagery; a difference of technique. The realities are the same."[65]

One question before the electorate concerned the support that blacks would be willing to give a Republican like Callaway when faced with the presented Democratic choice. Callaway very candidly admitted that the election strategy of the Republican Party in the 1966 gubernatorial race centered on trying to mobilize white conservatives to the GOP banner.[66]

Callaway won a plurality of the vote at 46.5 percent to Maddox's 46.2 percent. Arnall received just enough write-in votes (7.08 percent) to deny either candidate a majority.[67] In the event that no gubernatorial candidate received a majority of the popular vote, the state constitution called on the General Assembly to determine the next chief executive. In a special joint session of the state House and Senate, Democrat Lester Maddox was elected to be the next governor of Georgia by a vote of 182 to 66.[68] Given the partisan imbalance in the General Assembly at the time with 229 Democrats, 29 Republicans, and 1 Independent, this outcome came as no surprise.

Statistical analyses by the authors of precinct data from Fulton and Bibb (Macon) Counties estimate that the black vote was split 52 percent for Callaway, 38 percent for Arnall, and 7.9 percent for Maddox.[69] Another published analysis utilizing only data from Fulton County put black support for Callaway at 52 percent, Arnall at 46 percent, and Maddox at 3 percent (Bartley and Graham 1967). Clearly then, Callaway did receive just over a majority of the black vote in these urban areas; however, this appears to have been more of a default position on the part of blacks, given the fact that an avowed segregationist was in the race, as opposed to the GOP actively attempting to mobilize the black vote.

Perhaps more telling was the ability of a write-in candidate to achieve a notable percentage of the total vote, given the fact that, under Georgia law, the candidate's name had to be spelled correctly. By our estimates, less than 5 percent (4.5 percent) of white registrants in Fulton and Bibb Counties chose the write-in option, lending weight to the supposition that the black community was the major driver behind support for Arnall. It could be argued counterfactually that Callaway could have won a majority had this black support not gone to a write-in candidate.

The GOP did pick up two congressional seats in 1966 but failed to hold onto the Third District seat vacated by Callaway. In the legislature, the Republicans lost three House seats and two Senate seats.[70] There is little doubt that the GOP's inability to continue to build on the gains experienced in 1964, especially the loss for the state's highest office, most likely retarded Republican growth in the Peach State for some time.[71] In the following election cycle, advancement for the GOP was once again muted when Republican presidential candidate Richard Nixon was supplanted by Independent candidate George Wallace. Wallace won 42.8 percent of the popular vote in Georgia to Nixon's 30.4 percent.

Although the ability of the GOP in Georgia to organize, contest, and win elections left a lot to be desired in the wake of the 1966 election, the party's conservative stance on racial issues had all but crystallized at this point. Following the 1968 election, Bartley wrote:

Since 1964 the Republican Party in Georgia has rarely deviated from the political strategy associated with the Goldwater candidacy . . . the G.O.P. has sought to combine the economic conservatism and "good government" programs that have appealed to the more affluent urbanites with the social and ideological conservatism that has attracted the support of lower status whites (1970, 89–90).

In the aftermath of the civil rights era, it would be the Georgia Democrats who would move slowly over time in a leftward direction, eventually mirroring the national party and leaving the GOP as the party of racial conservatism in Georgia. Of course, the leftward shift for state Democrats is explained in large part by the exodus of white conservatives and the infusion of increasing numbers of black citizens into their ranks.

In order to demonstrate the increasing importance of black Georgians to the Democratic Party, we collected over-time data on registration and voting for this group. The top section of Figure 4.2 plots black voting behavior in Fulton (Atlanta) and Bibb (Macon) Counties during presidential elections. We have data for Fulton County from 1952 to 1976 and Bibb County from 1948 to 1972.[72]

For both counties, there was a discernible shift between the 1960 and 1964 elections, where a precipitous drop in the percentage of blacks voting for the Republican presidential candidate can be observed. The graphical pattern is a fair representation of a *critical* realignment among blacks in Georgia. Following the new pattern established in 1964, black voting for Republican presidential candidates never returned to its previous level. In Fulton County, the average black vote for Republican presidential candidates prior to 1964 was 56 percent. From 1964 through 1976, this figure dropped to 3.3 percent. During Goldwater's run, only 1 percent of black voters in Fulton County were predicted to have voted Republican. The bottom panel charts the Georgia Republican Party based on factional control. The shift from the Eisenhower to the Goldwater faction exactly corresponds to the noted realignment among black voters from Republican to Democratic voting. As outlined previously, this fact was in no way a coincidence.

Although civil rights legislation may have signaled a change in positions of the national parties on the race question, we cannot leave out the very real effects produced by the VRA, namely the enfranchisement of a large portion of the black population in the state. As the 1964 presidential election provided a breakpoint for the shift in black voting behavior from competitive numbers for the Republicans to overwhelming support for Democrats, it must also be noted that the 1960s also marked the beginning of increasing numbers of blacks entering the Georgia electorate. These new registrants

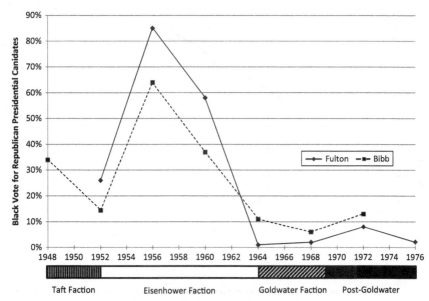

FIGURE 4.2 Black Voting Patterns and Factional Control of GOP in Georgia, 1948–1976

supplied mounting numbers of Democratic partisans and made blacks an increasingly important coalition within the state Democratic Party.

Figure 4.3 displays black registration as a percentage of total registration in Fulton County over a fifty-year time frame. From our first observation in 1958, these numbers increased monotonically for almost thirty years, from 21 percent to 46 percent in 1986.[73] By 1986 then, blacks made up almost half of the total Fulton County electorate. A similar pattern can be noted in the increase in black registration at the state level that was demonstrated in chapter 2 (see Figure 2.7, Georgia panel). Without a doubt, the VRA helped to provide the raw material for a new, and what would become a critical, coalition housed within the Democratic Party.

Clearly, 1964 is the focal point for party change in Georgia, and much of the flashpoint can be traced directly to LBJ's push for landmark civil rights legislation and the ongoing struggle over public school integration ignited by the *Brown* decision. Even before this event, the Kennedy Administration's stance on civil rights had begun to evoke a strong reaction from conservative Republicans, chief among these being Arizona Senator Barry Goldwater. As documented, the "Draft Goldwater" movement drew white conservatives from the South who were starkly opposed to the national Democratic position, not only on race but on other matters such as the *Great Society* as well. In Georgia, these conservatives may have been initially drawn to the GOP by Goldwater and the national political scene, but we should note that these

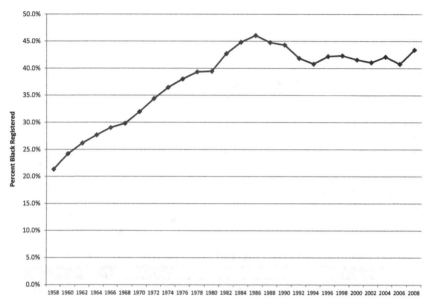

FIGURE 4.3 Racial Compostion of the Fulton County Electorate, 1958–2008

individuals were also responsible for taking over the state party apparatus. So, although national politics may have provided an impetus for two-party change in the South, such change would not have been possible without action at the state level and below.

Although the seminal events of 1964 converged to begin the process of two-party development in Georgia, it is no secret that it was literally decades before this process fully played out. The eventual movement from one-party Democratic dominance to genuine two-party politics very much resembled the *issue evolution* process described by Carmines and Stimson (1989), where the race issue produced a new equilibrium between the Republican and Democratic parties. This dynamic process, however, took decades to completely sort itself out within the Georgia political context.

## Conclusion

Having examined the transformation of the Republican Party in Virginia and Georgia, we can now draw some associations between these two cases, as well as locate what we have learned within the context of relative advantage theory. As predicted by our theory, these case studies provide a great deal of historical evidence that both white conservatives and blacks were acting in their own political self-interests. For white conservatives, this meant taking advantage of the existing GOP party machinery as an alternative outlet to an increasingly left-tilting national Democratic Party (especially on the race question). For black Southerners, many of whom were newly enfranchised, such a calculation meant aligning themselves with a party (at least on the national level) that more and more represented their interests.

Of course, these two political events themselves should in no way be viewed as independent phenomena. The fact that black registrants were increasingly identifying and voting Democratic was in no way lost on white conservatives, who could envisage at some point in the future a much more liberal state Democratic Party as a result. On the other hand, the hard-right turn of the Republican Party as it was repopulated with conservatives meant for blacks the loss of political opportunity within the GOP.

It should also be noted that, although national events and personalities may have contributed to the alteration of the Southern party landscape, the transformation at the state level and below was produced by—and could only have been produced by—actions on the part of Southerners operating in their own local context, whether that be white conservatives transferring their allegiance to the GOP or blacks identifying and voting as Democratic partisans.

This fact is certainly highlighted by our two case studies where the road taken to contemporary political convergence between the Virginia and Georgia state party systems varied greatly along the way. In Georgia, white conservatives rapidly seized control of the state Republican Party during the 1964 election cycle. In Virginia, the struggle between moderates and conservatives within the state GOP extended well into the 1970s. Rates of black voter registration, the relative size of the black electorate, and the allegiance of this group to the Democratic banner also varied greatly both between these two states and over the course of time as well.[74]

Although the case studies presented in this chapter have chronicled in great detail the transformation of the Virginia and Georgia Republican Parties in response to events of the civil rights era, they cannot provide systematic empirical verification for the theory of relative advantage as the causal mechanism producing the noted political changes that engulfed the region. It is to this task that we now turn. The next three chapters provide empirical confirmation of relative advantage theory as it applies to Republican growth, using state-, county-, and individual-level data over time. An additional chapter analyzes changes in black mobilization at the state and county levels within this same theoretical framework.

# Republican Growth

| Putting Relative Advantage
to the Test

*State-Level Republican Growth in the*
*Modern American South*

THE THEORY OF RELATIVE *advantage* is, at the very least, a plausible explanation for the interrelationships between the two most significant components
of the transformation of modern Southern politics: the growth of the GOP
and the political mobilization of African Americans. We examine the case for
relative advantage as it relates to the development of the Republican Party in
the region in a series of steps. In this chapter, we begin the empirical assessment of the theoretical claims we make with regard to Republican growth by
focusing on a regionwide examination of this phenomenon. In chapter 6, we
assess the extent to which relative advantage explains county-level Republican growth in two states for which we have the necessary data, Louisiana and
North Carolina. Finally, in chapter 7, we examine relative advantage for white
Southerners at the individual level.

To reiterate, we argue that the size of the Republican Party in the South
grew, over the time period of our analysis, because the benefits of voting
and identification with the Republican Party for whites, in comparison to
Democratic affiliation, increased.[1] So, from a political standpoint, the relative advantage of the Republican Party increased during this period, but the
extent to which this was the case varied considerably across the Southern
states.

Note that the theory of relative advantage involves more than the mere
presence of significant partisan cleavages. According to the relative advantage perspective, transformation of the party system also requires a *catalyst*.
This catalyst may take the form of a deviation in policy orientations and/or
ideological positions held within existing political structures brought about

by the effective mobilization of a new electoral constituency, such as African Americans in the South in the latter half of the twentieth century. Citizens identify with and vote for candidates of political parties for a variety of reasons. The factors that influence peoples' choices of one party or the other include (1) the relative competitiveness of the party in an array of political arenas, and (2) the consistency of each party's political objectives with a citizen's own political objectives. In the South, white support for the Republican Party grew relative to the Democratic Party because

1. Republicans were able to field competitive candidates in an increasing number of elections at the local, state, and national levels, resulting in a waning of the significance of the Democratic Party nomination process; and
2. The electoral mobilization of the black population—an almost uniformly Democratic electorate—precluded the continued control of the Democratic Party machinery by conservative whites. As the local Democratic Party became more difficult to control, the party apparatus itself became relatively less valuable.

The development of a viable Republican Party was a novel aspect of postwar politics in the South. The absence of active and significant two-party competition in the South was one of Key's primary criticisms of the region's political system during the first half of the twentieth century. According to Key, the lack of interparty competition stunted the growth and development of viable party organizations in the South.[2] Over the past half-century, however, the Southern GOP has become an organizational equal of, and sometimes superior to, the Democratic Party in the region (see, for example, Maggioto and Wekkin 2000).

The theory of relative advantage predicts that state-level Republican strength relative to that of the Democratic Party is partly a function of the ability of the GOP to offer a platform for the nomination and election of candidates to pursue policy objectives. We argue that the mechanisms of interparty competition are paramount for explaining the rise of the GOP in the South. In an effort to examine the devices that induced two-party competition and, as a result, viable Republican parties at the state level, we include measures designed to test the importance of party competition at various officeholding levels.

In this respect, the theory of relative advantage is consistent with proponents of the *bottom-up* perspective of Republican growth. Scholars have been preoccupied with the pattern of two-party emergence in the South for at least forty years. One prominent theory posits that two-party competition in the region began as a product of support for Republican presidential candidates (see Lamis 1988 or Aistrup 1996 for support of this theory of party change). Success at the presidential level then filtered down to statewide offices (i.e., governor, U.S. senator), which, in turn, led to increased levels of voting for GOP congressional candidates. Finally, this *top-down* process culminated in GOP viability at the substate level (i.e., state legislative seats). In *The Rise of Southern Republicans*, Black and Black (2002) highlight the importance of presidential campaigns, especially Reagan's, in producing a realignment at the congressional level in the region. Likewise, other research has uncovered a link between GOP state party election strategies and recruiting candidates to run in legislative districts with a tendency to vote for Republican presidential candidates (Bullock and Shafer 1997).

Others, however, have challenged the *top-down* theory of party change in the region (Aldrich 2000 and Aldrich and Griffin 2000). Using a series of Granger causality tests, these studies demonstrated that GOP electoral successes at the national level are a direct product of, or are caused by, prior victories at the state level. Likewise, success in state legislative races was a precursor to winning U.S. House elections, so there is evidence that state GOP party-building efforts were the result of a highly complex process operating at multiple levels.

As theorized, state-level Republican Party strength relative to that of the Democratic Party is in part associated with the ability of the GOP to offer an alternative platform for nomination and election of candidates to pursue policy objectives. The mechanisms of interparty competition are paramount in explaining the rise of the GOP in the South. Given the prior emphasis on, and disagreement about, Republican Party formation in the postwar South, it is imperative that we properly model this political dynamic. So that we might understand the forces that induced two-party competition and viable Republican parties at the state level, we include measures intended to assess the importance of party competition at different officeholding levels.

The theory of relative advantage also highlights the impact of racial dynamics on the growth of the Republican Party. However, in contrast to Key (1949) and a host of subsequent research, we argue that it is black *mobilization*, not simply black *context*, that drove GOP growth in the South. Initially, Southern conservatives opposed the development of the Republican Party. However, once disenfranchised African American voters returned to the political arena, Southern conservatives shifted strategies and began to build a local Republican Party that could serve as an organized political alternative to the Democratic Party, which was increasingly the party of choice for African

Americans (see Aistrup 1996; Aldrich and Griffin 2000; Maggioto and Wekkin 2000; and Rhodes 2000). As blacks moved into the Democratic Party in significant numbers, conservative white Southerners were forced to seek an alternative vehicle for their political ambitions and objectives. Similarly, to the extent that blacks were perceived as a threat, we would expect to see conservative white reaction to this to be greatest in those areas in which African Americans actually became a major force in local and state politics. We test the *black mobilization* hypothesis, as well as the more traditional and competing *black-belt* hypothesis.

Our empirical assessment of the implications of the theory of relative advantage also takes into account a variety of prominent alternative explanations. These include in-migration (Bass and De Vries 1976; Scher 1977; and Stanley and Castle 1988), various economic dynamics (Cobb 1999; Shafer and Johnston 2001, 2006; and Sosna 1987), and the religious conservatism of white Southerners (Green, et al. 1998, 2010 and Kellstedt 1989).

## Data and Methods

This section describes the data utilized, operationalization of the variables analyzed, and the methodology employed for the analyses presented in this chapter.

### Data

The data for this chapter come from a wide variety of published and unpublished sources, both hard copy and electronic. Most of the demographic and economic information was drawn from U.S. census reports. Data on black registration from 1976 through 2008 were compiled from the biennial report on voting and registration produced by the Census Bureau as well. Black registration figures for the earlier time period rely primarily on estimates and official figures compiled by the Southern Regional Council's Voter Education Project. The Glenmary Surveys of church membership along with reports from the Southern Baptist Convention served as our sources for religious denomination data in the Southern states. Statistics on election outcomes, vote totals, and seat contestations at various officeholding levels were compiled from a long list of published sources including books, newspapers, state blue books (both hard copy and electronic), and historical election returns from various state agencies and archives. A detailed compilation of all data sources utilized for this chapter can be found in Appendix A.

## Variable Operationalizations

The dependent variable, *Republican Strength*, is measured at the state level utilizing a method developed by David (1972). General election vote percentages for Republican candidates in gubernatorial, senate, and congressional elections were utilized to create a composite state-level index of GOP strength.[3] Following the construction of each GOP state index, a ten-year (five-time point) moving average was applied to smooth any sharp variations present in each series.[4] The David Index of Party Strength was the method of choice for Lamis (1988) in his detailed study of party change in the South.

As *Republican Strength* is measured over time for each of the individual Southern states, it is important to assess the extent to which this series is stationary. The standard modeling procedures that we implement below are intended for stationary variables, and the appropriate interpretation of the model coefficients and standard errors presumes that the dependent variable, in particular, does not contain a unit root. We estimate two standard unit root tests specifically designed for panel data to evaluate whether *Republican Strength* is stationary. Both of the Levin, Lin, Chu and the Im, Pesaran, Shin tests allow us to reject the null hypothesis that the variable is nonstationary. The results of these tests are reported in Table 5.1.[5]

Independent variables representing possible explanations for Republican Party growth in the South can be classified into three groups: political, economic, and demographic. Variables designed to tap political concerns include *Black Electoral Strength*, *% Black*, *Substate Party Competition*, as well as two sets of variables designed to represent the effects of presidential campaigns. The first of these variables taps into the potential influence of the political mobilization of African Americans in the region. *Black Electoral Strength* is calculated at the state level as the number of black registrants divided by the total number of registered voters. Operationalized as it is, our measure of African American electoral strength places African Americans

TABLE 5.1  TSCS Unit-Root Tests for GOP Strength

| TEST | TEST STATISTICS |
| --- | --- |
| Levin, Lin, and Chu | $-2.47^{***}$ |
| Im, Pesaran, and Shin | $-2.005^{**}$ |

NOTES: For both tests, a significant test statistic allows for the rejection of the null hypothesis that the series is nonstationary.
$^{*}p < .10;\ ^{**}p < .05;\ ^{***}p < .01$

within the context of the existing electorate—a much more precise method for estimating the potential influence of blacks as an electoral presence than alternative indicators (i.e., the percentage of blacks registered to vote).

To control for the size of the overall African American population in each state, we include a variable tapping the number of blacks in the population divided by the total state population in the model (% *Black*). Although African Americans are a ubiquitous presence in the Southern political scene, their numbers are not uniform throughout the region. Most studies of Southern politics, therefore, include some control for the relative size of the black population (see, for example, Nye and Bullock 1993).

In order to examine competing claims that two-party emergence in the region was a product of a different set of distinct processes, we include a number of specific indicators in an effort to differentiate between the effects of party competition at the national level with those at a more localized, grassroots level. Given the important emphasis on presidential campaigns and state-level party growth in the South, we include two distinct sets of variables in an effort to capture this dynamic. The first indicator was based on the actual percentage of a state's vote captured by the Republican presidential candidate.[6] A second set of models was also estimated using a set of $n$-1 dummy variables designed to measure the effects of specific presidential campaigns. These variables were coded one during the presidential election year as well as for the subsequent off-year election (i.e., Goldwater 1964, 1966), with the 1960 Nixon campaign serving as the excluded base category.

In order to directly test the effects of substate party competition on state-level GOP growth, we include a measure designed to capture this process in our multivariate models. The viability of the Republican Party at the substate level in the South varied greatly both over time and among states. In order for our model to account for this fact, an index was created to measure the relative level of competitive strength for the GOP among the eleven states in our sample.[7] In creating such a measure, we draw directly from the work of Aistrup (1996) and Anderson (1997), making some modest alterations to their measures of GOP competitiveness.[8]

In a given election cycle, *Substate Party Competition* is calculated by summing the percentage of seats contested by the GOP in both the upper and lower houses in a state's legislative body, along with the percentage of seats won by GOP candidates, again in both houses. This figure is then divided by four to yield an index ranging from zero to one—with the former an indicator of essentially no two-party competition and the latter a sign of complete Republican dominance. In the models presented in Table 5.3, *Substate Party*

*Competition* is lagged behind the dependent variable by one election cycle—with the idea that competitive gains made by the GOP at the subnational level will not translate into concomitant Republican Party gains at the state level until the following election cycle.

A competing explanation for growth of the Republican Party focuses on the extensive economic changes that forever altered the region. In order to examine the Southern transformation from an economy based intensively in agricultural production to one increasingly dominated by manufacturing today, we include a measure tapping the percentage of the workforce employed in the agricultural sector. *Agricultural Employment* is measured as the number of a states' workers employed in the farming and agricultural sector of the economy divided by the total workforce of the state. According to the economic transformation theory, one should expect to see increases in GOP strength in states where the percentage of workers employed in agricultural pursuits is declining. A second variable designed to model economic change is also included in the analysis. *Per Capita Income* measures the changes in a state's relative income level over time. Operationalized as the nominal income of a state in relation to the size of its population, this measure of wealth is a direct correlate with the growth of the Southern economy. Rapidly expanding income levels should translate into ever-increasing numbers of Republican Party loyalists.

As indicated, our model also includes a set of demographic factors thought to be associated with GOP growth in the South. *In-migration* is measured as the proportion of a state's population that is comprised of white residents born outside the Southern region. To the extent that Republican growth is at least partially driven by the in-migration of white Republican sympathizers, it should be captured by this variable. A final demographic variable is designed to represent the proportion of a state's population who are members of an evangelical Protestant denomination.[9] Specifically linked to GOP growth, *Evangelical Protestantism* is hypothesized to be positively related to Republican strength at the state level (see Appendix B for more detailed information concerning variable construction).

## Method

In order to model Republican growth in the region, we utilize a time series cross-sectional methodology (TSCS) that provides us with the leverage to distinguish between the various temporal and cross-sectional forces that might have shaped the growth of the GOP in the South. Analyses of the entire region preclude the examination of subregional demographic, economic, and political dynamics that might influence Republican growth.

Likewise, analyses based on individual states—even when grouped with other one-state studies—tend to ignore regionwide trends that played important roles in partisan development. This chapter takes a middle-of-the-road approach in order to avoid the shortcomings of these two, more limited, methods.[10]

More specifically, we estimate a dynamic panel model with the Southern state serving as our unit of analysis, producing a total of eleven cross sections over a forty-eight-year period—from 1960 through 2008.[11] We are utilizing one of the more commonly accepted techniques in political science to model TSCS data with a continuous dependent variable, the Beck and Katz (1995 and 1996) procedure for generating parameter estimates using ordinary least squares (OLS) regression with the inclusion of a lagged dependent variable in the model to help ameliorate issues related to autocorrelation. The issue of heteroskedasticity in this technique is addressed by the use of clustered robust standard errors.

Although widely accepted, recent scholarship has called for extensions on the Beck and Katz method. Wilson and Butler (2007) caution against utilizing panel models that fail to explicitly take into account unobserved unit (cross-sectional) heterogeneity. Ignoring the issue of unit heterogeneity when it does exist can result in incorrectly estimating the size and/or direction of slope coefficients in the model. For our study, it is not logical, nor realistic, to assume that all eleven states should share a common intercept ($a$) or starting point for *Republican Strength* in 1960. To alleviate this concern, it is suggested that fixed effects be incorporated in panel models using the Beck and Katz approach. We follow this course of action by including $n$-1 state dummies for the models presented. Wilson and Butler further explain that utilizing fixed effects within a TSCS context acts to sweep *away the cross-sectional variation, [leaving] only longitudinal variation within* [states] (2007, 120). Using this approach then will allow us to isolate the over-time effects in our substantive variables of interest as they relate to Republican growth in the region.[12]

In addition to helping ameliorate the statistical issue of serial correlation, the inclusion of a lagged dependent variable within a TSCS framework can also play a substantive role. Using a dynamic panel setup helps to model *persistence* in the dependent variable series. By comparing the coefficient of the lagged dependent variable with those of the other key independent variables, we can partition the extent to which GOP growth is a product of the substantive regressors in our models, as opposed to change produced from movement in the dependent variable series from previous time periods. In this manner, we can statistically derive the extent to which GOP growth in the South is dependent on past patterns of success or failure (Wawro 2002).

# Results

The dramatic growth of the Southern wing of the Republican Party is widely discussed, but it is still easy to underestimate the sheer magnitude of the partisan transformation that the region experienced during the past half-century. What we saw in the data on self-reported partisanship from the American National Election Studies presented in chapter 2, we also saw in our *Republican Strength* variable based on the David index. In 1960, approximately 10 percent of Southern voters aligned with the Republican Party. In 2008, the average was well over 50 percent, resulting in a GOP electorate in 2008 that was more than *five times* larger than it was in 1960. The scope and magnitude of the Southern shift to the Republican Party was simply unprecedented in American political history.

This dramatic growth was not, however, uniform across the Southern states. As you can see from the boxplots in Figure 5.1, there is considerable variation in the growth of the Republican Party among the Southern states. Figure 5.1 illustrates the distribution in our measure of Republican support across the Southern states from 1960 to 2008. A score of 30 percent on this measure—what we refer to as the GOP strength index—indicates that 30 percent of voters consistently supported Republican candidates.[13] Although the Republican Party had a significant following (20 percent or higher) in states such as Florida, North Carolina, Tennessee, and Virginia as early as 1960, Republicans in Georgia and Louisiana were far more difficult to find (less than 5 percent of the voting population). In Mississippi, Republicans were all but invisible (less than 1 in 100).

Prior to the Reagan era, although the Republican Party grew significantly—from 10 percent of the voting population to 37 percent in 1980—the variations among the states continued to persist. In 1978, approximately one in eight voters in Louisiana supported the Republican Party; in Tennessee, nearly half of all voters consistently supported Republican candidates. During and after the Reagan era, the GOP continued to grow, though at a somewhat slower pace than it did during the 1960s and 1970s, but the state variation in support for the GOP decreased dramatically from 1980 to the present. What was once a thirty-point gap between the most Republican and least Republican states has now been more than cut in half. The standard deviation for GOP support in 2008 was little more than a quarter of the standard deviation in 1978.

Before proceeding to a discussion of the results of our multivariate analyses, we will examine the relationship between black mobilization and Republican growth through a series of Granger causality tests specifically designed for use

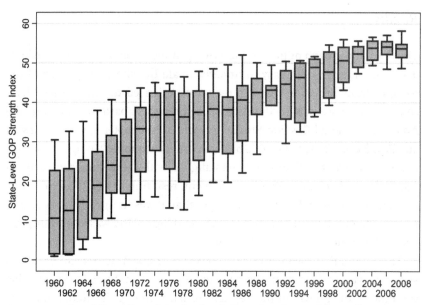

FIGURE 5.1 Republican Growth in the South-State Boxplots, 1960–2008

with TSCS data (for technical specifications and step-by-step instructions for implementing the tests reported here, see Hood, Kidd, and Morris 2008). We begin by evaluating the extent to which

$$Black\ Mobilization_{(i,t-k)} \xrightarrow{Granger\ causes} GOP\ Strength_{(i,t)}$$

for the eleven states in our sample. A series of F-statistics based on lag lengths of three time periods (i.e., t-3) are reported in Table 5.2A. The $F_1$ test statistics examine the hypothesis that there is no causal relationship between black mobilization and GOP growth for any of the states in our sample. As noted in the table, the $F_1$ test statistic at one lag (t-1) is statistically significant, indicating that, for at least some of the states in our sample, black mobilization does Granger-cause Republican growth. $F_1$ test statistics for subsequent lags are not significant, casting doubt on the causal relationship of these two variables beyond a one-lag time period.

Having established that a relationship does exist, we generated a second set of test statistics in order to determine if a common (homogeneous) causal process is present across all eleven Southern states. A statistically significant $F_2$ test statistic indicates that the causal process is heterogeneous, while an insignificant test statistic supports a homogeneous causality process. We again calculate these tests out to three lag lengths. Looking at Table 5.2B reveals that black mobilization Granger-causes Republican growth across all the states in our sample. Having statistically established

TABLE 5.2A  TSCS Granger Tests: $F_1$ Test Statistics

| BLACK MOBILIZATION GRANGER-CAUSES GOP STRENGTH | $F_1$ |
|---|---|
| Lags | |
| t–1 | 2.076** |
| t–2 | 1.394 |
| t–3 | 1.136 |

NOTES: $F_1$ Critical Values
*$p < .10$; **$p < .05$

TABLE 5.2B  TSCS Granger Tests: $F_2$ Test Statistics

| BLACK MOBILIZATION GRANGER-CAUSES GOP STRENGTH | $F_2$ |
|---|---|
| Lags | |
| t–1 | .807 |
| t–2 | .584 |
| t–3 | .682 |

NOTES: $F_2$ Critical Values
*$p < .10$; **$p < .05$

that a common causal process between these two variables of interest exists, it is now necessary to turn to the specification of a multivariate model in order to determine if this relationship will stand up to the addition of control variables. If the relationship between these two variables remains even after the inclusion of substantive controls, we can be much more confident in our findings.

In chapter 3, we argued that our theory of relative advantage provides a logical and compelling explanation for the explosion of Southern Republicanism from 1960 to the present. More specifically, we identified *Substate Party Competition* and *Black Electoral Strength* as the dual engines of this Republican growth. We hypothesize that, as blacks mobilized and, almost uniformly, entered the Democratic Party, conservative white Democrats' control of the party was threatened by a growing coalition of more liberal whites and African Americans. In response to their waning influence in the Democratic Party, conservative whites moved to the Republican Party. To evaluate this contention, we test the following hypothesis:

$H_1$: *Black Electoral Mobilization* is positively related to *Republican Strength*.

We also argue that the relative competitiveness of the Republican Party and its candidates in state and local races had an independent (but reinforcing) effect on Republican growth. As Republican candidates became increasingly competitive for significant political offices, the rolls of Republican Party supporters grew as well. To evaluate this claim, we test the following hypothesis:

$H_2$: *Substate Party Competition* is positively related to *Republican Strength*.

At the regional level, we know that these three variables—*Republican Strength*, *Black Electoral Strength*, and *Substate Party Competition*—grew substantially over the past fifty years. What we do not know is whether or not these variables are empirically related. More specifically, we don't know the substantive relationships between these variables at the state level—a much more reasonable level of analysis than the entire region.

We also assess the extent to which *top-down* dynamics influenced the growth trajectory of the Southern Republican Party (see Aistrup 1996 and Black and Black 2002). We include a presidential vote variable in one model and a set of presidential election dummy variables in another in order to examine the impact of electoral dynamics at the presidential level on partisan dynamics at the state level. A positive and significant coefficient for the *Presidential Vote* variable would suggest some top-down influence on Republicanism. Significant coefficients for the individual presidential elections would also suggest some top-down influence on GOP growth, though, depending on the nature of the election, the influence could be positive or negative. For example, we might expect Reagan's 1980 and 1984 campaigns to be positively related to Republican gains at the state level in subsequent election cycles. The hypotheses to test for the presence of a *top-down* party-building influence for the Republican Party in the region can be more formally stated as the following:

$H_3$: The Republican share of the presidential vote is positively related to *Republican Strength*.
$H_4$: Successful Republican presidential campaigns are positively related to *Republican Strength*.

Again, the competing *bottom-up* theory is examined using the hypothesis labeled $H_2$ (see above).

Although we are particularly interested in the effect of increased party competition and black mobilization on Republican growth, we cannot ignore more traditional explanations for the increase in Southern Republicanism. We include control variables—as previously described—to account for these existing perspectives. More specifically, these controls assess the viability of the following hypotheses:

> *Racial Threat Hypothesis* (Key 1949; Black and Black 1987, 2002):
> $H_5$: Black context is positively related to *Republican Strength*.
> *Class Transformation Hypothesis* (Lublin 2004; Shafer and Johnston 2006):
> $H_6$: Income growth is positively related to *Republican Strength*.
> $H_7$: The size of the agricultural sector is inversely related to *Republican Strength*.
> *Evangelicalism Hypothesis* (Green et al. 2010; Kellstedt 1989):
> $H_8$: The proportion of evangelical Protestants is positively related to *Republican Strength*.
> *In-migration Hypothesis* (Lublin 2004; Scher 1997):
> $H_9$: White in-migration from outside the Southern region is positively related to *Republican Strength*.

To assess the empirical support for these various hypotheses, we implement the TSCS models described above with two different specifications for presidential election effects. The results of our models are presented in Table 5.3.[14] Even when accounting for all of the standard alternative explanations for Republican growth in the South, there is substantial evidence for the two primary hypotheses derived from the theory of relative advantage:

1. Black mobilization is strongly and positively associated with the growth of Republicanism.
2. Substate party competition is also strongly and positively associated with Republican growth.

The statistical significance of *Black Electoral Strength* and *Substate Party Competition* is mirrored by the substantive impact of black mobilization on Republican growth. In Figure 5.2, we have plotted the impact of *Black Electoral Mobilization* on *Republican Strength* for the state in which the effect was smallest (Texas), the state in which the effect was largest (Mississippi), and the average effect for all states in the region.[15] Given that the increase in Republicanism for the time frame of our analysis went from 12 percent to 52 percent, the average trend line suggests that more than a quarter of the increase in Republican growth was due to the direct effect of increases in black mobilization.

*Substate Party Competition* also plays a substantively important role in the growth of Southern Republicanism. In Figure 5.3, we have plotted the impact

TABLE 5.3 Explaining State-Level GOP Party Growth in the South, 1962–2008

| | MODEL 1 | MODEL 2 |
|---|---|---|
| Constant | -.1363 (.0345) | .0624 (.0351) |
| *Political:* | | |
| Republican Strength$_{t-1}$ | .8493** (.0277) | .8720** (.0256) |
| Substate Party Competition$_{t-1}$ | .1108** (.0199) | .0709** (.0156) |
| Presidential Vote | .00021 (.00013) | — |
| Black Electoral Strength | .1258** (.0316) | .1218** (.0370) |
| % Black | .1583 (.1163) | .1236 (.0956) |
| Goldwater 1964 | — | .0090* (.0039) |
| Nixon 1968 | — | .0138 (.0071) |
| Nixon 1972 | — | .0113 (.0098) |
| Ford 1976 | — | -.0078 (.0099) |
| Reagan 1980 | — | .0082 (.0085) |
| Reagan 1984 | — | -.0137 (.0107) |
| Bush 1988 | — | .0172 (.0086) |
| Bush 1992 | — | .0117 (.0108) |
| Dole 1996 | — | .0262 (.0131) |
| Bush 2000 | — | .0385* (.0156) |
| Bush 2004 | — | .0367 (.0174) |
| Bush 2008 | — | -.0269 (.0190) |
| *Demographic:* | | |
| In-Migration | .0344 (.0446) | -.0412 (.0627) |
| Evangelical Protestants | .4355* (.1422) | .2519 (.1492) |
| *Economic:* | | |
| Per Capita Income ($1,000) | -.0005 (.0004) | -.0012 (.0006) |
| Agricultural Sector Employment | .0058 (.1246) | -.0661 (.1000) |
| $R^2$ | .979 | .981 |
| N | 264 | 264 |

NOTES: OLS Coefficients with fixed effects and robust standard errors clustered by state in parentheses.
*$p < .05$ (two-tailed test); **$p < .01$ (two-tailed test)

of *Substate Party Competition* for the state in which the effect was smallest (Arkansas), the state in which the effect was largest (Tennessee), and the average effect for all Southern states. Again, given that the increase in Southern Republicanism for the time frame of our analysis rose from 12 percent to 52 percent, the average trend line suggests that more than half of the increase in Republican growth was due to the direct effect of an increase in the prior substate competitiveness of Republican candidates.[16] The evidence at hand strongly supports the contention that black electoral mobilization led directly to Republican growth in the South. The results of our extended

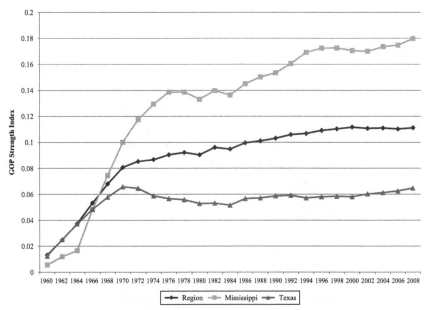

FIGURE 5.2 The Effect of Black Registration on Republican Growth in the South, 1960–2008

models also provide strong empirical support for the *bottom-up* theory of two-party development in the South over that of the *top-down* school. We conclude that state-level GOP growth was, in part, propelled by Republican success at lower officeholding levels. This is compelling evidence for the *bottom-up* perspective.

The coefficient for the lagged value of *GOP Strength* is also positive, statistically significant, and close to 1 (.85 to .87). This statistical result closely mirrors the almost monotonic growth in GOP strength over the time period of our study (see again Figure 5.1). Viewed in this light, Republican success in prior election cycles creates an ever-growing base of support for future years. When or where the momentum of this positive growth will be slowed or altered remains a question for the future.

Overall then, we see that *Black Electoral Strength* and *Substate Party Competition*—as predicted by the theory of relative advantage—are responsible for the preponderance of the increase in Southern Republicanism over the past half-century. The dramatic impact of black mobilization and increased interparty competition is even more striking when one realizes that no other single variable was significant in both sets of model estimates. We find no empirical support—in either the presidential vote model or the model that includes dummy variables for each of the presidential elections—for the *Racial Threat* hypothesis or the *Economic Growth/Class-Based* hypothesis.

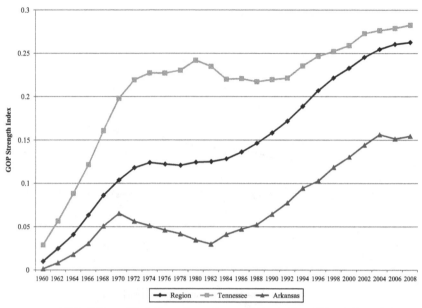

FIGURE 5.3 The Effect of Sub-State Party Competition on Republican Growth in the South, 1960–2008

We also fail to find any support for the in-migration hypothesis. Clearly, there is considerable state-level variation relating to in-migration, and in-migration levels have also varied over the years, but we find no support for the contention that this variation—either across states or across time—is related to the strength of the GOP in the South.

Finally, there is mixed support for the evangelicalism hypothesis. Although *Evangelicalism* is statistically significant ($p < .05$) and signed appropriately in Model 1, it is not significant (and its coefficient is considerably smaller) in Model 2 of Table 5.3. *Evangelicalism* is also consistent in both of the GMM-IV models, but the coefficients vary considerably (see Table C.5.1). Given the inconsistency of these results, we can make no firm conclusion regarding the impact of evangelicalism on state-level GOP growth in the South. Still, there is some limited evidence that evangelicalism played a role in the growth of Southern Republicanism, and we will continue to assess the potential effects of evangelicalism in subsequent chapters.

## Discussion and Conclusion

So, what explains the variation in Republican growth that we see across the Southern states over time? The theory of relative advantage predicts a direct relationship between black mobilization and Republican growth. An additional expectation of relative advantage theory is the presence of a direct relationship between party competition and Republican growth. We find strong statistical support for both propositions. From a substantive viewpoint, slightly more than half of the growth in Republicanism in the South over the last half-century is directly attributable to the effects of these two variables. Conversely, we find only mixed support for the contention that the growth of Southern Republicanism is due to evangelicalism, and we find no support for the contention that the explosion in Republican growth in the South was fueled by racial threat, economic growth or class politics, or in-migration. Likewise, there is almost no statistical support indicating that presidential campaigns acted as a growth catalyst for the GOP in the region (the *top-down* school).

As we found in our earlier study of the late twentieth-century South, political factors begat political change well into the twenty-first century. Although there is no doubt that regional in-migration and economic transformation were ongoing phenomena during the period of time under study, these factors—along with other demographic variables such as black context and evangelicalism—did not appear to have a consistent and direct effect on the growth of Southern Republicanism over the time period analyzed. We find no reason to believe then, that economic or demographic change alone, however profound, would have broken the long-held constant in Southern politics of one-party Democratic dominance, absent these political changes. Our findings and conclusions contrast sharply with the body of existing literature on the growth of the Republican Party in the South.

Even with a basic understanding of the political dynamics of the growth of Southern Republicanism, a number of important questions remain: First, what factors fostered (or constrained) the mobilization of the black electorate? To what extent did political organizations such as the Southern Regional Council boost mobilization, and did the efforts of white extremists (e.g., civil rights violations) restrict black political mobilization? What factors explain the wide variance in substate Republican competitiveness? Did a variety of local factors boost competitiveness in specific regions; or did national party efforts in particular locales boost competitiveness; or is it some mixture of the two? In addition, an exhaustive effort should be undertaken to understand the link between the effect of economic and demographic change in the region and the corresponding political alterations that led to two-party politics. To fully understand the transformation of the Southern party system—and party systems more generally—we must find answers to these important questions.

Although it has been a prominent aspect of the literature on Southern politics since Key's *Southern Politics in State and Nation*, the absence of any empirical support for the racial threat hypothesis is not so surprising when one remembers that Key's original characterization of this perspective was intended for a political context in which African Americans were excluded from electoral politics. For conservative whites in a polity that disenfranchised blacks, the primary threat—as Key described it—was violence. In this political context, Key provided a compelling logic for the relationship between black context and white conservatism. In a political environment in which African Americans are mobilized and effective participants in the electoral system, the nature of the threat to white conservatives—now a political threat (the loss of control of the Democratic Party to African Americans and liberal whites)—has changed. In modern Southern politics, a primary motivating factor for white movement to the Republican Party, as relative advantage theory suggests, is black mobilization, not black context. Simply put, Key's threat, while relevant to the time about which he was writing, is no longer a driving force in Southern politics. This has been true for some time—at least as long as African Americans have been effectively re-enfranchised in the South. What is surprising was the length of time it has taken us to realize the time-bound and contextually dependent nature of Key's original (and important) insight.

Frankly, we were surprised by the weakness of the economic hypothesis for Republican growth. It is plausible, and others have found some empirical support for a relationship between economic growth and Republican expansion in the South (Lublin 2004 and Shafer and Johnston 2006). Failure to account for the impact of substate party competition and black mobilization may provide one explanation for the earlier results, but another explanation may be that the state is not the ideal unit of analysis for discerning the effect of economics and income growth on partisanship. One might argue that such an effect is much more likely to manifest itself at the county level or at the individual level. One could also make a similar argument for the likely effect of the racial threat hypothesis and GOP growth. Using the state as the unit of analysis has a long and storied history in Southern politics scholarship. Still, these are legitimate empirical questions worthy of further study. Using county-level and individual-level analyses, we address both of these claims in subsequent chapters.

Though the data reflect the dynamics predicted by the theory of relative advantage, we still lack a full understanding of the relationship between black mobilization and Republican growth. Data limitations make it difficult (but not impossible) to examine this dynamic at the substate level, so further work remains to be done on this issue. We also still lack a full characterization of the individual-level dynamic, or dynamics, that produce the aggregate-level results reported. What factors are at work at the county and individual levels that tie black mobilization to Republican growth—and, in some states, Republican growth to black mobilization—in the South? These questions are addressed in subsequent chapters.

| Relative Advantage and Republican
Growth at the Substate Level

IN THIS CHAPTER, WE explore Republican substate growth in the South using Louisiana and North Carolina. For our theory to have wider utility, it should be able to explain GOP expansion in the South across more than one context. In brief, we specify a similar set of analyses as those constructed in chapter 5, this time using parishes or counties as the unit of analysis.[1] This chapter serves as a test of *relative advantage* theory using a smaller geographic division and a slightly different dependent variable. We are fortunate as well to be able to analyze a state from each of the recognized subregions of the South: Louisiana as a representative of the Deep South and North Carolina as an example of a Rim South state.

Both Louisiana and North Carolina require registration by party and, in addition, both also collect data on registration by race.[2] Unlike the state-level analyses previously presented, Republican growth is now measured by GOP registrants as a percentage of total registrants. Fortunately, we have unbroken annual data for both of these states going back to 1966, the year following the implementation of the VRA. Using party registration data, if anything, should provide a much more conservative test of the theory of relative advantage, given the fact that changes in party registration (or identification) always lag behind alterations in voting behavior. White Southerners showed a propensity to vote for GOP candidates long before identifying or registering as Republicans.

Figures 6.1 and 6.2 present a series of boxplots for Republican registration in Louisiana and North Carolina over time. A quick glance at these two figures reveals two very different patterns for over-time GOP growth in these states. The growth in the Bayou State is impressive, beginning with a median value of only .6 percent in 1966 and increasing to 22.8 percent in

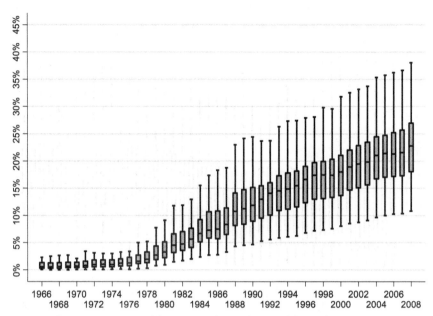

FIGURE 6.1 Louisiana Republicans-Parish Boxplots, 1966–2008

2008. Looking at Figure 6.1, we can see that Republican registrants across all parishes were close to nonexistent for a decade through 1976, when the percentage of GOP registrants began a slow, monotonic rise over the next 30 years. As evidenced by the extent of the box and whiskers in the earlier part of the time series, there was very little variance in GOP registrants across parishes (the entire plot remained under the 5 percent threshold until 1977). After 1977, the degree of variance between parishes increased, as evidenced graphically by elongation of both boxes and whiskers across subsequent years.

North Carolina began the post-VRA time series with a median value of 11.1 percent, one indication that the GOP party machinery was more developed in the Tar Heel State compared with Louisiana (see Figure 6.2). Over time, the median for Republican registrants in the state shows a slow, monotonic rise ending in 2008 at 31 percent. The pattern of GOP registration in North Carolina is also characterized by a much wider degree of dispersion across the entire time series, demonstrated graphically by the size of both the box and whisker set for each year. For example, even in 1966 the 1-percent-to-99-percent range for GOP registrants is 68.3 percent. By the end of the time series, this range had narrowed to some degree but was still a considerable 55 percent.

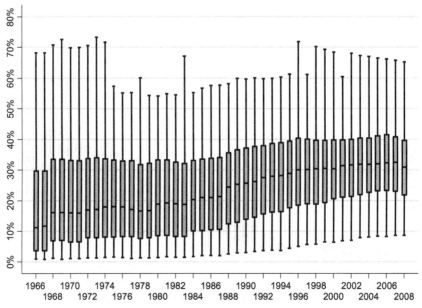

FIGURE 6.2 North Carolina Republicans-County Boxplots, 1966–2008

## Theoretical Underpinnings

As in chapter 5, we are looking for evidence that our theory of relative advantage has applicability beyond the state-level context. As a quick review, our theory stipulates that the rise in Republican registration in Louisiana and North Carolina in the post-VRA era was a direct product of the ability of the black populace to participate in the political process. Within a parish or county, we should see increasing numbers of whites registering as Republicans where there was a relative advantage to doing so, namely, in those parishes or counties where larger numbers of (re)enfranchised black citizens were registering and identifying as Democrats. This produced a crowding-out effect for white conservatives and the influence they could exert on Democratic Party politics. So, the value of identifying as a Democrat for white conservatives should decrease over time as the ability of this group to use the Democrat Party to nominate candidates and pursue policy objectives was diminished. For white conservatives, and much later white moderates, the Republican Party represented a ready-made, viable alternative to the increasing intraparty competition that characterized the post-VRA Democratic Party.

Our theory indicates that the presence and extent of black political mobilization should be the drivers behind the shift of white conservatives with regard to registering and identifying as Republicans. As such, our models include a direct measure of black mobilization at the parish or county level to act as a direct test of relative advantage theory. In the pre-civil rights era, such a threat to white political hegemony might have been defined simply by the size of the local African American population. Key's *black-belt hypothesis* however, is not an adequate manner for conceptualizing the political up-heaval created by the VRA and other constitutional and statutory changes in this area. The size of the black population may still exert some degree of causal influence on the rate of Republican registration, and we therefore include such a measure in the empirical models found in Tables 6.1 and 6.2. As Key was writing before the widespread re-enfranchisement of African Americans in the region, the size of the African American population in the post-civil rights era may actually be viewed as having a negative relationship with GOP registration. Clearly, with almost all black Southerners registering and identifying as Democrats, the relative size of the African American pop-ulation could effectively be viewed as a ceiling or cap on the size of GOP registration within a specific parish or county.

The rise of viable substate two-party competition in the South varied con-siderably across the eleven states of the region. Some states like North Caro-lina actually contained local Republican Party organizations, a residual dating back to the Civil War and the Reconstruction era. In other states, es-pecially those in the Deep South, there was virtually no formal Republican Party in any organizational sense of the word outside of a very small group of citizens seeking political patronage. These post office Republicans in the Deep South were seldom involved in traditional party-building activities such as recruiting and promoting candidates to run for office. Not only should Republican Party registration be affected by the size of black mobili-zation within the parish or county, but also by the extent of the existing orga-nizational development of the Republican Party within the state. For those states where the Republican Party maintained some local party organization, we should see increases in GOP registration earlier, compared with those states where the GOP was essentially anemic or nonexistent. Such would seem to fit the data in the cases of Louisiana and North Carolina, which ex-hibit very different patterns in terms of the rise of Republican registration at the substate level (see again Figures 6.1 and 6.2).

In our search for empirical evidence bearing on the theory of relative advantage, we cannot ignore other prominent theories related to the rise of the Republican Party in the region. Other explanations for GOP growth include demographic change (especially in-migration) (Bass and De Vries 1976; Scher 1977; and Stanley and Castle 1988), economic development

(Cobb 1999; Shafer and Johnston 2001, 2006; and Sosna 1987), and religion (Green et al. 1998, 2010 and Kellstedt 1989). In order to determine the extent to which relative advantage theory provides an empirical explanation for the rise in GOP party registration in Louisiana and North Carolina, we simultaneously control for the presence of competing causal mechanisms posited by other scholars. Only in this manner can we be reasonably assured that political mobilization on the part of blacks is the primary, or at least one of the primary, empirical explanations for the increase in Republican Party activity at the substate level.

## Political Backdrops

### North Carolina Party Systems

More than any other state in the South, North Carolina contained a viable Republican Party element during the pre-civil rights era. The Republican Party in the Tar Heel State, however, was confined primarily to the Appalachian Mountain spine running through the western section of the state (see the 1966 panel in Figure 6.3). The GOP successfully ran candidates for local offices, but statewide electoral success was beyond reach during this period of time.[3]

Following the success of a fusion party around the turn of the twentieth century that included a coalition of populists, Republicans, and blacks, measures were taken to reassert Democratic dominance that included the disenfranchisement of African Americans (Eamon 2008 and Bass and De Vries 1976).[4] The presence of a viable Republican group within the state produced a fairly strong bifactional system within the Democratic Party, as opposed to a free-for-all multifactional affair. Key (1949) described a Democratic Party during this time as being split into two factions called the *organization* and the *anti-organization*. Fault lines between these two groups fell largely along economic lines.

The *organization* faction largely resembled the typical conservative "Bourbon Elite" found in other areas of the South: very pro-business, anti-tax, and bent on maintenance of the racial caste system. Bass and De Vries (1976) report that this faction largely dominated the North Carolina political scene through the middle of the twentieth century. It is interesting to note that this element was geographically based in the middle of the state in the Piedmont region. Unlike other Southern states where the most reactionary politics was housed in black-belt areas, the Piedmont did not contain the highest concentrations of blacks. Instead, the black belt in North Carolina ran through the coastal plain/tidewater region in the eastern portion of the state (Key 1949). This was the geographic center of the *anti-organization* forces and also the most heavily Democratic area of the state up to the present day. From 1948 through the mid-1970s, this progressive faction was typically the more dominant (Bass and De Vries 1976 and Fleer 1994).

Some mark the election of Republican Governor James E. Holshouser Jr. in 1972 as the demarcation line for genuine two-party politics in North Carolina. This was also the same year that conservative icon Jesse Helms was elected to a U.S. Senate seat. Certainly, compared to Louisiana, viable two-party competition was occurring approximately two decades earlier in North Carolina. What changed? A confluence of political, social, and demographic transformations worked to alter the party landscape of North Carolina.

Though labeled by many, including V. O. Key, as being progressive on racial matters, this issue nonetheless played a key role in realigning conservative Democrats to the GOP.[5] Going back to the 1968 presidential contest, Luebke (1998) indicated that George Wallace's vote share was positively related to county-level black registration. Although Wallace was running as an independent candidate, this relationship was a sure indicator that North Carolina conservatives had de-aligned from the Democratic Party and were willing to respond to racially conservative cues. Likewise, Helms's racially conservative Senate campaigns attracted many disaffected white Democrats, known as *Jessecrats*.

The Piedmont provided fertile ground for the cultivation of new GOP converts, especially those classified as economic conservatives. Rapid urbanization and economic growth beginning in the 1970s, along with numbers of white in-migrants, provided the raw material necessary for GOP growth. Textile mills, furniture factories, and tobacco gave way to financial services and high tech in the research triangle area and the corresponding urban crescent that runs from Raleigh down through Charlotte (Eamon 2008 and Luebke 1998). This transformation, which accelerated in the 1990s, ushered in an era of decided two-party competition on a statewide basis. Today, the two parties mirror the ideological divide present at the national level, with the GOP representing economic, racial, and social conservatism. Race and religion are the two most prevalent cleavage lines, with whites and evangelical Protestants representing core groups in the Republican Party and blacks and mainline white Protestants undergirding Democratic ranks. Although the recognized economic schism does exist between the two parties, it is not nearly as pronounced in North Carolina as in other states (Prysby 2010).

In terms of electoral success, an interesting pattern has emerged in the post-civil rights era where Republicans have experienced a far greater level of success at the federal level, and Democrats have maintained a substantial string of victories for state constitutional and legislative offices (Prysby 2010). For example, North Carolina has elected only two Republican governors in the last century. On the other hand, except for Barack Obama's narrow victory in 2008, North Carolina voted Republican in every presidential election since 1968 sans one, native Southerner Jimmy Carter's 1976 run. Since 1972, Republicans have won ten of fourteen U.S. Senate elections, with the congressional delegation typically split evenly between the two parties.

More recently, the GOP has begun to make significant substate gains, capturing a majority in both chambers of the state legislature in 2010 for the first time since 1898.[6] In addition, the Republican Party has almost achieved parity in control of county commissions with the Democrats.[7] In terms of party affiliation, a statewide poll from November 2010 indicated that 44 percent of North Carolinians identified as Democrats, 38 percent as Republicans, and 17 percent as Independents.[8] Certainly, North Carolina appears to remain one of the more electorally competitive states in the region for the near term.

Figure 6.3 maps the growth in North Carolina GOP registrants in ten-year increments, beginning in 1966 and continuing through 2006. The percentage of Republican registrants is displayed at the county level beginning with the 1966 time period. The bulk of Republican strength in this time period resided in the Appalachian mountain chain, with a number of counties containing 30 percent or more GOP registrants. Conversely, Democratic strength was housed in the eastern sections of the state. This initial level of GOP strength is a far cry from what existed in Louisiana in the same time period (see Figure 6.4). Over time, as levels of Republican registration remained stable in the mountain area, there was a slow diffusion across the state eastward through the Piedmont, into the coastal plain, and finally into the tidewater area. By 2006, only one-fifth of the counties in North Carolina contained fewer than 20 percent GOP registrants, compared with 1966 when fully three-fifths fell into this category.

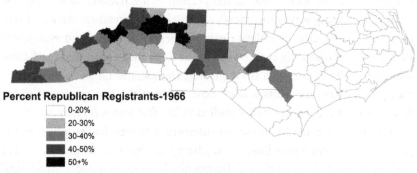

Percent Republican Registrants-1966

▢ 0-20%
▨ 20-30%
▨ 30-40%
■ 40-50%
■ 50+%

FIGURE 6.3 Republican Registrants in North Carolina, 1966–2006

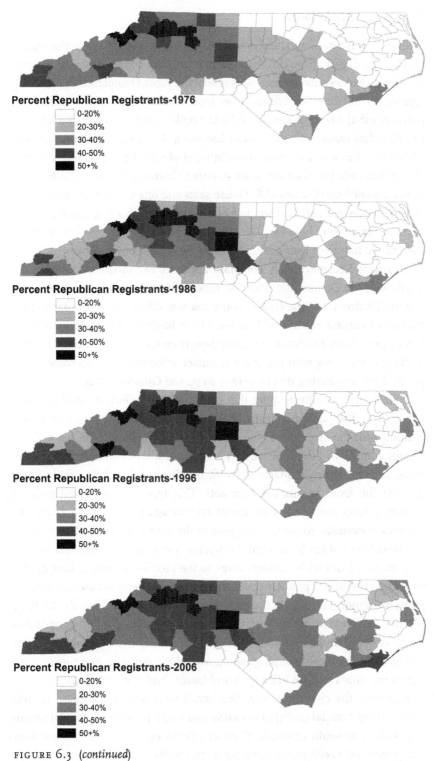

**Percent Republican Registrants-1976**

- ☐ 0-20%
- ▨ 20-30%
- ▨ 30-40%
- ▨ 40-50%
- ■ 50+%

**Percent Republican Registrants-1986**

- ☐ 0-20%
- ▨ 20-30%
- ▨ 30-40%
- ▨ 40-50%
- ■ 50+%

**Percent Republican Registrants-1996**

- ☐ 0-20%
- ▨ 20-30%
- ▨ 30-40%
- ▨ 40-50%
- ■ 50+%

**Percent Republican Registrants-2006**

- ☐ 0-20%
- ▨ 20-30%
- ▨ 30-40%
- ▨ 40-50%
- ■ 50+%

FIGURE 6.3 (*continued*)

## Louisiana Party Systems

The South is no monolith, as key differences exist across states in the region. In this regard, perhaps none is more distinctive than Louisiana. Until recently, we would also describe Louisiana as one of the most Democratic states in the region, second only to Arkansas on most indicators of partisan strength (Grosser 1982). Over the course of the last half-century, however, the Republican Party has made major strides in Louisiana. In 1960, the Democrats held all federal offices and all state constitutional offices. In the state legislature, Republicans did not hold any seats in either chamber. By 2010, the Republicans controlled six of seven U.S. House seats and one U.S. Senate seat. At the state level, the governor's office, five of six executive offices, and a majority in the state house were held by GOP officeholders—a remarkable feat given the entrenched nature of Democratic Party politics in the Bayou State.

Following Reconstruction, Louisiana appeared like much of the rest of the South with the Democratic Bourbon Elite taking control of the state's party system. During this time frame, Louisiana was effectively a one-party state, having all control resting with conservative business interests within the Democratic Party. Known as the second-party system in Louisiana, the white working class along with the black populace effectively had no voice in the political process during this time (Key 1949 and Grosser 1982).

Unlike other Southern states that continued to be characterized by Bourbon control, the party system in Louisiana underwent a radical change beginning with the election of Huey Long to the governorship in 1928. From this time until 1963, the state party system could still be characterized as one-party, but very strongly bifactional with the dividing line being that of economics: the *haves* versus the *have-nots*. This type of class-based political system, pitting the good-government faction against the Long populists, failed to materialize to the same degree in the South outside of Louisiana.

The collapse of the bifactional third-party system was created in large part as a reaction from white conservatives to the race issue. Parent (2004) also writes that the largest political sea change in the state revolved around the civil rights movement. Writing in the early 1980s, Grosser labeled this the *No Party* era. In a similar vein, others described the state party system in the 1970s and 1980s as being multifactional in nature, with a fairly weak Republican Party included among these groupings along with black, populist, and conservative Democrats (Bass and De Vries 1976 and Landry and Parker 1982).

Following the civil rights era, Democrats were able to maintain control with a strong biracial coalition of blacks and white populists, many of whom were Cajuns in south Louisiana (Bass and De Vries 1976). The race question that generated a realignment among whites in the Protestant north did not have the same resonance for those whites of French or southern European heritage (Bolner 1982 and Parent 2004). Even in the early 1980s, Grosser (1982) still indicated that there was no evidence of a Republican majority in the state. During this time, blacks became a major base of support for the Democratic Party and the number of black elected officeholders increased tremendously (Parent and Perry 2010). For example, Parent reports that black officeholding went from 33 to 333 in ten years (1968 to 1978).

By the mid-1990s, Republicans had made concerted gains in officeholding at multiple levels, with the most high-profile election being that of Mike Foster to two terms as governor. Parent and Perry (2010) describe the period from 1996 to 2005 as competitive two-party politics, so perhaps we can also characterize this as a new party era, supplanting the previous period of party disorganization following the civil rights movement.

The largest shift preceding genuine two-party politics involved the movement of white Catholics in the southern part of the state away from the Democratic Party. Cultural issues, like abortion, appear to have had some bearing on the realignment of this group to the GOP. The current party coalitions in Louisiana now resemble those at the national level, with the GOP receiving support from the business community, middle-class suburbanites, and social conservatives (the "Religious Right") often found in the rural areas of the state. The Democratic Party is composed of a coalition of blacks, blue-collar laborers, and white progressives in urban areas (Parent 2004 and Parent and Perry 2010). As indicated earlier, the more recent trend in the state involves continuing Republican gains in terms of voter registration and officeholding, especially state constitutional and legislative offices.

Figure 6.4 provides a series of snapshots in ten-year increments beginning in 1966 that map the growth of the Louisiana GOP. In this case, we are plotting the percentage of Louisianans registered as Republican at the parish level. In 1966, only a single parish (Caddo) contained more than 5 percent Republican registrants, with the remaining parishes falling below the 5 percent level. Ten years later, not much had changed, with only three additional parishes falling into the 5–10 percent range. By 1986, however, the GOP presence had greatly expanded across the state, especially in the north. During this time period, a number of parishes in the Catholic south continued to defy the pattern of Republican growth found elsewhere in the state. Rapid growth then continued to be evident in 1996 and again in 2006 as Republican identification increased, to varying degrees, across the entire state. By 2006, at least 10 percent of registrants in every parish were Republican.

Our goal in this chapter is to explain how and why these patterns of GOP growth emerged in North Carolina and Louisiana. To do so, we make use of

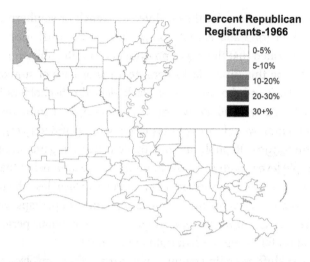

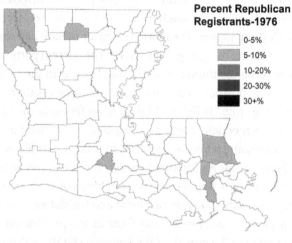

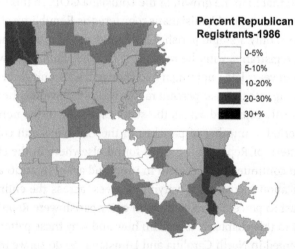

FIGURE 6.4 Republican Registrants in Louisiana, 1966–2006

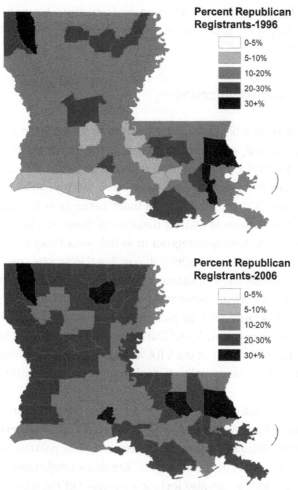

FIGURE 6.4 (*continued*)

multivariate models designed to simultaneously account for demographic, economic, and political changes over time. In addition, we also account for factors related to the unique political geography of these states through the inclusion of substantive variables related to geography.

## Data

The data for the analyses presented in this chapter come from a number of primary sources. Party and racial registration data were collected directly from state entities including state archive libraries, the Louisiana Secretary of State, and the North Carolina State Board of Elections. Demographic and economic data were derived from various years of the U.S. Census, and data on religious adherence again came from the Glenmary Studies. A detailed listing of the data sources utilized for this chapter can be found in Appendix A.

## Variable Operationalization

The dependent variable, *Republican Registrants*, for both the Louisiana and North Carolina analyses is operationalized as the number of Republicans by parish/county divided by the number of total registrants. We are fortunate to have these data on an annual basis from 1966 through 2008. Although we could measure GOP growth using an index based on vote outcomes (as in chapter 5), this variable is a direct measure of those in Louisiana or North Carolina who were willing to register or switch (over time) their registration to the Republican Party. If anything, using Republican voter registration is a much more conservative measure of Republican growth, as registration lagged behind alterations in voting patterns. In addition, these registration figures provide a fairly accurate picture of the number of Republican identifiers at the parish or county level.[9] Our time series for these two states begins just after implementation of the VRA and should, therefore, capture the effects of increased black political mobilization related to this landmark legislation.

Our primary independent variable of interest, *Black Electoral Strength*, is the number of black registrants as a percentage of total registrants. According to relative advantage theory, this measure of black political power should be positively related to the percentage of Republican registrants in the parish or county. In addition, we also include a measure of the relative size of the black population in the parish or county. As in all Southern states, the percentage of blacks in the population varies greatly in spatial terms. North Carolina and Louisiana are not exceptions to this. The size of the black population within a parish or county can also be thought of as a ceiling on the maximum size of the GOP in a given area.

Additional control variables in the models presented in this chapter include median household income adjusted for inflation. This measure is our primary means of assessing the economic hypothesis as it relates to Republican growth. Parishes or counties with higher income levels relative to others should see greater numbers of GOP registrants. Republican increases following World War II have also been linked to urbanization, and we include a variable, *Percent Urban*, to control for this possibility. We also control for the size of non-Southern in-migration into these counties and parishes relative to the total parish/county population. Although the scholarly literature is mixed on the role in-migration played on Republican growth, on the whole we would expect that this variable should be positively related to the number of GOP registrants.[10]

Finally, we measure the effect of religion using historic church denomination data. *Percent Evangelical* is operationalized as the number of adherents in specified evangelical Protestant denominations over the total parish/county population. Linked to social conservatism, we hypothesize that this measure is positively correlated with GOP growth. For Louisiana, we also specify a separate model that includes a variable to measure the percentage of Catholic adherents within each parish. The Protestant-Catholic divide approximates the north/south political subregions in Louisiana. As discussed previously, Republican registration should be negatively associated with the measure of Catholicism.

In North Carolina, we include an additional control variable designed to tap into the importance of military bases within the Tar Heel State. Measured as the number of active military personnel as a percentage of the total population within the county, this is formulated to capture a potential source of Republican identifiers and is also linked in a secondary fashion with economic growth. North Carolina is rife with military installations including Camp Lejeune, Fort Bragg, Cherry Point MCAS, and Pope Air Force Base, to name a few. The state ranks third after Texas and California in terms of the percentage of active-duty military personnel at 9.9 percent of the nationwide total.[11] In addition, military retirees often settle near bases, and this could be another source of potential GOP identifiers in such counties. Appendix B contains additional detailed information on variable operationalizations.

## Methodology

Our modeling strategy is very similar to that employed for the state-level models described in chapter 5. In this case, we pool counties/parishes across years to create a panel model designed to explain GOP growth using the percentage of Republican registrants as our dependent variable. More specifically, we model partisan change in Louisiana and North Carolina in separate models, using parishes or counties as the unit of analysis. The time span for both models ranges annually from 1966 through 2008. These models are estimated using OLS, contain a lagged dependent variable and fixed effects, and employ robust standard errors. In addition, we also report alternative model estimates using a GMM instrumental variable framework in Appendix C.[12]

## Results

Growth patterns for Republican registration have already been discussed from a descriptive standpoint (see again Figures 6.1 and 6.2). Our task now involves testing a series of multivariate models designed to provide Causal explanations for these observed growth patterns in Louisiana and North Carolina. After implementing two separate unit-root tests specially designed for use with panel data, there was evidence that our dependent variable series for both North Carolina and Louisiana may not be stationary. In order to correct for this issue, we transformed the dependent variable for both states by taking the natural log of each series. Reapplying the unit-roots tests following these transformations, the series were determined to be stationary.[13]

Our next task will be to examine the relationship between Republican registration rates and black mobilization using a series of Granger causality tests, which are again specifically designed for use with panel data.[14] For the sixty-four parishes in Louisiana and the one hundred counties in North Carolina, we evaluate the extent to which

$$\textit{Black Mobilization}_{(i,\,t\text{-}k)} \xrightarrow{\textit{Granger causes}} \textit{GOP Registration}_{(i,\,t)}$$

The results for both North Carolina and Louisiana demonstrate that there is strong evidence, in a binary sense, of a causal relationship between black mobilization and rates of Republican registration. Additional testing reveals that the nature of this relationship is *heterogeneous*, or exists for some subset of parishes and counties in the two states under analysis.[15] Given the substate diversity within these two states, it would be of some surprise had this process been determined to be effectively the same (*homogeneous*) across all sixty-four parishes and one hundred counties in our study. We now turn to the specification of multivariate models designed to determine whether the observed Granger relationship between black mobilization and GOP registration holds as a general pattern across our unit of analysis with the addition of key control variables.

The results of our multivariate models are located in Table 6.1 for North Carolina and Table 6.2 for Louisiana, respectively. We first turn our attention to the models designed to explain partisan change in North Carolina. One of our primary variables of interest, *Black Electoral Strength*, is positively and significantly related to the level of GOP registrants at the county level, while *Percent Black* is negatively and significantly associated with our dependent variable.[16] In addition, the lagged value of GOP registrants is positively and significantly related to levels of Republican Party registrants in the present time period.

TABLE 6.1 Explaining County-Level GOP Registration in North Carolina, 1966–2008

|  | MODEL |
| --- | --- |
| Constant | −.1031 (.0715) |
| Log GOP Registrants$_{t-1}$ | .8657** (.0189) |
| Black Electoral Strength | .3994** (.1112) |
| Percent Black | −.9912** (.1894) |
| In-Migration | −.1164** (.0319) |
| Evangelical Protestants | −.0386 (.0477) |
| Percent Military | −.2169 (.2063) |
| Percent Urban | .0998** (.1894) |
| Median Household Income ($1,000) | .0016* (.0007) |
| $R^2$ | .98 |
| N | 4,200 |

NOTES: OLS Coefficients with fixed effects and robust standard errors clustered by county in parentheses.
DEPENDENT Variable (*GOP Registrants*) is logged.
*$p < .05$ (two-tailed test); **$p < .01$ (two-tailed test)

Turning to the other covariates in the model, we see that in-migration to the Tar Heel State is negatively linked to Republican growth. This finding is, however, in line with one recent study that found contemporary in-migration in North Carolina was actually linked to higher levels of unaffiliated registrants and Democratic voting in the 2008 presidential election (Hood and McKee 2010). On the other hand, urbanization and income levels are both positively associated with GOP party registration. This pattern more closely aligns with traditional explanations for Republican growth in the post-World War II South. It should be noted as well that North Carolina has experienced higher levels of income growth and also contains many more highly urbanized areas compared to Louisiana. Neither active-duty military personnel nor the percentage of evangelical Protestants, however, appears to have any apparent relationship with GOP party registration levels.

We now turn to a discussion of the findings for our parish-level model of Louisiana, which are located in Table 6.2. Model 1 in Table 6.2 contains a variable designed to measure the percentage of Catholic adherents within each parish, and a second model replaces this indicator with one that measures evangelical Protestant membership levels. As with the North Carolina model, *Black Electoral Strength* is significant in both models and signed in a positive direction.[17] Again, this is an indication that the percentage of black registrants within a parish is positively related to the growth in GOP registrants. Although we are using OLS, remember that the dependent variable is

TABLE 6.2 Explaining Parish-Level GOP Registration in Louisiana, 1966–2008

| | MODEL 1 | MODEL 2 |
|---|---|---|
| Constant | .4042** (.0588) | .3436** (.0726) |
| Log GOP Registrants$_{t\text{-}1}$ | .9556** (.0047) | .9550** (.0048) |
| Black Electoral Strength | .4101** (.1437) | .3801* (.1468) |
| Percent Black | −1.3321** (.2395) | -1.286** (.2415) |
| In-Migration | .5462** (.0878) | .5517** (.0929) |
| Evangelical Protestants | — | .1107 (.1313) |
| Catholic | −.0680 (.0764) | — |
| Percent Urban | −.0823** (.0214) | −.0840** (.0215) |
| Median Household Income ($1,000) | −.0043** (.0588) | −.0041** (.0008) |
| R² | .98 | .98 |
| N | 2,688 | 2,688 |

NOTES: OLS Coefficients with fixed effects and robust standard errors clustered by parish in parentheses.
DEPENDENT Variable (*GOP Registrants*) is logged.
*$p$ < .05 (two-tailed test); **$p$ < .01 (two-tailed test)

logged, which somewhat complicates the interpretation of the magnitude of effects related to individual coefficients. A substantive interpretation for *Black Electoral Strength* is offered at the end of the current section.

Moving on to the remaining covariates, one can see that the percentage of black residents within the parish is negatively and significantly related to the level of Republican registrants. With blacks identifying overwhelmingly as Democrats, this should come as no surprise, and this indicator can be seen as a natural ceiling or cap on GOP identifiers in a given geographic locale. The coefficient representing the lagged value of GOP registrants is also positive and significant, an indicator that the level of GOP registrants in the previous year is a close approximation of the value in the present time period, allowing for some small degree of positive growth. This finding closely approximates the boxplots displayed in Figure 6.1.

The relationship between the percentage of non-Southern in-migrants within each parish and GOP registration was positive and statistically significant. For the Bayou State at least, the movement of non-Southerners into the state over time helped to bolster GOP party registration figures. Two variables that were negatively related to GOP registration were the level of urbanization and median household income. While the existing literature links these factors to increased Republican growth, our models indicate that this was not the case at the parish level in Louisiana. Louisiana contains comparatively fewer large, urban parishes, and those that do qualify under this definition (i.e., Orleans Parish and Caddo Parish) tend to also contain large numbers of black residents. Growth in GOP identification then took place in more comparatively rural parishes with lower income levels. This finding is certainly interesting given the emphasis by some placed on wealth being the primary driver behind partisan change in the region (see, for example, Shafer and Johnston 2001). Finally, neither of the two indicators of religious adherence, *Percent Catholic* or *Percent Evangelical Protestant*, were significant predictors of GOP registration levels.

We must take a number of issues into consideration as we interpret the magnitude of the effect for *Black Electoral Strength*, the first being the fact that our dependent variable is in logarithmic form. In econometrics, when none of the covariates are logged, this specification is known as a log-level model. For coefficients in this type of model, a one-unit change is interpreted as a percentage change in the dependent variable. This property is known as the *semi-elasticity* of $y$ as it relates to $x$, or $\%\Delta y/\Delta x$ (see Wooldridge 2000). For the models presented in Tables 6.1 and 6.2, the direct effect of a one-unit increase in *Black Electoral Strength* in North Carolina is four-tenths of a percentage point (.4 percent) increase in the dependent variable. Increasing black registration by one unit in Louisiana will result in approximately the same percentage increase in the value of GOP registrants, at .41 percent.

In order to capture the full effect of *Black Electoral Strength*, we need to calculate both the direct and the indirect effects of this indicator through the lagged dependent variable. Again, this functional form is known as an impulse-response function and is discussed in more detail in chapter 5.[18] Figure 6.5 provides a substantive interpretation for the effect of *Black Electoral Strength* on the percentage of Republican registrants using Mecklenburg County (Charlotte) in North Carolina and Caddo Parish (Shreveport) in Louisiana as examples.

Looking at Figure 6.5, one can see that, minus a handful of time periods, *Black Electoral Strength* contributed to a positive rate of growth for both Mecklenburg County and Caddo Parish over the time period of our analysis. The highest levels of increase occurred in 2008 for Mecklenburg County at 1.9 percent and in 1972 for Caddo Parish at 3.4 percent; the former certainly the result in large part of the *Obama Effect*. Year to year, most rates of increase were modest in nature, averaging .8 percent for Mecklenburg and 1.3 percent for Caddo annually. It should be noted that, while the percentage increase in Republican registration for any given year may not appear sizeable (i.e., 1 percent), the cumulative effects over long periods of time can be quite substantial. The empirical evidence and interpretation of the models presented

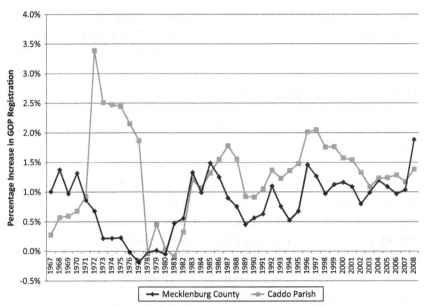

FIGURE 6.5 The Effects of Black Electoral Strength on Republican Registration

provide clear evidence that the political mobilization of blacks at the county level in North Carolina and the parish level in Louisiana led to concomitant increases in GOP registrants.

## Discussion and Conclusion

In this chapter, we attempted to explain over-time change in Republican registration at the substate level for Louisiana and North Carolina from 1966 through 2008. We were especially interested in testing our theory of relative advantage outside of the state-level context utilized in chapter 5. The results revealed strong evidence for our theory, as black political mobilization was a statistically significant predictor of Republican registration rates in both post-VRA Louisiana and North Carolina. In fact, black mobilization was the only consistent predictor of GOP registration across the models presented, which span a forty-two-year post-VRA time period.

In these models, we also endeavored to test competing hypotheses of two-party growth, namely the economic development, demographic change, and religious cleavage theories of party change. For both Louisiana and North Carolina, we found no direct evidence that evangelical Protestantism was a contributing factor to Republican growth at the substate level. It is interesting to note that Catholicism in Louisiana (Table 6.2, Model 2) was also not significant. Although these religious indicators were not significantly related to Republican registration at the substate level over the time period of our study, this is not to say that evangelicalism is not an important cleavage point between the present-day Republican and Democratic parties in the South.

The level of Catholicism should have been a fairly close approximation of the south Louisiana political subregion characterized by the French Acadian culture and higher levels of populism (see Bass and De Vries 1976 for more description). During a large segment of the post-civil rights era, white Cajuns often joined with blacks to form a highly viable biracial Democratic electoral coalition. Democratic strength, theoretically then, should have been closely correlated with the number of Catholics in southern Louisiana; however, this was not the case empirically.

For the remaining two theories, there was mixed evidence. Looking first at changes related to demography, we saw that non-Southern in-migration was positively related to GOP registration rates in Louisiana, but was a negative predictor in North Carolina. Again, this may point to differing patterns of in-migration in the Rim South versus the Deep South. On the other hand, the degree of county-level urbanization was a positive predictor of GOP registration in North Carolina, but a negative one in Louisiana. As for the economic development hypothesis, there was again a differential relationship across the two states under analysis—positive for North Carolina and negative for the Louisiana.

These results are interesting and point to the fact that states comprising the South can be very diverse, compared to one another and internally as well. In addition, the relationship between two-party development and demographic and economic change appeared to differ across states. For Louisiana, GOP growth appeared more prevalent in less urbanized, lower-income parishes with higher levels of non-Southern natives. In the Tar Heel State, wealthier, more urbanized counties tended to exhibit more GOP growth. But the influx of in-migrants tended to exert a dampening effect in North Carolina. As mentioned previously, the two states analyzed are representative of the two prevalent political subregions in the South. At least for the analyses presented, the noted differences between Louisiana and North Carolina may be representative of differing causal mechanisms for these two states, evidence that some prevalent theories of two-party development in the region may be valid for some geographic divisions, but not for others.

In summary, we have presented empirical evidence in this chapter to support the theory of relative advantage as a driver of political change in the South, this time at the parish and county levels for two states. As black citizens were (re)enfranchised and moved into the political arena as active participants, overwhelmingly as Democratic partisans, whites were forced to share the existing party structure with these newcomers. The more pronounced this crowding effect was (the larger the proportion of blacks as a percentage of the local electorate), the more compelling the reason was for white conservatives, and later moderates, to defect to a political party where they could implement their policy objectives. This pattern has now been demonstrated to hold across multiple geographic units (states and parishes/ counties) for extended periods of time while controlling for competing theories and unobserved unit heterogeneity. In chapter 7, we look for evidence of relative advantage as a driver of Republican identification at the individual level.

## CHAPTER 7

An Examination of the Theory
of Relative Advantage at the
Individual Level

## Introduction

Partisan political dynamics do not occur only at the state level. Although there is a long tradition of state-level analysis in Southern politics—going back to Key (1949) at least—any theory of partisan dynamics, such as the theory of *relative advantage*, should provide insights into party politics at the substate and individual levels of analysis as well. In chapter 6, we examined the role of black mobilization in the growth of Republicanism at the substate level in Louisiana and North Carolina, one state from the Deep South and one state from the Rim South. In these two states—the only states for which suitable data were available—the evidence strongly indicates that black mobilization was one of the primary, if not the most important, driving force in the local-level growth of the GOP; this is additional and compelling support for the theory of relative advantage.

In this chapter, we focus on the individual-level dynamics of GOP growth. Again, using the theory of relative advantage, we attempt to explain both elite and mass partisan behavioral dynamics in the Southern context. We provide strong empirical evidence in support of relative advantage's ability to explain party-switching among GOP party activists (from the Democratic Party to the Republican Party) as it relates to the size of the black voter registration at the county level, and strong empirical evidence explaining Republican identification at the mass level as it relates to the size of the mobilized black electorate, especially among individuals in the Deep South states and, to a lesser extent, among younger people.

## Theoretical Perspectives on Individual-Level Partisan Attachment

As we have noted earlier, scholars studying partisan change in the South have walked down four paths, some wider and others narrower. Perhaps the widest path is the one that explains partisan transformation in the South as a gradual process driven by the changing attachment of white conservatives from the Democratic Party to the Republican Party. A large body of scholarship has traced the gradual transformation of the white Southern electorate from the Democratic Party to the Republican Party, which all the while maintained its conservative ideological footing (see, for example, Sundquist 1983; Black and Black 1987, 2002; and Carmines and Stanley 1990). McKee (2009) describes this process as one of *issue evolution*, and in that sense the ideology of Southern whites does not change; it has been and still is conservative. Rather, influenced by party elites, the place of specific issues has evolved slowly and moved from association with one party to the other. For the South, the issue of race and racially conservative policies was transferred from the Democratic to the Republican Party over the course of several decades in the mid-twentieth century (Carmines and Stimson 1980; Carmines and Woods 2002; and Sundquist 1983).

Another path has focused on economic changes in the South and the impact they have had on partisan identification. This explanation holds that the New Deal cleavages over economic and social welfare policy—long overshadowed in the South by the policies of racial segregation—found their way to the South once blacks had been effectively enfranchised. The result was a Southern politics that began to look a lot like the politics of the rest of the country, where Republican support for lower taxes and smaller government attracted increasing support from middle- and upper-class conservatives. Then, as the South's economic transformation continued apace, and as the South became more suburban and middle class (due in part to white in-migration and black out-migration), the shift to Republicanism continued (Ladd and Hadley 1978; Sundquist 1983; Black and Black 1987, 2002; Lamis 1990; and Nadeau and Stanley 1993).

A third path has focused on cultural and social issues and the tendency over time for white evangelical Christians to identify increasingly as Republicans and less so as Democrats. For decades, the South had been the most conservative region of the country on most social, cultural, and lifestyle issues, and these issues have become a central focus of the Republican Party since the 1980s (Black and Black 2002; Green et al. 2002; and Green et al. 2003). This convergence has resulted in increased Republican identification on the part of white evangelicals and serves as an electoral boost of energy for Republican candidates in the South, especially in the context of the *culture wars* that have ensued since the late 1960s (Jelen and Chandler 2000).

A final path focuses on race and the effects of racial attitudes on white partisan preferences. The relationship between white conservatism (and Republicanism) and the size and proximity of the black population, Key's (1949) "black-belt hypothesis," is well documented (for example, see Aistrup 1996; Black 1976; Black 1978; Giles 1977; Giles and Buckner 1993, 1996; Giles and Evans 1986; Giles and Hertz 1994; Glaser 1994; Matthews and Prothro 1966; and Wright 1977). However, the passage of the VRA in 1965 marked a shift in how Key's hypothesis should be viewed by scholars.

In chapter 3, we noted that Key's hypothesis was based upon the presumption of a physical threat to whites from a de jure disenfranchised black population. Whites who lived in proximity to large populations of blacks voted Democratic because the Democratic Party, in turn, maintained the system of disenfranchisement and segregation. However, in the post-VRA South, the perceived threat shifted, becoming less a physical one (although certainly some of that perception lingered) and more of a political one as de jure disenfranchisement gave way to mass enfranchisement. The theory of relative advantage would thus suggest a direct link between black electoral mobilization (into the Democratic Party) and white identification with the Republican Party: As black political power settled in the previously white and conservative Democratic Party, the nascent Republican Party provided white conservatives with greater strategic opportunity.

In fact, a wealth of evidence at the elite level of the Republican Party makes it clear that blacks were perceived as increasingly electorally threatening. Barry Goldwater's vow to "go hunting where the ducks are" was a statement about electoral strategy, not fear of physical violence. Richard Nixon's "Southern Strategy," which had dominated Republican presidential politics in the South since 1968, was also about electoral strategy. The literature, however, does present a mixed set of results when it comes to the effect of race on partisan change. For instance, a body of scholarship emerged in the 1970s arguing that race had not played a primary role in increased Republican identification (see Beck 1977; Campbell 1977a, 1977b; and Wolfinger and Arseneau 1978). This was followed by a body of scholarship in the 1980s and 1990s that placed race in a list of issues that had contributed to gains in Republican identification (see Petrocik 1987; Stanly 1988; Black and Black 1987, 1992, 2002; Lamis 1999; and Watson 1996).

If, in fact, the post-VRA South saw a shift in perceptions of blacks away from a physical threat and toward a political (electoral) threat, then the theory of relative advantage suggests that we should expect to see such a shift among those who perceived this new threat more clearly and had a strategic opportunity to respond. This would have been the case for partisan activists and elites. For this group, the differential change in the benefits of identifying with and working for the Republican Party trumped those of the Democratic Party. The Republican Party, the theory suggests, would become increasingly more electorally viable, and the Democratic Party would become increasingly less so.

Unlike activists who would be keenly attuned to take advantage of differential changes in the benefits of identifying and working for the Republican Party, the perceptions of ordinary voters were not as clear and may also have been mediated by other factors. For instance, as Shafer and Johnston (2006) point out, the absence of issue cleavages that was the legacy of the pre-civil rights political system of the South benefited Democrats by allowing them to maintain a "big tent" party. Conservative white voters, then, would still see the relative advantage in Democrats over shifting to Republicans even after the VRA and the development of a more coherent Republican Party message. However, as the Republican political elite were able to highlight the increasingly distinctive party positions and create clearer issue cleavages, an increasing number of conservative whites found strategic reasons to switch partisan preferences. Given the durable nature of partisan affiliation (Carmines 1991 and McKee 2009), the development of issue cleavages takes time. Older white conservatives who had identified as Democrats and voted that way all their lives (perhaps with the exception of presidential voting beginning in 1964) were less likely to switch, but younger conservative whites who did not have that same history were more likely to respond to issue cleavages and identify with the Republican Party.

We would not, however, expect to see the post-VRA perception of blacks as a political threat to be uniform across the region. Partisan change began immediately after the passage of the VRA, with all five Deep South states voting Republican at the presidential level for the first time (Carmines and Stimson 1989). With African Americans constituting a larger proportion of the population in the Deep South than in the Rim South—and thus representing a greater potential electoral threat in the Deep South— conservative whites in the Deep South were more likely to see the strategic advantage of switching to the Republican Party than their conservative white counterparts from the Rim South states.[1] Again, relative advantage theory leads us to expect the attractiveness of the Republican option to be a function of the relative size of the black (and overwhelmingly Democratic) electorate.

In the next section, we test these propositions by assessing the empirical evidence for the theory of relative advantage at the individual level. To do this, we examine a wide array of individual-level data rarely, if ever, seen in the research on the growth of Southern Republicanism.

## Elite-Level Analysis

### Data

In order to empirically explore the theory of relative advantage at the elite level, we make use of two unique datasets collected to study party activists, both Republican and Democratic, across the South. The primary sources for this component of our study come from surveys of county-level party officials conducted in 1991 and 2001. Officially known as the Southern Grassroots Party Activists Studies, these surveys provide us with a unique opportunity to study the behavior of party activists, primarily county chairs and members of county executive committees, across the South (Clark and Prysby 2005 and Hadley and Bowman 1993). The 1991 survey included 4,857 GOP party officials, and the 2001 survey included 3,557 GOP party officials.

As these elites have already self-selected into leadership positions within the Republican or Democratic parties, there is little to examine in terms of the choice of party identification, which is the focus of our mass-level analyses in the following section. Both surveys, however, included a series of questions that probed whether these respondents had ever switched parties and, if so, what reasons had prompted them to switch. Our analysis for this section focuses specifically on comparing those GOP activists who indicated that they had at one time been Democrats with those who had been lifelong Republicans. In this context, the theory of relative advantage would lead us to expect that those elites faced with increased competition within the Democratic Party due to black political mobilization may have been led to seek another avenue to accomplish political goals. White Democratic Party activists, especially those who are ideologically conservative, should have been more likely to switch to the Republican Party in such a context. More specifically, we hypothesize:

> $H_1$: White GOP activists in counties with higher levels of black mobilization should be more likely to be party-switchers.

## Variable Operationalization

Our dependent variable for both the 1991 and 2001 analyses is a binary indicator coded one for those GOP activists who indicated that they had switched from the Democratic Party to the Republican Party and zero for those who reported they had always been Republican. The primary independent variable of interest, *Black Registration*, is a county-level contextual measure calculated as the percentage of blacks in the overall electorate. *Black Registration* should be positively associated with the probability of a GOP activist being a party-switcher and is a direct test of relative advantage theory.

We include a number of additional control variables in the two multivariate models designed to explain party-switching behavior among Republican activists. *Deep South* is a dummy variable designed to control for subregional differences in the South with Alabama, Georgia, Louisiana, Mississippi, and South Carolina coded one and the remaining six states coded zero. At the individual level, we also include measures for gender (male = 1; female = 0), education level,[2] income,[3] and age (in years). We control for the ideological predisposition of the activist by including the traditional five-point scale where one is very liberal and five is very conservative.

Finally, as is well documented, specific religious beliefs and practices have been shown to have a strong association with Republican partisanship in the South. Along these lines, we include three separate religious indicators in an attempt to measure association with what has been termed the "Religious Right." *Evangelical Protestant* and *Born Again* are dummy variables designed to denote membership in an evangelical Protestant denomination and a respondent's self-identification as a born-again Christian. Finally, we measure religious commitment with the indicator *Church Attendance* (never = 1; a few times a year = 2; once or twice a month = 3; almost every week = 4; once a week = 5; more than once a week = 6).

## Methodology

As our dependent variable *Party-Switcher* is binary, we use logistic regression to estimate separate models for the 1991 and 2001 samples. We confine our analyses to include only white GOP party activists. Because these models include mixed-mode data, namely a county-level measure of black registration, we calculate robust standard errors by clustering on the county indicator. Failing to take clustering into account can result in standard errors that are biased in a downward direction, possibly leading one to commit a type-I error (Primo et al. 2007).

As black registration figures are not available for all the states in the South, we make use of the actual registration data for 1991 and 2001 from Florida, Georgia, Louisiana, North Carolina, and South Carolina and impute the values for this variable for the remaining six states in the analysis.[4] We do have complete coverage for a close proxy to black registration in the form of the black voting-age population (VAP). Black VAP is utilized as our chief measure to impute values for black registration for which actual data were not available. Again, we would argue that data on black registration are a superior measure compared to black VAP in terms of empirically evaluating relative advantage theory, in that the former are an approximation of black political power as opposed to a measure of potential power.

## Empirical Results

Before delving into the results of our multivariate models, it is instructive to examine some basic descriptive statistics concerning GOP party activists. To begin, 28.1 percent in 1991 and 23.9 percent in 2001 of the GOP activists reported that they had switched parties. Table 7.1A lists the self-reported reasons these individuals gave for switching parties. Almost 100 percent of the respondents in both study years indicated that they switched to the GOP because it was *more likely to take the right stand on issues*. The only other category that more than a majority of switchers viewed as being important in their decision calculus was the view that the Republican Party offered more appealing candidates (76.1 percent in 1991 and 70 percent in 2001).

When asked what was the *most important* reason for having changed their party affiliation, approximately 85 percent in both years reported that it was the GOP's stance on issues (see Table 7.1B). Although these surveys do not allow us to probe further as to specific types of issues, it is obvious that, for most of these elites, the issue congruence between themselves and the Republican Party was the primary factor that necessitated the need to change party affiliation.

The results from our multivariate models of party-switching among GOP activists are presented in Table 7.2. At first glance, one may note that there is a remarkable amount of congruency across the two models. Our primary variable of interest, *Black Registration*, is both positive and statistically significant for both years. GOP party activists residing in counties with higher proportions of blacks in the local electorate are more likely to have switched to the Republican Party. This finding is congruent with what would be predicted by relative advantage theory. In a situation where ideologically conservative white Democratic elites were facing an increasing presence of black

TABLE 7.1A  GOP Party Activists' Self-Reported Reasons for Switching Parties

|  | 1991 | 2001 |
|---|---|---|
| Better/Appealing Candidates | 76.1 | 70.0 |
| Better Issue Positions | 96.8 | 97.8 |
| Friend Persuasion | 7.5 | 12.4 |
| Personal Opportunities | 11.1 | 9.8 |
| Better Organized Party | 35.9 | 34.4 |

NOTE: Entries are percentages.
DATA: 1991 and 2001 Southern Grassroots Party Activists Surveys.

TABLE 7.1B  GOP Party Activists' Self-Reported Most Important Reason for Switching Parties

|  | 1991 | 2001 |
|---|---|---|
| Better Candidates | 10.3 | 9.9 |
| Better Issue Positions | 84.4 | 85.2 |
| Friend Persuasion | 2.2 | .9 |
| Personal Opportunities | 1.3 | .9 |
| Superior Party Organization | 1.8 | 3.1 |

NOTE: Entries are percentages.
DATA: 1991 and 2001 Southern Grassroots Party Activists Surveys.

registrants and black party activists, they found it to their benefit to change their party allegiance to the GOP.

Across both models, males were more likely to have switched parties, and those who indicated they were born-again Christians from the 1991 sample also showed a statistically significant probability of party-switching behavior. Age was also found to be positively associated with the propensity of GOP activists to indicate they had altered their party allegiance. This finding makes sense as older activists were more likely to have identified as Democrats in the past when the region was characterized by one-party politics.

The effect of our measure of county-level black political mobilization on the probability of GOP party activists to indicate they were party-switchers is presented in Figure 7.1. We simulate the probability that a GOP activist switched parties across varying levels of county-level black registration, holding the remaining independent variables at their mean or modal values.[5] For the 1991 model, probabilities are plotted with *Black Registration* ranging from 0 percent to 60 percent and for 2001, the range was 0 percent to 75 percent (the actual ranges were 0–60.4 percent and 0–76.5 percent respectively).

TABLE 7.2  Models Predicting Party-Switching among GOP Activists

|  | 1991 | 2001 |
|---|---|---|
| Black Registration | .9116* (.3599) | .9248** (.3382) |
| Deep South | −.0835 (.1046) | −.0540 (.1209) |
| Male | .2365** (.0783) | .2734** (.0977) |
| Education | −.0141 (.0404) | .0535 (.0538) |
| Income | −.0026 (.0194) | .0116 (.0366) |
| Age | .0130** (.0032) | .0177** (.0036) |
| Ideology | .0429 (.0463) | .0177 (.0700) |
| Evangelical Protestant | .1088 (.0970) | −.0126 (.1249) |
| Born Again | .2116* (.0926) | .1003 (.1117) |
| Church Attendance | −.0236 (.0303) | −.0300 (.0315) |
| Constant | −2.0102** (.3550) | −2.7139** (.4289) |
| N | 4,002 | 2,913 |

NOTES: Entries are logistic regression coefficients with robust standard errors clustered by county in parentheses.
$^*p < .05$; $^{**}p < .01$ (two-tailed test)
DATA: 1991 and 2001 Southern Grassroots Party Activists Surveys.

The patterns for both the 1991 and 2001 samples are very similar, with the probability of switching monotonically increasing as the percentage of blacks in the electorate increases. For the 1991 sample, a GOP activist residing in a county where the electorate did not contain any black registrants (0 percent) had a .256 probability of being a party-switcher, compared to .373 for an activist where 60 percent of the electorate was black—a 12-point increase. In 2001, GOP activists in counties with no black registrants had a probability of switching of .212 compared to .351 in counties where 75 percent of the electorate was comprised of black citizens. Across this range, the likelihood of switching is approximately 14 points higher.

## Mass-Level Analysis

### Data

In order to study relative advantage theory as it relates to mass political behavior, we rely on two data sources: the American National Election Studies (ANES) (cumulative dataset) and the Southern Focus Polls (SFP). Using these two data sources allows us to examine the effect of black political mobilization on the Republican Party identification of white Southerners. These data sources are the only longitudinal studies that provide comprehensive political and socio-demographic information on respondents, along with

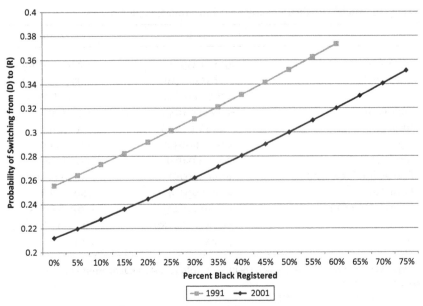

FIGURE 7.1 Party Switching among GOP Activists

detailed geographic identifiers. In this case, we know a respondent's county of residence and are, therefore, able to accurately model the local political environment. In addition, these data sources also provide us with sizeable numbers of respondents from the American South. Our analyses of mass-level political behavior span the post-civil rights era running from 1972 to 2008 for the ANES[6] data and the entire time period for the SFP data, from 1992 to 2001.

As with our analyses of Republican Party elites, the theory of relative advantage indicates that, as conservative whites faced increasing competition at the local level from black political mobilization, there would be a greater probability of defection to the Republican Party. More specifically, we hypothesize:

H$_2$: Whites residing in counties with higher levels of black mobilization should be more likely to identify as strong Republicans.

In addition, we have reason to believe that the effects of black mobilization may be mediated by two other factors: subregion and age. It is well documented that black mobilization is likely to be more pronounced in the Deep South and may, therefore, have a more sizeable effect on the strength and direction of white partisanship.[7] Formally, we hypothesize:

H$_3$: Whites residing in Deep South counties with higher levels of black mobilization should be more likely to be strong Republicans.

We also know that some conservative whites who grew up identifying with the Democratic Party may find it difficult to switch parties, even those who may have altered their voting behavior. Compared to their older counterparts, younger white Southerners should show higher levels of strength and association with the Republican Party in areas experiencing higher levels of black mobilization or:

H$_4$: Younger whites residing in counties with higher levels of black mobilization should be more likely to be strong Republicans.

## Variable Operationalization

The dependent variable from both data sources is the traditional seven-point party identification scale with a value of one denoting respondents who are strong Democrats and seven those who are strong Republicans.[8] As with the elite-level analysis, our primary variable of interest is designed to measure black political mobilization. Again, *Black Registration* is measured as the percentage of the total county electorate composed of black registrants. We also include a second contextual measure, *Deep South*, which is designed to differentiate between the two geographic subregions of the South. These variables should be positively related to a respondent's strength of identification with the Republican Party.

For both analyses of the SFP and ANES data, we include a number of controls such as *Age* (in years); *Education*[9]; *Income*[10]; whether the respondent was born in the South (*Native Southerner*); and ideological predispositions measured on the traditional seven-point scale (1 = extremely liberal; 7 = extremely conservative). For the ANES analysis, we include a dummy variable to denote union membership on the part of the respondent (*Union Membership*) and for the SFP models, there are two additional religious-based measures. *Attendance* is a measure of self-reported attendance at religious services (1 = never; 2 = several times a year; 3 = two–three times a month; 4 = once a week; and 5 = more than once a week), and *Baptist* is a binary indicator coded one for those respondents who reported their denominational affiliation as Baptist.[11]

As indicated in the aforementioned hypotheses, we also specify two additional models (for both datasets) where the effects of *Black Registration* are mediated by age and subregion. To accomplish this, we create two interactive terms where *Black Registration* is multiplied by *Deep South* and an age dummy where respondents who are forty years of age and under are coded one. For the model testing the age effect, we remove the interval-level age variable and replace it with an *Under-41 Age Cohort* indicator.

## Methodology

The analyses for all models presented in this section of chapter 7 are estimated using ordered logit as they all rely on the same seven-point party identification scale. As *Black Registration* is a county-level contextual measure, we again make use of clustered robust standard errors.[12] In addition, all models are restricted to include only white and, when possible, non-Hispanic respondents. Both the models that rely on the ANES and the SFP include a set of *n-1* year-specific dummy variables to control for temporal factors related to our data. As with the mass-level analysis, we again were forced to impute some values for *Black Registration* as this data did not exist for all the Southern states included in our models (see endnote 4).

## Empirical Results

We first discuss the results of our models designed to analyze data from the SFP, which are presented in Table 7.3. The first column presents the model estimates for the additive model. In this case, *Black Registration* does not exert any independent statistical effect on the partisanship of white Southerners. We do find that older respondents along with those who are native to the region and women are less likely to identify as strong Republicans. Income and education levels, conservatism, and greater attendance at religious services are significantly and positively related to the seven-point party identification scale.

Columns 2 and 3 of Table 7.3 present the results of our interactive models. Model 2 examines the hypothesis that whites residing in a Deep South state will be more likely to identify with the GOP as levels of black registration in their county also increase. The interactive term in this model is positive and statistically significant, an indication that local levels of black registration do, indeed, have a differential impact based on subregion.

The results of Model 2 for black registration, subregion, and the interactive terms are translated into predicted probabilities that are presented in Figure 7.2. In the figure, we examine the probability that a respondent will identify as an Independent who leans Republican, a weak Republican, or strong Republican based on whether they reside in the Rim South or the Deep South and on the level of black political mobilization at the county level

TABLE 7.3 Models Predicting Party Identification among White Southerners, 1992–2001

| | MODEL 1 | MODEL 2 | MODEL 3 |
|---|---|---|---|
| Black Registration | −.0523 (.2731) | −.6347 (.3766) | −.1198 (.3584) |
| Deep South | .0775 (.0704) | −.1408 (.1212) | .0975 (.0712) |
| Under-41 Age Cohort | — | — | .5751** (.0797) |
| Age | -.0207** (.0018) | −.0210** (.0018) | — |
| Black Registration * Deep South | — | 1.2568* (.5496) | — |
| Black Registration * Under-41 Age Cohort | — | — | .0667 (.4217) |
| Education | .0850** (.0284) | .0859** (.0285) | .0924** (.0287) |
| Income | .1084** (.0153) | .1085** (.0153) | .1242** (.0156) |
| Gender | −.1520** (.0544) | −.1483** (.0543) | −.1597** (.0544) |
| Native Southerner | −.1501** (.0517) | −.1468** (.0517) | −.1270* (.0516) |
| Ideology | .4586** (.0187) | .4585** (.0187) | .4516** (.0182) |
| Baptist | .0248 (.0597) | .0271 (.0594) | .0315 (.0597) |
| Church Attendance | .0507* (.0201) | .0511** (.0200) | .0408* (.0199) |
| Intercept 1 | −.8115** (.2061) | −.8871** (.2111) | .4099* (.2031) |
| Intercept 2 | .4060* (.2059) | .3326 (.2110) | 1.6208** (.2039) |
| Intercept 3 | .8937** (.2065) | .8211** (.2113) | 2.1063** (.2061) |
| Intercept 4 | 1.2846** (.2076) | 1.2124** (.2122) | 2.4952** (.2076) |
| Intercept 5 | 1.8140** (.2079) | 1.7422** (.2123) | 3.0220** (.2086) |
| Intercept 6 | 2.9815** (.2119) | 2.9105** (.2157) | 4.1872** (.2145) |
| N | 5,328 | 5,328 | 5,328 |

NOTES: Entries are ordered logit coefficients with robust standard errors clustered by county in parentheses. Year-specific fixed effects included but not shown.
*$p < .05$; **$p < .01$ (two-tailed test)
DATA: Southern Focus Polls, 1992–2001.

(this measure ranges from 0 percent to 60 percent, which closely mimics the actual range for these data).[13]

Looking at Figure 7.2, one can see that the probability of a white Southerner identifying as a Republican leaner does not vary by subregion or level of black political mobilization. Across the range of possible values for *Black Registration*, the probability of identification for this category is essentially static at approximately .13. When one examines weak and strong Republicans, however, there are discernable differences both between subregion and across levels of black registration. First, weak and strong Republicans in the Rim South actually see a decline in the probability of identification within these categories as levels of black registration increase. Conversely, we do see

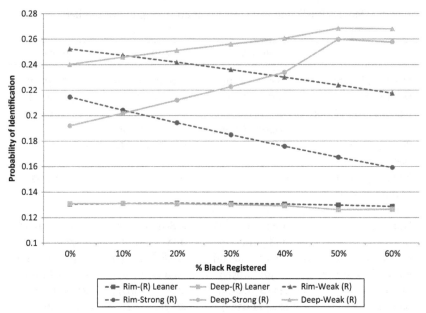

FIGURE 7.2 Republican Identification for White Southerners by Subregion and Level of Relative Advantage

DATA: Southern Focus Polls, 1992–2001.

the expected relationship emerge for Deep South whites, with the probability of identification for weak Republicans increasing from .24 to .27 as the scale moves from 0 percent to 60 percent black registration. Likewise, an even greater shift is observed for strong Republicans in the Deep South, where a probability differential of approximately 7 points is realized (.19 versus .26) across the range of values for black registration. In a county where the electorate is composed of 60 percent black registrants, whites in the Deep South are 10 points more likely to identify as strong Republicans than their counterparts in the Rim South (.26 versus .16). Likewise, the probability of identification as a weak Republican is about 5 points higher at the maximum level of black registration for the Deep South versus the Rim South.

Returning to Table 7.3, Model 3 examines the interaction effect between age cohort and *Black Registration*. In this case, the interaction term is positive as hypothesized but fails to reach conventional levels of statistical significance. The age cohort dummy is positive and significant, denoting that those forty and younger have a higher probability of GOP identification compared with older respondents. This finding is not a surprise given the fact that many older respondents would have grown up in a time where the only option in terms of party affiliation was the Democratic Party. We also know that for some Americans, party affiliation is an *unmoved mover*; once a particular label is adopted, it becomes difficult to alter, even after voting patterns may have shifted in response to changes in the ideological positioning of parties on specific issues. This finding, however, is in no way mediated by the context of black political mobilization.

We now turn to the results generated from the analyses involving the ANES, which are presented in Table 7.4. Looking at Model 1 where *Black Registration* is included as only an additive term, we fail to see any independent effect on the partisanship of white Southerners. Again, a number of individual-level factors such as education, income, and conservatism are positively associated with the strength of Republican Party affiliation. Conversely, age, union membership, and being a native Southerner are negatively associated with our dependent variable.

Model 2 explores the interaction of *Black Registration* with *Deep South*. The interaction term in this case is both positive and significant as hypothesized, with those whites residing in the Deep South more likely to be affected by increasing levels of black mobilization compared to whites in the Rim South. Unlike the models that utilized the SFP data, we do find support for the hypothesis that the impact of black political mobilization is also mediated by age as evidenced by the positive and significant result for the interaction term in Model 3. As the percentage of blacks registered in the electorate grows, whites in the forty-and-under age cohort are increasingly likely to identify as Republicans.

Simulated probabilities for the interaction terms in Models 2 and 3 are plotted graphically in Figures 7.3 and 7.4 respectively. Figure 7.3 examines the changes in probability for three categories of Republican identification based on subregion of residence and the level of black registration. Looking at the figure, one can see that the probability of identification as Independent-leaners, weak Republicans, and strong Republicans for Deep South residents increases over the plotted range of black registration (see the solid lines). The probability estimates for Rim South residents, conversely, are all negatively sloped over this same range (see the dashed lines). As an example, the probability of a Deep South respondent identifying as a strong Republican changes from .09 to .15 as the scale for black registration moves from 0 percent to 60 percent. Across the same range, the probability for a Rim South respondent decreases 4 points from .12 to .08. At approximately 20 percent black registration, the probability of identifying as a strong Republican in the Deep South just surpasses the probability of such identification in the Rim South.

Figure 7.4 plots predicted probabilities for various types of GOP identification across a range of values for black registration by age cohort. The figure graphically demonstrates that the effects of black registration are clearly mediated by

TABLE 7.4  Models Predicting Party Identification among White Southerners, 1972–2008

| | MODEL 1 | MODEL 2 | MODEL 3 |
|---|---|---|---|
| Black Registration | −.1428 (.4501) | −.7953 (.4809) | −.6745 (.5518) |
| Deep South | −.0182 (.0976) | −.3408 (.2017) | −.0122 (.0998) |
| Under-41 Age Cohort | — | — | .3573** (.1100) |
| Age | −.0151** (.0023) | −.0155** (.0022) | — |
| Black Registration * Deep South | — | 1.8045* (.9225) | — |
| Black Registration * Under-41 Age Cohort | — | — | 1.0286* (.5174) |
| College Degree | .1683* (.0761) | .1697* (.0764) | .1485 (.0777) |
| Income | .1524** (.0288) | .1545** (.0287) | .1756** (.0294) |
| Female | −.0761 (.0604) | −.0762 (.0614) | −.0865 (.0599) |
| Native Southerner | −.6190** (.1205) | −.1501** (.0517) | −.5969** (.1195) |
| Ideology | .6011** (.0422) | .6003** (.0420) | .5972** (.0419) |
| Union Member | −.4841* (.2219) | −.4936* (.2200) | −.4915* (.2231) |
| Intercept 1 | −.2890 (.2649) | −.3718 (.2672) | .5848 (.2639) |
| Intercept 2 | .9657** (.2550) | .8842** (.2558) | 1.8379 (.2540) |
| Intercept 3 | 1.5185** (.2680) | 1.4377** (.2696) | 2.3909 (.2691) |
| Intercept 4 | 2.0912** (.2654) | 2.0116** (.2667) | 2.9638 (.2674) |
| Intercept 5 | 2.8032** (.2814) | 2.7248** (.2824) | 3.6763 (.2896) |
| Intercept 6 | 3.9077** (.2928) | 3.8306** (.2940) | 4.7829 (.3019) |
| N | 4,058 | 4,058 | 4,058 |

NOTES: Entries are ordered logit coefficients with robust standard errors clustered by county in parentheses. Year-specific fixed effects included but not shown.
*$p < .05$; **$p < .01$ (two-tailed test)
DATA: American National Election Studies, 1972–2008.

age, with younger respondents more likely to respond to competition in their local political environment by identifying as GOP adherents. Although the effects of age cohort on Republican partisanship are not as pronounced as those uncovered by subregion, they do exhibit a similar set of patterns. Again, the slopes of the predicted probabilities for the under-forty-one cohort across increasing values of black registration are all positive, whereas they are negative for the over-forty age cohort. The probability of identifying as a strong Republican for those in the younger age cohort at the maximum value for black registration is .16, compared with .07 for older respondents—a 9-point gap. A substantial gap also exists for weak Republicans, where the probability of identification for younger residents is .20, compared with .11 for those in the older age cohort.

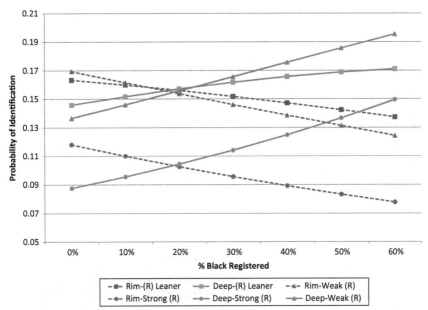

FIGURE 7.3 Republican Identification for White Southerners by Subregion and Level of Relative Advantage

DATA: American National Elelection Studies, 1972–2008

## Conclusion

Overall, we find substantial support for the behavioral expectations of both party elites and average citizens suggested by the theory of relative advantage. First, among Republican Party elite who were once Democratic identifiers, the relationship between party-switching and local black registration rates is positive and statistically significant. The likelihood of a Republican Party activist having switched to the Republican Party from the Democratic Party increases dramatically as the proportion of the black electorate in the activist's county increases. In terms of the theory of relative advantage, as the potential opportunities and rewards related to activism in the Democratic Party decrease given the increased presence of black registrants in the Democratic Party, white conservative Democrats make a strategic move out of the Democratic Party and into the Republican Party, where the potential opportunities and rewards are greater.

In terms of mass political behavior, there is a positive and statistically significant relationship between Republican Party identification and the relative level of black electoral strength in Deep South states, as well as suggestive evidence of a similar relationship for younger white Southerners throughout the South. Unlike party elites, where the potential opportunities

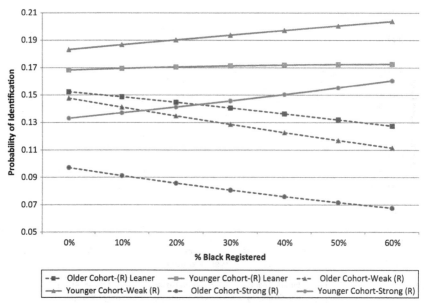

FIGURE 7.4. Republican Identification for White Southerners by Age Cohort and Level of Relative Advantage

DATA: American National Elelection Studies, 1972–2008

and rewards are related to organizational leadership positions and policy positions, for the mass public, the theory of relative advantage suggests that a strategic shift from the Democratic Party to the Republican Party among white conservatives would be related to greater electoral and policy comfort. Thus, the potential opportunities and rewards are less tangible for the mass public than for the partisan elite, but no less important.

# Black Mobilization

| Relative Advantage in a Post-VRA World

*Black Voter Registration in the Modern South*

THE THEORY OF *RELATIVE advantage* was originally developed to explain the growth of the Republican Party—and the variation in this growth across states and time—in the South. In the preceding chapters, we have outlined and explained the theory and examined the supporting evidence in various contexts including state, county, and individual levels. There is substantial evidence in support of the theory of relative advantage at the state level. Although not designed to explain substate- and individual-level Republican growth, the logic of the theory does naturally extend to these contexts, so while the additional evidence for the theory manifest in the substate- and individual-level data is significant, it is not especially surprising.

According to the theory of relative advantage, the key determinant of GOP growth in the American South (along with substate party competitiveness) is black mobilization. Again, a significant amount of evidence at the state, substate, and individual levels indicates that as African Americans joined the electorate (and the Democratic Party), the ranks of the Southern GOP grew accordingly. At the individual level, we demonstrated that whites, in particular, responded to increased black mobilization by growing more attached to the Republican Party. A logical question then becomes, what drives black mobilization?

Relative advantage theory should be as equally useful in predicting the strategy pursued by Southern African Americans in response to changes in the political environment as it is for white conservatives in the region. The theory suggests that patterns of political activity will differ across the Rim South and the Deep South (for the reasons suggested above). Relative advantage implies that in the Deep South—the subregion with the largest African American population and, prior to the growth of the Republican Party, the most conservative Democratic partisans—black mobilization will be driven (at least in part) by the exodus of white conservatives from the Democratic Party. More specifically, in the Deep South, our theory suggests that the growth of the Republican Party will concomitantly drive black mobilization.

## Explaining Black Mobilization in the South

Figure 8.1 presents a series of boxplots representing African American registration for the eleven Southern states from 1960 through 2008. In the Southern context, two facts about black mobilization (which we measure in terms of voter registration) are clear from even the most cursory study of the data. First, black mobilization has grown dramatically since the early 1960s, as evidenced in Figure 8.1. Less than 30 percent of the African American population in the South was registered to vote in 1960; by 2008, nearly three-quarters of the African American population was registered to vote. Even if we focus solely on the post-VRA era, the increase in African Americans on the voting rolls is substantial. In 1966, less than half of Southern blacks were registered to vote.

Second, growth in black mobilization has varied dramatically by state. In Arkansas, the percentage of African Americans registered to vote has risen from 37.7 percent in 1960 to 52 percent in 2008. In Mississippi, the percentage

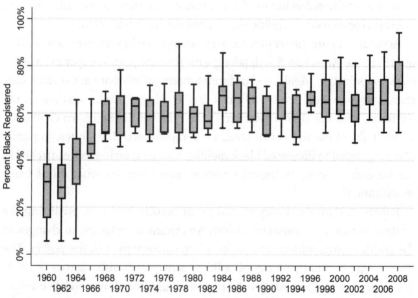

FIGURE 8.1  State-Level Black Registration Boxplots, 1960–2008

of registered blacks has risen from less than 6 percent to nearly 82 percent. More generally, it is relatively easy to see that the growth in the extent of African American mobilization varies significantly across subregions in the South. The Deep South has simply seen much greater political mobilization in its African American community than has the Rim South. In 1960, less than 20 percent of blacks in the Deep South were registered to vote, compared to 40 percent in the Rim South. By 2008, 70.1 percent of African Americans were registered to vote in the Rim South, but in the Deep South, nearly 80 percent of African Americans were registered to vote. While black registration was more than *quadrupling* in the Deep South, it was not even *doubling* in the Rim South.

Although the difference between the rates of mobilization in the Rim South and the Deep South are not as dramatic if we limit ourselves to the post-VRA era, it is still significant. From 1966 to 2008, the voter registration rate of African Americans grew by more than 77 percent (from 44.8 percent to 79.6 percent). During the same time period, the registration growth rate in the Rim South was just over 30 percent (from 53.7 percent to 70.1 percent). Clearly, distinctive dynamics were driving black mobilization in the two subregions of the American South.

No standard treatments of mobilization (or any treatments focusing specifically on African American mobilization) provide an explanation for this dramatic subregional discrepancy. Resource-oriented models (see Conway 2000; Verba and Nie 1972; and Wolfinger and Rosenstone 1980) suggest that variation in mobilization rates should mirror the variation in socioeconomic variables such as income or education.[1] Among African Americans specifically, there is clear evidence that poverty depresses mobilization (see Harris, Sinclair-Chapman, and McKenzie 2005) and those living in depressed areas tend to participate at significantly lower rates than blacks in more prosperous areas (Cohen and Dawson 1993).

Given this literature, it is at least a little surprising that recent black registration rates are significantly higher in the Deep South than in the Rim South, even though blacks in the Rim South have higher income levels.[2] Similarly, though the growth in African American mobilization in the Deep South has dwarfed the growth in the Rim South, the incomes of black households in the Rim South have risen more during the 1960–2008 time period (over $23,000) than the incomes of black households in the Deep South (less than $21,000 for the same time period). At first glance (at least), variation in resources does not explain the difference in political mobilization.[3]

A second important component of the literature on black mobilization—the *empowerment* thesis (Bobo and Gilliam 1990; Browning, Marshall, and

Tabb 1984; Leighley 2001; and Harris, Sinclair-Chapman, and McKenzie 2005)—is not particularly well suited to explain the growth in black registration rates in the South. In their path-breaking work, Bobo and Gilliam provide an authoritative definition of "political empowerment" with the following:

> By political empowerment—or political incorporation, as some have called it (Browning, Marshall, and Tabb 1984)—we mean the extent to which a group has achieved significant representation and influence in political decision making (1990, 378).

Bobo and Gilliam (1990) go on to argue that it is just this type of political success that drives black mobilization:

> We hypothesize that where blacks hold more positions of authority, wield political power, and have done so for longer periods of time, greater numbers of blacks should see value in sociopolitical involvement. We expect, then, that the greater the level of empowerment, the more likely it is that blacks will become politically involved (1990, 379).

There is considerable evidence that empowerment plays an important role in the extent to which African Americans participate in a variety of political acts and activities. These range from donating money to political campaigns and attending campaign meetings to contacting local officials and participating in various community activities (see Bobo and Gilliam 1990 and Harris, Sinclair-Chapman, and McKenzie 2005). But when the focal activity is registering to vote, it is difficult to see how empowerment can precede—in a causal sense—the focal mobilization activity. This is particularly true in the American South. If empowerment is understood as "significant representation and influence in political decision making" (Bobo and Gilliam 1990, 378), and it is measured by the prevalence of black elected officials (particularly mayors, state legislators, and members of Congress), then the manifestation of black empowerment cannot logically precede the presence of a significant number of registered black voters. When mobilization is viewed in terms of voter registration, then the mobilization itself must precede (or have historically preceded) empowerment.

If theories focused on resources—or "economic distress" (Harris, Sinclair-Chapman, and McKenzie 2005, 1145)—or empowerment provide little or no leverage on the question of subregional black mobilization in the South, then how do we understand this rather puzzling empirical fact? What if African Americans responded to the potential political opportunities created by an exodus of conservative white Southerners from the Democratic Party in much the same way conservative white Southerners responded to the political pressures created by the mobilization of African Americans?

In some of our early empirical assessments of the theory of relative advantage, we were concerned about the possibility of a feedback loop between GOP growth and black mobilization. Using a specially designed Granger test of causality for TSCS data, we were able to empirically test for such a possibility.[4] The evidence for the presence of a feedback loop—black mobilization producing GOP growth, which in turn boosted black mobilization—was present, but limited to the Southern states with the highest percentage of African Americans in the population (the Deep South along with North Carolina). Previously, we could not explain the presence of the effect—why did GOP growth have an impact on black mobilization?—or the limited manifestation of the effect—why is the effect limited to the Deep South? It was not until we considered an extension of the theory of relative advantage to this relationship that we were able to explain *both* phenomena: (1) the presence of a GOP growth effect on black mobilization and (2) its presence only in the Southern states with the highest percentages of African Americans.

Why might we expect to see GOP growth driving—at least in part—black mobilization in the Deep South but not in the Rim South? Two significant distinctions between the Deep South and the Rim South are important here. First, the states of the Deep South have historically had significantly larger African American populations (in relative terms) than the states of the Rim South. Over the 1960–2008 time period, African Americans made up slightly less than 17 percent of the population in the Rim South states. In the Deep South, African Americans made up more than 30 percent of the population. In fact, every single state in the Deep South during this time period had a larger African American population than the Rim South state with the largest African American population (North Carolina). This demographic disparity between the Deep South and the Rim South is easily seen in Figure 8.2, which plots the average black population by state from 1960 through 2010.

Second, Democrats and the Democratic Parties in the states of the Deep South were traditionally more racially conservative than Democrats and the Democratic Parties in the states of the Rim South. Students of Southern politics have long argued that black context is directly associated with white conservatism (Black 1978; Black and Black 1987; Key 1949; and Keech 1968), the most famous characterization of this relationship being Key's "black-belt hypothesis" (1949). So, in just those situations in which a mobilized black population would likely have the most impact on electoral outcomes (because of the relative size of their voting bloc), they would be joining state-level

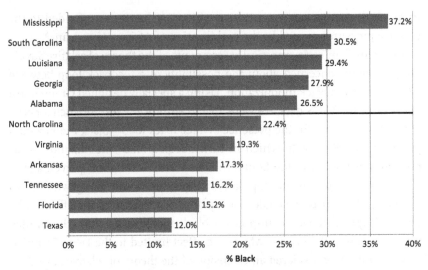

FIGURE 8.2 Mean Black Population by State, 1960–2010

parties—at least in the early part of our time period—that are most conservative on racial issues.[5]

When examining GOP growth with the theory of relative advantage, we
are trying to understand what would lead a Democrat to become a Republican. When examining black mobilization, the issue is what would lead an
African American to register to vote—the first significant step toward political mobilization. To bring the theory of relative advantage to bear on this
question, we also assume that the decision to mobilize is a decision to
become a Democrat. This is not a trivial assumption. Theoretically, we might
look at the decision about whether or not to register/mobilize as one with
*three* basic options: remain unregistered and immobilized, register to vote
and identify as a Democrat, or register to vote and identify as a Republican.
During the post-Reconstruction era, however, the Republican Party was
rarely thought of as a significant and viable option for African Americans.

All else being equal, the incentive to register (and subsequently to vote)
for African Americans is directly related to the *potential* size of the politically
active African American population in a state. In places where the African
American population is, at least potentially, a sizeable voting bloc, returns for
participation are greater than in those places where the relative size of the
African American population is significantly smaller. But if white Democrats
in areas with the largest black populations are also the most racially conservative Democrats, then all is not equal. The inherent advantage of a larger
potential voting bloc is thwarted by the ideological extremism of the dominant voting bloc in the party. Simply put, it would take a larger number of

black voters to form a *decisive* voting bloc in a conservative Democratic Party (e.g., Deep South) than in a moderate Democratic Party (e.g., Rim South).

Given these dynamics, the theory of relative advantage applied to the phenomenon of black mobilization (specifically registration) in the South suggests that patterns of political activity will differ across the Rim South and the Deep South (for the reasons described above). Our theory also suggests that in the Deep South—the subregion with the largest black population and, prior to the growth of the Republican Party, the most conservative Democratic partisans—black mobilization will be driven (at least in part) by the exodus of white conservatives from the Democratic Party. In the Deep South, our theory suggests that the growth of the Republican Party will drive black mobilization. More specifically, we hypothesize:

$H_1$: The relative size of the black population is directly related to the extent of black mobilization.

$H_2$: The impact of the relative size of the black population on black mobilization will be greater in the Rim South than in the Deep South.

$H_3$: GOP growth will foster increased black mobilization in the Deep South. It will have little or no effect in the Rim South.

In the next section, we discuss alternative explanations for black mobilization in the South. This is followed by a description of our empirical analysis. We then report results from two separate analyses—one focusing on the state level and another on the substate level in Louisiana and North Carolina—that provide clear evidence for the contention that Republican growth has spurred increases in black registration in the Deep South but not in the Rim South— just as the theory of relative advantage would lead us to expect.

As we noted above, individual-level models of political participation tend to focus on resource-based approaches to explaining registration and voting. Demographic factors such as age, education, income, and occupation—the socioeconomic status or SES variables—often correlate highly with registration and voting (see Verba and Nie 1972; Bennett and Bennett 1986; Conway 2000; and Wolfinger and Rosenstone 1980). The relationship between SES and voting also holds for African Americans (Tate 1991).[6] It is important to note that there is some disagreement about the specific causal relationship between SES and voting. Some argue that a direct relationship exists between SES and participation, whereas others contend that SES influences participation only indirectly (by influencing the extent to which citizens have "civic skills") (see Brady, Verba, and Schlozman 1995 and Verba, Schlozman, and Brady 1995 for a description of this debate). Nevertheless, no one seriously argues that SES plays no role in the individual-level choice process regarding political participation.

For our study, in which the cross-sectional unit of analysis is a state, income is the most meaningful SES variable. Studies focusing on African Americans, however, often find either a weak relationship between income and voting or voter registration or no relationship at all (Cohen and Dawson 1993 and Tate 1991, 1993). Likewise, these studies show that the relationship between family income and political participation is generally quite weak (if it exists at all) (Cohen and Dawson 1993 and Tate 1991, 1993). Given these conflicting strains of literature, we do not have an a priori expectation regarding the existence of a relationship between income and black registration, but we do include income in our model and expect that, if a relationship does exist, it would be positive.

The political context in which elections occur is also likely to influence registration rates. As elections generate greater interest among the general population, or as the outcome of the election takes on greater importance, we would expect registration rates to increase. From previous research, we know that presidential elections tend to generate significantly greater public interest than off-year elections, and that this increased interest results in a boost in turnout. We should find the same dynamic at work in our sample, so we expect registration rates to be higher during presidential election years than in years when voters are not selecting a president.

H$_4$: Black mobilization will be greater in years in which a presidential election is held than in other years.

Previous research also suggests that the presence of a prominent African American candidate on the ballot tends to contribute to higher registration (and turnout) rates among African Americans. The archetypal case is Jesse Jackson's first run for the White House in 1984. President Obama's election year is also likely to fit into this category. There is little doubt that the Jackson candidacy led to an increase in African American registration nationwide (see Tate 1991, 1993 and Walton 1997). Although the specific reasons for this increase are not fully clear—extensive organizational efforts to register voters is one likely explanation—the evidence strongly supports the presence of an effect at the national level and in the Southern states.[7]

H$_5$: The Jackson campaign in 1984 will be positively associated with black mobilization.
H$_6$: The Obama campaign in 2008 will be positively associated with black mobilization.

We now move to a discussion of the data and methods used to test our hypotheses.

## Data and Methods

Two of the variables used for the state-level analysis—*Republican Strength* and *Percent Black*—were used in previous analyses and are described in detail in chapter 5. At the county/parish level, we use actual registration data, as in chapter 6, to operationalize GOP strength. For the substate analyses, *Republican Strength* is measured as the number of registered Republicans as a percentage of total registrants for each county or parish. *Black Income* is taken directly from census data and is measured as black median family income adjusted for inflation.[8] *Jackson 1984* and *Obama 2008* are simply dummy variables for those relevant election years. *Presidential Election Year* is a dummy variable coded one for each presidential election year (1968, 1972, . . . 2008). With the exception of our measure of *Republican Strength*, the variables utilized for the state- and the county-level analyses are identically measured.

A significant deviation from our previous analysis is our treatment of black registration. In models of GOP growth, we included the variable *Black Electoral Strength*, which is defined as the percentage of African Americans among all registered voters. Note that this variable taps not only the extent to which the black population is mobilized, but also the relative size of the African American component of the voting age population. Obviously, efforts to boost black mobilization—regardless of their effectiveness—will have little or no impact on the relative size of the African American component of the population. In this chapter, therefore, we focus on the percentage of the African American voting age population that is registered to vote. We refer to this variable as *Black Mobilization*, which is measured specifically as

Black Registration/Black Voting Age Population.

As in chapter 5, we estimate a dynamic time series cross-sectional model, with the state serving as the unit of analysis. Beginning with the first post-VRA election (1966), this produces a total of eleven cross sections over a forty-three-year period—from 1966 through 2008.[9] Again, we utilize one of the more commonly accepted techniques in political science to model TSCS data with a continuous dependent variable. As suggested by Beck and Katz (1995, 1996), we generate parameter estimates of black mobilization using ordinary least squares (OLS) regression with the inclusion of a lagged dependent variable in the model to help ameliorate issues related to autocorrelation.[10]

The county-level analysis is based, as in chapter 6, on data from Louisiana and North Carolina, the only two Southern states for which we have voter registration data by party and race from the mid-1960s to the present. The time period of the analysis is the same as for the state-level analysis. Obviously, the number of cross sections varies across states. While there are one hundred counties in North Carolina, there are only sixty-four parishes in Louisiana. We have complete data for all of the county/parish variables with the exception of black income.[11] For this reason, the models that include a measure of black income are based on a sample that is slightly smaller for both Louisiana and North Carolina.

For both the state and substate analyses, we include fixed effects in order to deal with the possibility that these geographic units have distinctive—and unobserved—characteristics that influence the baseline level of black mobilization. To further address the inferential complications generated by the potential presence of heteroskedasticity, we also make use of robust standard errors clustered by state, county, or parish, given the circumstances.

In addition to helping ameliorate the statistical issue of serial correlation, the inclusion of a lagged dependent variable within the TSCS setup can also play a substantive role (see chapter 5 for a more detailed discussion on this topic). Using such an approach allows us to statistically derive the extent to which black mobilization is dependent upon previous levels of black mobilization. Given the fact that election roles are not purged on an annual basis, the inclusion of a lagged dependent variable in this particular context is substantively crucial.

Finally, because we are unable to reject the possibility of the presence of autocorrelation in our fixed-effects estimates, we estimate a GMM instrumental variable model with fixed effects (IV-FE) again with clustered standard errors.[12] The results at the state and substate level are robust across both types of model specifications (see also endnote 15). A detailed description of data sources and variable operationalizations are located in Appendices A and B respectively.

## Findings

### State-Level Analysis

The results from our FE and IV-FE models are presented in Table 8.1. Note that, although we were unable to rule out the possibility of non-trivial autocorrelation in the FE models,[13] the substantive and, to a large extent, the statistical results are comparable across these various model specifications. The first finding to note indicates that prior GOP growth is strongly and positively related to black mobilization, but only in the Deep South. There is no evidence of a relationship between prior GOP growth and black mobilization in the Rim South.

Second, note that the size of the black population—the *potential* mobilized population—is positively associated with black mobilization in five of the six models. We can also see that the effect of population size on mobilization is significantly greater (from a substantive and a statistical standpoint) in the Rim South than in the Deep South. These results are also consistent with our hypothesized expectations.

The effects of GOP growth on black mobilization in the Deep South are more than statistically significant; they are substantively significant as well. Figure 8.3 highlights the substantive effect of GOP growth on black mobilization, and we can see that it is dramatic.[14] The figure indicates black mobilization rates increasing monotonically over time from 9.6 percent in 1966 to 22.5 percent by 2008. The effect related to GOP strength then accounts for nearly a quarter of black mobilization by the end of our time frame. Though we have no empirical evidence to suggest that GOP growth has affected black mobilization outside the Deep South, the substantive impact of the effect in the Deep South is quite dramatic.

Consistent with previous research on black mobilization rates, we also see evidence of a "political context" effect. Registration rates are consistently higher in presidential election years, and we see that black mobilization was higher during the first Jackson candidacy (1984) and the year President Obama was elected (2008). Somewhat surprisingly, we find no evidence of an income effect on black mobilization. It is worth noting the consistency of each of these results across the Rim South and the Deep South. Where relative advantage theory suggests distinctive results in the Rim South and the Deep South, we find them. When no distinction is expected, one does not materialize.

Given the size of the coefficients for contextual effects associated presidential elections and the Jackson and Obama campaigns, the effect of GOP growth clearly dwarfs the substantive impacts of these other factors. In the Deep South, we cannot avoid the conclusion that the primary impetus to black mobilization was the growth of the Republican Party. Is the same dynamic obviously at work at the substate level? We turn to that question in the next section.

## Substate-Level Analysis

Although relative advantage theory provides a rationale for state-level effects in the South, that does not preclude the possibility of local-context effects throughout the South. Given the wide variation in the size of the black populations in

TABLE 8.1 Explaining Black Mobilization in the South, 1966–2008

| | DEEP SOUTH | RIM SOUTH | DEEP SOUTH | RIM SOUTH | DEEP SOUTH | RIM SOUTH |
|---|---|---|---|---|---|---|
| Constant | .0424 (.3110) | -.2467 (.1440) | | | | |
| Republican Strength$_{t-1}$ | .1852* (.0894) | -.1008 (.1473) | .1714** (.0777) | -.0850 (.1176) | .1419** (.0773) | -.1310 (.1164) |
| Black Mobilization $_{(t-1)}$ | .4932*** (.1060) | .7401*** (.1014) | .5268*** (.0944) | .7964*** (.0818) | .5315** (.0922) | .8023*** (.0800) |
| % Black | .8581 (.9604) | 2.281** (1.022) | .9198* (.5894) | 2.227*** (.7697) | .8354* (.5778) | 1.860*** (.7663) |
| Black Income | -.0013 (.0017) | .0014 (.0022) | -.0015 (.0016) | .0010 (.0016) | -.0014 (.0016) | -.0008 (.0015) |
| Jackson 1984 | .0601* (.0295) | .0456** (.0181) | .0609** (.0284) | .0472** (.0247) | .0644** (.0280) | .0516** (.0242) |
| Presidential Election Year | .0253 (.0197) | .0536** (.0127) | .0254** (.0116) | .0549*** (.0108) | .0206* (.0118) | .0497*** (.0108) |
| Obama 2008 | | | | | .0561** (.0290) | .0604*** (.0254) |
| Estimation Procedure | FE | FE | IV-FE | IV-FE | IV-FE | IV-FE |
| R² | .62 | .38 | .65 | .61 | .66 | .63 |
| N | 110 | 132 | 110 | 132 | 110 | 132 |

NOTES: *p < .10; **p < .05; ***p < .01, one-tailed tests (except for constant).

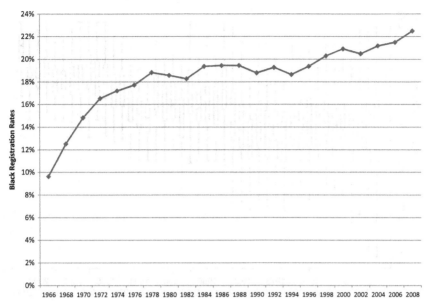

FIGURE 8.3 The Effect of GOP Growth on Black Mobilization in the Deep South, 1966–2008

counties within each of the Southern states, there is at least some reason to think (and relative advantage theory suggests) that county-level GOP growth might well be influenced by the level of black mobilization—especially in those counties with larger black populations. Unfortunately, county-level data on black mobilization (percentage of blacks registered to vote) and Republican strength across the time period of our analysis (or any reasonably comparable time period) is very limited. In fact, only two states collect sufficient data for a feasible analysis of the impact of GOP growth on black mobilization—North Carolina and Louisiana, a Rim South state (albeit one with a historically high African American population) and a Deep South state. Using the only satisfactory county-level data available to us, we investigate the local-level impact of GOP growth on black mobilization in Louisiana and North Carolina.

First, we note that in both Louisiana and North Carolina, not only has the average level of black mobilization *increased* dramatically since the passage of the VRA, but the variation among counties in both states has *decreased* dramatically (see Figures 8.4 and 8.5). Notice that while at least some counties in Louisiana and North Carolina had very high rates of black mobilization since the mid-1960s, the floor of black mobilization has risen consistently since that time.

The substate level results for Louisiana and North Carolina presented in Table 8.2 are strikingly similar to the state-level results for the Deep South.[15]

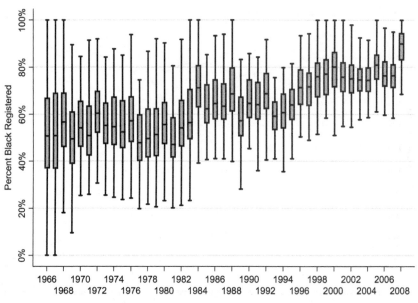

FIGURE 8.4  North Carolina Black Registration-County Boxplots, 1966–2008

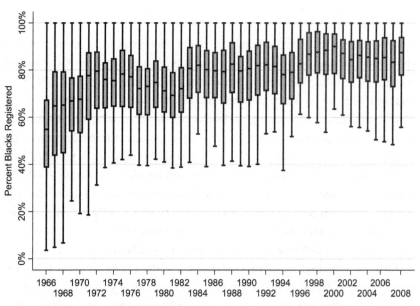

FIGURE 8.5  Louisina Black Registration-Parish Boxplots, 1966–2008

GOP growth clearly has a substantively and statistically significant effect on black mobilization. As the Republican Party grew in each of these states, the levels of black political mobilization—measured in terms of the percentage of voting age African Americans registered to vote—grew as well. We also see, as expected, presidential election years boosting black mobilization, as did the candidacies of Jesse Jackson (in 1984) and President Obama. Somewhat surprisingly, we find a significant, but negative, income effect. At this point, we unfortunately have no explanation for this counterintuitive result.

To more clearly demonstrate the substantive effect of GOP growth on black mobilization, we have selected one representative county from North Carolina (Wake) and one representative parish from Louisiana (Caddo) and graphed the estimated effect of Republican growth on black mobilization based on the coefficient estimates from our substate models.[16] In each case, we chose a relatively large county/parish (from a population standpoint)[17] and one that had neither an especially large nor an especially small African American population. These effects are presented in Figure 8.6.

In both Caddo Parish and Wake County, the trajectory of the substantive impact of GOP growth on black mobilization mirrors the state-level effect we see in the Deep South. While the effect was relatively small in the late 1960s and early 1970s, it was quite substantial during the last two decades. Though the effect is somewhat larger in Wake County, it is still clear that in both Wake County and Caddo Parish, *the* driving force behind black mobilization is Republican growth.

## Discussion and Conclusion

The impetus for the development of relative advantage theory arose out of the absence of a compelling explanation for the growth of Southern Republicanism over the past half-century. Yet the implications of the strategic behavior that underlies the theory of relative advantage are not limited to the behavior of white Southern conservatives; relative advantage suggests at least a partial explanation for African American political behavior, particularly in regard to electoral mobilization. Clearly, just as white conservatives strategically viewed the Republican Party as a mechanism to regain political influence following the enfranchisement of blacks into the electorate, African Americans also responded strategically to increases in Republican strength through heightened mobilization on their own part in an effort to counter GOP advances. To the extent that African Americans acted on a perceived "linked fate" (Dawson 1994), this strategic behavior is likely to be even more prevalent.

In this chapter, we assess the extent to which the implications of relative advantage theory manifest itself in the behavior of African Americans at the state and substate levels in Louisiana and North Carolina. We find strong

TABLE 8.2 Explaining County-Level Black Mobilization in Louisiana and North Carolina, 1966–2008

| | LOUISIANA | LOUISIANA | NORTH CAROLINA | NORTH CAROLINA |
|---|---|---|---|---|
| Republican Strength $_{t-1}$ | .0683*** | .1065*** | .5074*** | .4155*** |
| | (.0155) | (.0195) | (.0367) | (.0380) |
| Black Mobilization $_{(t-1)}$ | .8516*** | .8240*** | .7211*** | .7181*** |
| | (.0193) | (.0231) | (.0207) | (.0144) |
| % Black | .1432*** | .1920*** | .1455*** | .2841*** |
| | (.0451) | (.0511) | (.0485) | (.0401) |
| Black Income (in thousands) | | -.002*** | | -.003*** |
| | | (.0008) | | (.0008) |
| Jackson 1984 | .0154*** | .0114*** | .0943*** | .0941*** |
| | (.0035) | (.0036) | (.0082) | (.0071) |
| Presidential Election Year | .0070*** | .0105*** | .0506*** | .0494*** |
| | (.0024) | (.0026) | (.0028) | (.0021) |
| Obama 2008 | .0189*** | .0174*** | .0778*** | .0838*** |
| | (.0048) | (.0052) | (.0066) | (.0058) |
| Estimation Procedure | IV-FE | IV-FE | IV-FE | IV-FE |
| $R^2$ | .85 | .81 | .72 | .79 |
| N | 2,624 | 2,488 | 4,100 | 3,672 |

NOTES: *$p < .10$; **$p < .05$; ***$p < .01$, two-tailed tests.

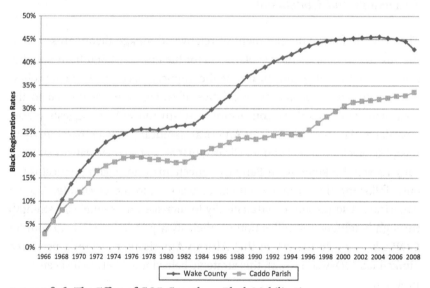

FIGURE 8.6 The Effect of GOP Growth on Black Mobilization

support—at both levels of analysis—for what is perhaps the most surprising aspect of relative advantage theory: the fact that GOP growth drove black mobilization in areas of the South where whites have traditionally been the most conservative and where African Americans have been most numerous (i.e., the Deep South states or counties/parishes located within black-belt regions within a particular state). What we now have is an integrated explanation of the two most significant aspects of the transformation of the Southern party system—an explanation that, at every turn, has passed empirical muster.

SECTION FOUR

# Conclusion

| Summary and Concluding Thoughts
*Disintegration of the Solid South*

IN THE MIDDLE OF the last century, during the congressional elections of 1950, not a single Southern Republican won a Senate race, and only two Southern Republicans won seats in the House of Representatives. The two Southern Republican victors were both from Tennessee, a Rim South state. B. Carroll Reece won the election from the first congressional district with considerably less than 50 percent of the vote in a three-person race in which the Independent came in second. Reece's district was in upper east Tennessee and included the tri-cities area, a traditional stronghold of what Key referred to as "mountain Republicans." The other Tennessean was Howard Baker. The future senator and Ronald Reagan's chief of staff won a close election for the House seat in the second congressional district by less than 3,300 votes. Baker also served a district in east Tennessee. In an era of mass black disenfranchisement in the region, there were no African American members of Congress from the South during this period of time.

Some sixty years later, there are not only far more Republicans in the congressional delegations from the South, there are also far more African Americans. Following the 2010 elections, Democrats held fewer than 30 percent of the congressional seats in the Southern states. Of the twenty-two Senate seats in the South, only three are held by Democrats. A majority of Southern Democratic House members are African American or Hispanic, and only one House seat in the Deep South is held by a white Democrat (John Barrow–GA).

In chapter 2, we provided an extensive depiction of this transformation, showing, in particular, that GOP growth was both temporally and spatially not uniform across the region. In certain regions in some states, bands of Southern Republicans were politically active before 1950. Other areas had, for all intents and purposes, no Republican Party at all until the 1970s. We also showed that by the beginning of the twenty-first century, Southern Republicanism was ubiquitous in every state in both the Rim South and the Deep South.

The growth in Southern Republicanism was matched by a similar growth in the mobilization of the black population. In 1960, fewer than 30 percent of voting age African Americans in the South had registered to vote. By 2008, nearly three-quarters of all voting-age African American Southerners had registered to vote. Although there is evidence that black mobilization was growing before the passage of the VRA in 1965 (see Timpone 1995), there is little question that the VRA provided the impetus for this broad and dramatic increase in voter registration.

The mobilization of the African American population was a regionwide phenomenon in the South over the past half-century, but as we showed in chapter 8, the extent of black mobilization was not uniform across states and counties. The data clearly indicate that some areas experienced significantly greater mobilization than others. It is also apparent that mobilization occurred more rapidly in some areas than in others. The areas with the largest increase in mobilization, however, were not often the same areas in which mobilization increased most rapidly.

As the existing literature would suggest, we see that black mobilization spiked with significant political events, such as the Jackson campaign in 1984 and the Obama campaign and election in 2008. But other patterns in black mobilization are not easily explained by existing research. In chapter 8, we highlighted the fact that we find no evidence of a positive relationship between income and black mobilization at either the state or the substate level. There is little reason to think that the particular type of political participation on which we focus—registering to vote—is likely to be primarily a function of black empowerment, another important aspect of the research on black political participation.

The theory of *relative advantage* outlined in chapter 3 helps us understand this dramatic Southern transformation. It also provides a logic that highlights the intersection of the two pillars of the disintegration of the "Solid South"—the mobilization of African Americans and the growth of the GOP. As African Americans flowed into the electorate (and overwhelmingly the Democratic Party), white conservatives bolted for the Republican Party. Although the competitiveness of the Southern Republicans and the organizational strength of the Republican Party in the South had an independent impact on subsequent GOP growth, we saw a strong relationship between black electoral strength and GOP growth even when accounting for variation in the strength of other factors. In chapter 4, we illustrated the dynamics of relative advantage with detailed case studies and a wealth of archival data.

We saw this dynamic in patterns of GOP growth clearly and consistently at the state level (in chapter 5) and at the county/parish level (in chapter 6). Somewhat surprisingly given the limitations of the data, we also found evidence of this dynamic at the individual level (although this effect was mediated). We also found that the mobilization of the African American electorate had a substantial effect on GOP growth in the face of controls for other traditional explanations, such as income growth, in-migration, and evangelicalism. Simply put, we found, as the theory of relative advantage predicted, that the growth of Southern Republicanism was *primarily* driven by racial dynamics, not class, demographic factors, or religion, as others have suggested. Though we are suggesting a distinctive dynamic, in this important respect our work mirrors Key's (1949) seminal text on Southern politics. At the midpoint of the last century, according to Key, Southern politics revolved around the issue of race. Southern politics in the early twenty-first century still revolves around the issue of race.

Much of the recent research on Southern politics—Lublin (2004) and Shafer and Johnston (2001, 2006) are prominent examples—argues that the role of race in modern Southern politics has been overemphasized and that the key to understanding the postwar partisan transformation in the South is class conflict driven by economic growth. We are not arguing that the economic transformation of the South did not play a role in the development of the Republican Party in the region, but it is not the key aspect of—or the primary mover behind—the growth of the Southern wing of the GOP. To understand the temporal and spatial dynamics of GOP growth in the region, we would argue that one must understand the politics of race. Stated succinctly, the partisan and political transformation of the South over the past half-century has, most centrally, revolved around the issue of race.

But is it possible that this racial dynamic has played itself out? If we are correct about the political dynamics that have gotten us to this point, then we may be very near the high-water mark of Southern Republicanism. Based on our analysis, the primary impetus for the growth of the Southern wing of the GOP was the increasing electoral strength of the African American population. A significant increase in black electoral strength would require one of the following: (1) a sizeable jump in the mobilization rate of the existing African American population, (2) a large increase in the relative size of the African American population, or (3) some non-trivial increase in *both* mobilization rates and population among African Americans.

With the release of the 2010 census data, demographers have highlighted a number of important trends related to the black population. The first of these involves black migration patterns within the United States. Increasingly, blacks born outside the South are moving to the region, reversing a longtime trend begun with the *Great Migration*.[1] This pattern, in part, has also resulted in an increasing share of the nation's black population residing in the region. By 2010, half of the black population (49.8 percent) was again living in the eleven-state South, up from a low of 45.1 percent in 1970.[2] Neither of these trends, however, has significantly altered the share of the black population within the region relative to other racial/ethnic groups. Table 9.1 displays the racial/ethnic composition of the South by decade beginning in 1950. Since 1970, blacks have comprised between 20.3 percent (1970) and 19.3 percent (2010) of the total population of the region—a remarkably stable pattern. The larger demographic trend to note from Table 9.1 is the sizeable drop in the non-Hispanic white population in the region, from 72.6 percent in 1980 to 58.3 percent in 2010, and the concomitant rise in the share of the Hispanic population, up nearly 11 percent over the same period of time.

Based on current demographic patterns then, we are likely to see neither a significant increase in black mobilization rates (which, according to census data are slightly higher than white mobilization rates) nor an increase in the relative size of the African American population in the South. The dynamic that has driven the growth of the Southern GOP to this point is unlikely to produce substantial further growth—at least among whites.

This prediction of a high-water mark for GOP growth among Southern whites is an important distinguishing characteristic of the theory of relative advantage. If, as others have recently argued, Southern Republicanism is primarily driven by class dynamics, then, as income rises among whites, we

TABLE 9.1 Racial/Ethnic Composition of the American South, 1950–2010

| DECADE | WHITE | BLACK | HISPANIC |
|--------|-------|-------|----------|
| 1950 | 75.1% | 24.9% | — |
| 1960 | 77.1% | 22.7% | — |
| 1970 | 79.3% | 20.3% | — |
| 1980 | 72.6% | 19.4% | 7.0% |
| 1990 | 70.2% | 19.0% | 9.2% |
| 2000 | 64.1% | 19.2% | 13.1% |
| 2010 | 58.3% | 19.3% | 17.6% |

NOTES: Entries are the percentage of total population in the eleven-state South comprised of each group. The Census Bureau did not collect population data on Hispanic ethnicity until 1980. Source: Decennial U.S. Census data.

should expect to see further Republican growth within this population segment. Which factors will drive future party system change obviously remains to be seen.

But even granting that racial dynamics, more specifically the relationship between black and white Southerners, have driven Republican growth to this point, the future of the Southern Republican Party is unlikely to unfold solely in terms of black and white. At the time of the passage of the VRA, the census did not even keep track of the size of the Hispanic population. Until 1970, the demographic distinctions were "white" and "nonwhite." Today, the future of the Southern party system may well depend on the attitudes and mobilization of Southern Hispanics. We provide a brief discussion of some of the possibilities associated with the growing political significance of the Hispanic population in the next section.

## The Growing Political Significance of Southern Hispanics

If the growth of Southern Republicanism and the mobilization of African Americans in the South are the two most significant political phenomena of the past half-century, then the most significant demographic phenomenon of the last twenty years is the widespread growth of the Hispanic population. In the early portion of the twenty-first century, the growth of the Southern Hispanic population is also shaping up to be one of the most important political dynamics as well (see again Table 9.1 for regional comparisons over time). While the South has had a small number of large, localized Hispanic communities for over a century (in Texas, for example), the dramatic region-wide growth of the Hispanic population is a late twentieth-century phenomenon. As Hispanics transform Southern demography, they have the potential to also transform Southern politics. To provide an idea of the potential for demographic and political change, consider the following: Texas is currently one of only four states where Anglos (non-Hispanic whites) do not represent the majority racial/ethnic group. By 2015, it is predicted that Hispanics will become a majority in Texas.[3]

Although Hispanics are not a monolithic group, in political or other terms, Hispanics not of Cuban origin tend to identify and vote Democratic more than a majority of the time.[4] Given the growth in this segment of the population, this trend should be troubling to the Republican Party in the region. Hispanics tend to be relatively conservative on social issues, but they are fairly liberal on economic matters. The former should benefit Republicans and the latter Democrats. So, unlike the black electorate, there does appear to be some maneuvering room for Republicans with this particular group. However, the party's current stance on the immigration issue has proven to be a stumbling block in the GOP's effort to court Hispanics. For a population segment with comparatively higher degrees of poverty and lower levels of educational attainment, the draw from economic issues would also seem to benefit the Democratic Party. Party registration figures from North Carolina indicate that approximately 40 percent of Hispanics identify as Democrats, compared to 28 percent Republicans, and 32 percent with no party affiliation (Bullock and Hood 2006). In short, existing research provides little guidance on the issue of which camp a majority of Hispanics may choose in terms of partisan affiliation.

A number of factors will work to mute the influence of Hispanics in the region for several decades into the future, even in Texas and Florida. Figure 9.1 presents the Hispanic share of the population for each Southern state along with the Hispanic voting- age population (VAP), using data from the 2000 and 2010 U.S. censuses. For every state except Texas, Florida, and Georgia, Hispanics comprised less than 5 percent of the total population in 2000. Note that even these small percentages represent substantial growth in a region where Hispanics were a negligible presence in many states before 1990. Total population estimates for 2010 show an increase in the number of states with a Hispanic population over 5 percent to six, all of which are located in the Rim South with the exception of Deep South Georgia. These 2010 estimates place the Hispanic population in Florida and Texas at 22.5 percent and 37.6 percent respectively.

Despite a growing presence throughout the region, recent research indicates that Hispanics will be slow to reshape the politics of the South. One recent study estimates that it could be the 2030s before growth in the Hispanic population alone would help Democrats reach parity with the GOP in Texas (Stanley 2008). A number of factors currently work to constrain the political influence of Hispanics in the region. One of these is the fact that the Hispanic population is, on average, currently younger than the non-Hispanic population. In Texas where Hispanics make up more than a third of the state's total population, this group comprises only about one-fifth of the VAP. Again, see Figure 9.1 for comparisons of the Hispanic VAP by state.

A second limiting factor relates to the issue of citizenship. A large percentage of Hispanics who have migrated to the South (with the exception of Florida and Texas) are not citizens and therefore cannot vote. Census estimates from the 2008 election cycle indicate that Hispanics comprised only 16 percent of the citizen VAP in Florida, compared to a 20.7 percent share of the VAP.

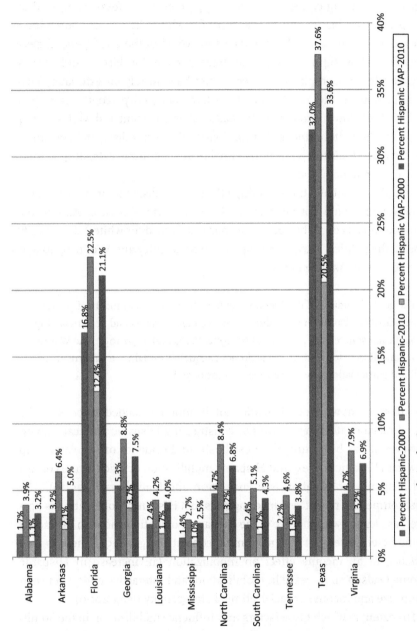

FIGURE 9.1 Hispanic Population by State

SOURCE: US. Census Bureau

Percent Hispanic-2000 ■ Percent Hispanic-2010 ■ Percent Hispanic VAP-2000 ■ Percent Hispanic VAP-2010

The potential for Hispanic political influence is also limited by the fact that Hispanic citizens in the South register and vote at lower levels than do blacks or whites. For the 2008 election, the Census Bureau put Hispanic registration among citizens to be to be 54.3 percent in Texas, compared to 73.7 percent for blacks and 73.6 percent for whites. The same source indicates that 37.8 percent of Hispanic citizens voted in the 2008 general election, far below 64.9 percent and 64.7 percent for blacks and whites respectively.[5] In Georgia, where we do not have to rely on estimates, Hispanic turnout in the 2008 general election was 59.6 percent. Again, this figure is far below turnout rates for blacks at 75.8 percent and whites at 77.4 percent.[6] The bottom line is that until such disparities dissipate, Hispanics will not reach their full political potential in any Southern state, despite their growing population base.

Still, the potentially transforming effects of a substantial increase in Hispanic voters should not be ignored. As in the case of African Americans, standard models of mobilization (primarily designed for whites) do not fully capture the political activity of Hispanics (see Leighley and Vedlitz 1999 and Leighley 2001). As Jang notes:

> The central finding of the literature is that the traditional models of political participation, based on individuals' socio-economic status and accompanying political resources (e.g., Verba and Nie 1972; Verba et al. 1978, 1995; and Wolfinger and Rosenstone 1980), alone do not adequately explain the patterns in political participation among Latinos . . . (2009, 512).

The most recent work on Hispanic mobilization has tended to focus on the role of racial context in spurring or constraining Hispanic political activity. However, it has been difficult to establish (find evidence of) a relationship between Hispanic context and Hispanic mobilization or black/white context and Hispanic mobilization (see Jang 2009 and Matsubayashi 2009). The most compelling recent evidence suggests that Hispanic mobilization is positively associated with the size of the Hispanic population and with the racial/ethnic heterogeneity of the geographic context (Jang 2009). There is also evidence of an income effect on mobilization (an increase in Hispanic income leads to an increase in mobilization) and interactive effects between group size and income or racial/ethnic heterogeneity (Jang 2009).

The extent to which these factors may influence mobilization in the Southern context remains to be seen. We also wonder if there are explicit political dynamics involved in the mobilization of Hispanics in the South. That the Hispanic population lacks a strong partisan vector—a clear preference for one party or the other—would suggest little change in the trend of Hispanic mobilization. However, if a strong partisan preference develops—that is, a large majority of mobilized Hispanics consistently demonstrates a preference for one party—then relative advantage suggests that Hispanic mobilization will increase accordingly. If Hispanic support coalesces around a single party, then we should see a significant increase in Hispanic mobilization. Why? Because the power of a cohesive Hispanic voting bloc coupled with an increase in mobilization is significantly greater than the value of mobilization for a bifurcated constituency. So, if the Hispanic population becomes more politically cohesive, we should also expect to see a concomitant increase in Hispanic mobilization.

Our earlier prediction that we are at (or very near) the high-water mark of Southern Republicanism is based on our understanding of black/white political dynamics. The future political development of the Hispanic population in the South could obviously have a significant impact on the subsequent trajectory of partisan politics. In fact, if the Hispanic population in the South coalesces around the Republican Party, we may be nowhere near the high-water mark of Southern Republicanism. If Hispanics coalesce within the Democratic Party, then we may have seen the zenith of the GOP in the American South.

## Race, Class, and the Engine of American Party Politics

As students of Southern politics, we would argue that regional politics should be studied for its own sake. But Southern politics is not isolated from the broader arena of American politics. Certainly no other region has undergone the dramatic partisan transformation experienced by Southerners during the past half-century, but the political implications of this transformation go well beyond Southern borders.

First, the level of ideological polarization in the American party system is simply inconceivable in the absence of the disintegration of the Solid South and the partisan transformation of Southern politics. Although scholars will certainly argue about the extent of ideological polarization (see, for example, Abramowitz 2011; Fiorina et al. 2010; Levendusky 2009; and Poole and Rosenthal 2007), Southern political dynamics enabled the development of whatever ideological polarization exists in the modern party system. We believe that this distinctive Southern contribution to our national party system is not fully appreciated.

But beyond this, we find the misinterpretation of the Southern partisan transformation problematic because of what it then mistakenly implies about the national party system. It is now commonplace to assume that the disintegration of the Solid South was the long overdue demise of a distinctive Southern politics. Basically, "the party system of the contemporary South has gradually come to resemble that of the country as a whole" (Bartels 2008, 94). From this perspective, the end of Democratic dominance resulted from (1) the waning significance of race, (2) the economic transformation of the South, and (3) the rise of a class-based politics. What is unclear, then, is why working- and middle-class Southern whites have shifted from their "natural" class home—the Democratic Party—to the Republican Party. Bartels also notes that the "decline in support for Democratic presidential candidates among white voters over the past half-century is *entirely* attributable to partisan change in the South" (2008, 78), a partisan change inconsistent with class-based explanations, at least for working- and middle-class whites.

Our theoretical and empirical focus here has been the South, and so we have no basis on which to decide whether the South is, in terms of partisan dynamics, indistinguishable from the rest of the United States. What we can say is that the Southern party system over the past half-century revolved around issues of race—not class. Much of the recent work on the American party system has clearly then underemphasized the crucial and distinctive role that race and racial dynamics have played.

Which leads us to what we consider the crucial question for the future of Southern politics (and possibly national politics): Whither Hispanics? The racial dynamics that produced the party system in the modern South are not likely to produce drastic changes any time soon. We do not expect a dramatic increase in the mobilization or the electoral strength of the African American population, and we should thus not expect a substantial increase in Republicanism among Southern whites. But if Hispanic Americans in the South coalesce around a single party—Democrat or Republican—the shift in the balance of power between the parties could well result in the development of a new party system. And if conjectures based on relative advantage theory are correct, once the transformation begins (when Hispanics begin a more-or-less permanent and consistent attachment to a single party), it could happen far more quickly than expected.

Although our focus is on the South and its politics, if the support of Southern Hispanics goes overwhelmingly to one party or the other, then spillover effects at the national level are all but unavoidable. Imagine the national-level ramifications of a Southern party system in which the Hispanic voting bloc could consistently deliver Florida, Georgia, North Carolina, and Texas—the four Southern states with the largest Hispanic populations—to their party's presidential candidate. How would the opposing candidate effectively combat such an Electoral College windfall? Needless to say, it would be difficult.

We are not there yet, and it is unclear when (or if) we ever will be. Race has left an indelible imprint on the region, and it would certainly be a mistake to ignore the potential future role of racial dynamics in Southern politics and, by implication, national politics. Just as the Southern novelist William Faulkner wrote, "The past is never dead. It's not even past."

| Data Sources

## Chapter 2

Figures 2.1 through 2.6

U.S. Census Bureau, Statistical Abstract of the United States: various years and editions, 1954 to 2010. Washington, DC (http://www.census.gov/compendia/statab/).

Figure 2.7

(See chapter 8 sources, State-Level Models, *Black Mobilization*.)

Figures 2.8 and 2.9

(See chapter 6 sources, *Percent Republican/Black Electoral Strength*.)

## Chapter 5

State-Level Republican Strength (Dependent Variable)/Presidential Vote

David, Paul T. 1972. *Party Strength in the United States, 1872–1970*. Charlottesville, VA: University of Virginia Press.
*Guide to U.S. Elections*, 3rd ed. 1994. Washington, DC: Congressional Quarterly Press.
*America Votes*. 1996, 1998, 2000, 2002, 2004, 2006, 2008. Washington, DC: Congressional Quarterly Press.

% Black

U.S. Department of Commerce. Bureau of the Census. [1960-Table 96; 1970-Table 20; 1980-Table 19; 1990-Table 19; 2000-Table QT-PL (American FactFinder)]. *General Population Characteristics*. Washington, DC: U.S. Government Printing Office.

## Black Electoral Strength

*VEP [Voter Education Project] News*. [1968-Vol. 2, no. 4; 1969-Vol. 3, no. 12; 1970-Vol. 4, nos. 1, 2]. Atlanta, GA: Southern Regional Council.

United States Bureau of the Census. [1976-Table 747; 1979-Table 840; 1980-Table 849]. *Statistical Abstract of the U.S.* Washington, DC: U.S. Government Printing Office.

U.S. Department of Commerce. Bureau of the Census. [1980-Table 5; 1982-Table 16; 1984-Table 2; 1986-Table 4; 1988-Table 2; 1990-Table 4; 1992-Table 4; 1994-Table 4a (electronic version); 1996-Table 4 (e.v.); 1998-Table 4 (e.v.); 2000-Table 4a (e.v.); 2002-Table 4a (e.v.); 2004-Table 4a (e.v.); 2006-Table 4b (e.v.); 2008-Table 4b (e.v.)]. *Current Population Reports: P-20 Series on Voting and Registration*. Washington, DC: U.S. Government Printing Office.

## In-Migration

U.S. Department of Commerce. Bureau of the Census. [1960-Tables 39 and 98; 1970-Table 50; 1980-Tables 75 and 85; 1990-Table P042 (American FactFinder); 2000-Table PCT63A (American FactFinder)]. *Census of Population, Place of Birth*. Washington, DC: U.S. Government Printing Office.[1]

## Agricultural Sector Employment

U.S. Department of Commerce. Bureau of the Census. [1960-Table 128; 1970-Table 167; 1980-Table 242; 1990-Table 151; 2000-DP-3 (American FactFinder)]. *General Population Characteristics*. Washington, DC: U.S. Government Printing Office.

## Per Capita Income

U.S. Department of Commerce. Bureau of Economic Analysis. 1989. *State Personal Income: 1929-1987*. Washington, DC: U.S. Government Printing Office.

U.S. Department of Commerce. Bureau of Economic Analysis, Regional Economic Accounts, State Annual Personal Income. 2010. SA1-3. Personal Income and Summary Estimates, 1969–2010 (http://www.bea.gov/regional/spi/).

## Substate Party Competition

### Electronic Data

Inter-University Consortium for Political and Social Research. STATE LEGISLATIVE ELECTION RETURNS IN THE UNITED STATES, 1968–1989 [computer file]. Fifth ICPSR ed. Ann Arbor, MI: Inter-university Consortium for Political and Social Research [producer and distributor], 1992.

### Books

Aistrup, Joseph A. 1996. *The Southern Strategy Revisited: Republican Top-Down Advancement in the South*. Lexington, KY: University of Kentucky Press. [Tables 4.1, 4.2, 4.3].

*The Book of the States,* 1960/1961–2008/2009. Lexington, KY: Council of State Governments.

Jewell, Malcolm E. and David M. Olson. 1982. *American State Political Parties and Elections,* 2nd ed. Homewood, IL: Dorsey Press. [Table 3.5].

Jewell, Malcolm E. 1967. *Legislative Representation in the Contemporary South.* Durham, NC: Duke University Press. [Table 4.1].


State Publications

*Tennessee Blue Book* (Electronic Edition): 1996, 1998; *Mississippi Blue Book:* 1995–1996, 1997–1998, 1999–2000; 2001–2002, 2003–2004, 2005–2006, 2007–2008, 2009–2010; *Georgia Official and Statistical Register:* 1966, 1968; *Arkansas Votes: 1968.*


Newspapers

*The Washington Post* (VA): 1959, 1961, 1963, 1965, 1967; *The Commercial Appeal* (MS): 1959, 1961; *Arkansas Gazette* (AR): 1960–66; *The Clarion Ledger* (MS): 1959.

*Original voting records/reports from government entities for the following states:* Mississippi: 1963, 1967; North Carolina: 1968, 1986, 1988; Virginia: 1959; and Georgia: 1960, 1962, 1964.

*Secretary of State/State Board of Elections Electronic Returns for the following states:* Alabama: 1998, 2000, 2002, 2004, 2006, 2008; Arkansas: 1996, 1998, 2000, 2002, 2004, 2006, 2008; Florida: 1994, 1996, 1998, 2000, 2002, 2004, 2006, 2008; Georgia: 1994, 1996, 1998, 2000, 2002, 2004, 2006, 2008; Louisiana: 1991, 1995, 1999, 2003, 2007; Mississippi: 1999, 2003, 2007; North Carolina: 1996, 1998; 2000, 2002, 2004, 2006, 2008; South Carolina: 1994, 1996, 1998, 2000, 2002, 2004, 2006, 2008; Texas: 1994, 1996, 1998, 2000, 2002, 2004, 2006, 2008; Virginia: 1995, 1997, 1999, 2001, 2003, 2005, 2007.


Evangelical Protestants

Sources for Evangelical Protestant Membership

*Churches and Church Membership in the United States, 1956.* New York: National Council of the Churches of Christ in the United States of America.

Bradley, Martin B., Norman M. Green Jr., Dale E. Jones, Mac Lynn, and Lou McNeil. 1992. *Churches and Church Membership in the United States, 1990.* Atlanta, GA: Glenmary Research Center.

Johnson, Douglas W., Paul R. Picard, and Bernard Quinn. 1974. *Churches and Church Membership in the United States, 1971.* Washington, DC: Glenmary Research Center.

Jones, Dale E. 2002. *Religious Congregations & Membership in the United States: 2000.* Nashville, TN: Glenmary Research Center [Electronic Data].

Quinn, Bernard, Herman Anderson, Martin Bradley, Paul Goetting, and Peggy Shriver. 1982. *Churches and Church Membership in the United States, 1980*. Atlanta, GA: Glenmary Research Center.

*Southern Baptist Handbook* [1960–1992]. Nashville, TN: Sunday School Board of the Southern Baptist Convention.

"Summary of Churches by State Convention [1993–2008]." Alpharetta, GA: North American Mission Board, Southern Baptist Convention (http://www.namb. net).

### Sources for State Population Estimates

U.S. Department of Commerce. Bureau of the Census. "Historical Annual Time Series of State Population Estimates and Demographic Components of Change, 1900 to 1990 Total Population Estimates" (www.census.gov/population/www/ estimates/st_stts.html).

U.S. Department of Commerce. Bureau of the Census. "State Population Estimates: Annual Time Series, July 1, 1990 to July 1, 1999" (www.census.gov/population/ estimates/state/st-99-3.txt).

U.S. Department of Commerce. Bureau of the Census. "Annual Estimates of the Resident Population for the United States, Regions, States, and Puerto Rico: April 1, 2000 to July 1, 2008 (NST-EST2008-01)" (http://www.census.gov/popest/states/ NST-ann-est2008.html).

## *Chapter 6*

### Percent Republican/Black Electoral Strength

Registration-related data was collected from annual reports produced by state agencies in Louisiana and North Carolina. These data were collected in both hard copy and electronic forms from the following entities: The North Carolina State Library; The North Carolina State Archives; The North Carolina State Board of Elections; The Louisiana Division-New Orleans Public Library; The Louisiana Secretary of State; and The Louisiana Department of Elections and Registration (now incorporated in the Secretary of State Division).

### Evangelical Protestants/Catholics

Sources for Evangelical Protestant and Catholic Membership come from various Glenmary Studies as follows:

*Churches and Church Membership in the United States, 1956*. New York: National Council of the Churches of Christ in the Unites States of America.

Bradley, Martin B., Norman M. Green Jr., Dale E. Jones, Mac Lynn, and Lou McNeil. 1992. *Churches and Church Membership in the United States, 1990*. Atlanta, GA: Glenmary Research Center.

Johnson, Douglas W., Paul R. Picard, and Bernard Quinn. 1974. *Churches and Church Membership in the United States, 1971*. Washington, DC: Glenmary Research Center.

Jones, Dale E. 2002. *Religious Congregations & Membership in the United States: 2000*. Nashville, TN: Glenmary Research Center [electronic data].

Quinn, Bernard, Herman Anderson, Martin Bradley, Paul Goetting, and Peggy Shriver. 1982. *Churches and Church Membership in the United States, 1980*. Atlanta, GA: Glenmary Research Center.

The remaining variables utilized come from various census reports as detailed below.

## Urban Residents

U.S. Department of Commerce. Bureau of the Census. [1960-Table 91; 1970-Table 134; 1980-Table 174; 1990-American Fact Finder; 2000-American Fact-Finder; 2006–2008-American Community Survey]. *Census of Population, Characteristics of the Population*. Washington, DC: U.S. Government Printing Office.

## % Military [North Carolina]

U.S. Department of Commerce. Bureau of the Census. [1960-Table 83; 1970-Table 119; 1980-Table 179; 1990-American FactFinder; 2000-American FactFinder; 2006–2008-American Community Survey]. *Census of Population, Characteristics of the Population*. Washington, DC: U.S. Government Printing Office.

## Median Household Income

U.S. Department of Commerce. Bureau of the Census. [1960-Table 86; 1970-Table 124; 1980-Table 180; 1990-American FactFinder; 2000-American FactFinder; 2006–2008-American Community Survey]. *Census of Population, Characteristics of the Population*. Washington, DC: U.S. Government Printing Office.

## In-Migration

U.S. Department of Commerce. Bureau of the Census. [1960-Table 82; 1970-Table 119; 1980-Tables 174,183; 1990-American FactFinder; 2000-American FactFinder; 2006–2008-American Community Survey]. *Census of Population, Characteristics of the Population*. Washington, DC: U.S. Government Printing Office.

## % Black

U.S. Department of Commerce. Bureau of the Census. [1960-Table 28; 1970-Tables 34, 38; 1980-Table 58-American FactFinder; 2000-American FactFinder; 2006–2008-American Community Survey]. *Census of Population, Characteristics of the Population*. Washington, DC: U.S. Government Printing Office.

*Chapter 7*

Black Registration

Sources for County-Level Black Registration and Total Registration by State (1972–2008):

*Alabama:* Charles S. Bullock III: 1972.

*Florida:* Florida Secretary of State: 1972–2008.

*Georgia:* Charles S. Bullock III: 1972; Georgia Secretary of State: 1980–2008.

*Louisiana:* Louisiana Department of Election and Registration and Louisiana Secretary of State: 1972–2008.

*Mississippi:* Charles S. Bullock III: 1972; The Institute of Politics in Mississippi: 1972.

*North Carolina:* North Carolina State Board of Elections: 1972–2008.

*South Carolina:* South Carolina State Election Commission: 1972–2008.

Bullock III, Charles S., Papers. Various Dates. Voter Registration Records. University of Georgia. Photocopies, Handwritten Tables, and Electronic Records.

DeLaughter, Jerry W., and Elaine F. Rainey. 1971. "Voter Registration in Mississippi." In *The Public Interest.* Jackson, MS: The Institute of Politics in Mississippi, Millsaps College.

Florida Secretary of State (1972–2008). Official Reports of Voter Registration by Race. Tallahassee, FL.

Georgia Secretary of State (1980–2008). Official Reports of Voter Registration by Race. Atlanta, GA.

Louisiana Department of Elections and Registration/Louisiana Secretary of State (1972–2008). Official Reports of Voter Registration by Race. Baton Rouge, LA.

North Carolina State Board of Elections (1972–2008). Official Reports of Voter Registration by Race. Raleigh, NC.

South Carolina State Election Commission (1972–2008). Official Reports of Voter Registration by Race. Columbia, SC.

Individual-Level Survey Data

Hadley, Charles D., and Lewis Bowman. Southern Grassroots Party Activists Project, 1991–1992: [Computer file]. 2nd ICPSR version. New Orleans, LA: Charles D. Hadley and Lewis Bowman [producers], 1993. Ann Arbor, MI: Inter-university Consortium for Political and Social Research [distributor], 1997. doi:10.3886/ICPSR06307

Clark, John A., and Charles Prysby. Southern Grassroots Party Activists Project, 2001 [Computer file]. ICPSR04266-v1. Greensboro, NC: John A. Clark and Charles Prysby [producers], 2005. Ann Arbor, MI: Inter-university Consortium for Political and Social Research [distributor], 2006-03-17. doi:10.3886/ICPSR04266

The American National Election Studies (www.electionstudies.org) Time Series Cumulative Data File [dataset]. Stanford University and the University of Michigan [producers and distributors], 2010.

The Southern Focus Poll (www.irss.unc.edu) 1992–2001 data files [dataset]. Odum Institute, University of North Carolina [distributor], 2011.

## Chapter 8

State-Level Models

Black Mobilization

Black Registration and Total Registration (1960–2008)

*Alabama:* U.S. Commission on Civil Rights: 1960; Voter Education Project: 1962–1970, 1974–1976; U.S Census Bureau, Current Population Reports, Voting and Registration: 1980–2008.

*Arkansas:* U.S. Commission on Civil Rights: 1960; Voter Education Project: 1962–1970, 1974–1976; U.S Census Bureau, Current Population Reports, Voting and Registration: 1980–2008.

*Florida:* Florida Secretary of State: 1960–2008.

*Georgia:* Voter Education Project: 1960–1970, 1974–1976; U.S. Census Bureau, Current Population Reports, Voting and Registration: 1980–1982; Georgia Secretary of State: 1986–2008.

*Louisiana:* Louisiana Department of Elections and Registration and Louisiana Secretary of State: 1960–2008.

*Mississippi:* U.S. Commission on Civil Rights: 1960; Voter Education Project, Newsletters and Reports: 1962–1970, 1974; U.S Census Bureau, Current Population Reports, Voting and Registration: 1980–2008.

*North Carolina:* U.S. Commission on Civil Rights: 1960; Voter Education Project: 1962–1964; North Carolina State Board of Elections: 1966–2008.

*South Carolina:* Voter Education Project: 1960–1962, 1966; U.S. Commission on Civil Rights: 1964; South Carolina State Election Commission: 1968–2008.

*Tennessee:* Voter Education Project: 1960–1970, 1974–1976; U.S Census Bureau, Current Population Reports, Voting and Registration: 1980–2008.

*Texas:* Voter Education Project: 1960–1970, 1974–1976; U.S Census Bureau: 1980–2008.

*Virginia:* U.S. Commission on Civil Rights: 1960, 1964; Voter Education Project: 1962, 1966–1970, 1974–1976; U.S Census Bureau, Current Population Reports, Voting and Registration: 1980–2008.

Southern Regional Council (1968, 2[4]; 1969, 5[12], 1970, 4[1–2]). *VEP* (Voter Education Project) *News*. Atlanta, GA.

Southern Regional Council, Voter Education Project (1968, 1970, 1971, 1974). "Voter Registration in the South" and other reports. Atlanta, GA.

U.S. Bureau of the Census. (1976, Table 747; 1979, Table 840; 1980, Table 849). *Statistical Abstract of the U.S.* Washington, DC: U.S. Government Printing Office.

U.S. Department of Commerce, Bureau of the Census. (1980, Table 5; 1982, Table 16, 1984, Table 2; 1986, Table 4; 1988, Table 2; 1990, Table 4; 1992, Table 4; 1994, Table 4a [electronic version (e.v.)]; 1996, Table 4 [e.v.]; 1998, Table 4 [e.v.]; 2000, Table 4a [e.v.]; 2002, Table 4a [e.v.]; 2004, Table 4a [e.v.]; 2006, Table 4b [e.v.]; 2008, Table 4b [e.v.]. *Current Population Reports: P-20 Series on Voting and Registration*. Washington, DC: U.S. Government Printing Office.

U.S. Commission on Civil Rights. 1959. *Report of the U.S. Commission on Civil Rights*. Washington, DC: U.S. Commission on Civil Rights.

U.S. Commission on Civil Rights. 1961. *Book 1: Voting*. Washington, DC: U.S. Commission on Civil Rights.

U.S. Commission on Civil Rights. 1968. *Political Participation*. Washington, DC: U.S. Commission on Civil Rights.

## Black Voting Age Population

(Used in the calculation of *Black Mobilization*)

U.S. Department of Commerce. Bureau of the Census. [1960-Table 20; 1970-Table 20; 1980-Table 19; 1990-Table 19; 2000-Table P5 (e.v.); 2010-Redistricting Data (e.v.)]. *General Population Characteristics*. Washington, DC: U.S. Government Printing Office.

## Republican Strength

(See chapter 5 sources, State-Level Republican Strength.)

## % Black

(See chapter 5 sources, % *Black*.)

## Black Median Family Income

U.S. Department of Commerce, Bureau of the Census. [1960-Table 65; 1970-Table 199; 1980-Table 61; 1990-Table 53; 2000-Table P-152B [e.v.]; 2005–2009-Table B19013B [e.v.] American Community Survey]. *General Social and Economic Characteristics*: Washington, DC: U.S. Government Printing Office.

## County-Level Models

### Black Median Household Income
**Louisiana and North Carolina**

U.S. Department of Commerce, Bureau of the Census. [1960-Table 88; 1970-Table 128; 1980-Table 186; 1990-Table 9; 2000-Table P-152B [e.v.]; 2005–2009-Table B19013B [e.v.] American Community Survey]. *General Social and Economic Characteristics*: Washington, DC: U.S. Government Printing Office.

## Republican Strength

(See chapter 6 sources, *Percent Republican*.)

## Black Mobilization

## Black Registration Data

(See chapter 6 sources, *Black Electoral Strength*.)

Black Voting Age Population

(used in the calculation of *Black Mobilization*)

U.S. Department of Commerce. Bureau of the Census. [1960-Table 27; 1970-Table 35; 1980-Table 45; 1990-Table 54; 2000-Table P5 (e.v.); 2010-Redistricting Data (e.v.)]. *General Population Characteristics*. Washington, DC: U.S. Government Printing Office.

% Black

(See chapter 6 sources, % *Black*.)

| Variable Operationalizations

*Chapter 5*

### State-Level Republican Strength (Dependent Variable)

For a given year, this index was calculated as follows:
(% Republican Vote [Senate Election] + % Republican Vote [Gubernatorial Election] +
% Republican Vote [Average Republican Congressional Vote])/3.[1]

### Presidential Vote

By state, the percentage of the vote won by the Republican presidential candidate. These figures were carried over for off-election years in the dataset.

### Presidential Campaign Dummies

A set of *n*-1 dummy variables was created to represent each presidential election, beginning with the 1964 Goldwater campaign and continuing through the McCain campaign of 2008. Each dummy variable took on a value of 1 during the presidential election year and the subsequent off-election year (Example: Goldwater campaign, 1964 and 1966 = 1; Else = 0). The 1960 Nixon campaign served as the excluded category.

### % Black

For each state in the analysis, % Black was calculated as follows:
Black Population/Total Population
It was necessary to interpolate estimates of black populations using the two actual sets of figures available. Using a technique very similar to one developed by Combs, Hibbing, and Welch (1984), we took the percent of the state population

labeled as black for each decade, subtracted the figure for the preceding decade, and then divided by ten (years). The aforementioned calculation allowed us to fill in the gaps (1960–1970; 1970–1980; 1980–1990; 1990–2000) using a linear growth pattern.[2] Extrapolations for 2001–2008 were performed using the same technique with Census Bureau population estimates cited below.

## Black Electoral Strength

For each state in the analysis, this variable was calculated as follows:[3]
Number of Blacks Registered to Vote/Total Number of Registered Voters

## In-Migration

In-migration was calculated for each state in our analysis as follows:
Number of White Residents Born outside the Southern Region[4]/Total
State Population
A straight-line linear interpolation/extrapolation method was used to create annual
    estimates.

## Agricultural Employment

This economic transformation variable was calculated using the following formula:
Number of Workers Employed in the Farming and Agricultural Sector of
the Economy/Total Employed Persons 16 and Older

## Per Capita Income

Per Capita Income was calculated as follows:
Total Personal Income (in Nominal $) by State/Total State Population

## Evangelical Protestant

This variable was calculated using the following formula:
Number of Evangelical Protestant Adherents/Total State Population
The scheme used to classify Protestant denominations as *evangelical* is found in
    Green et al. 1996, 188–89. The number of evangelical Protestant adherents in
    a state was calculated using Southern Baptist membership figures as a base.
    Southern Baptists constitute well over a majority of evangelical Protestant
    membership in all of the states in our analysis, and membership information
    for this denomination is available on an annual basis. Membership figures for
    the remaining evangelical denominations were gathered from national sur-
    veys conducted by the Glenmary Research Center. Because these surveys were
    not conducted annually, we used a linear interpolation technique (described
    above) to create annual estimates of non-Southern Baptist evangelical Protes-
    tant membership.

## Substate Party Competition

This variable is a four-part index calculated every other year as follows:
[(Percentage of State Legislative Seats Contested by GOP in the Lower House) + (Percentage of State Legislative Seats Contested by GOP in the Upper House) + (Percentage of State Legislative Seats Won by GOP in the Lower House) + (Percentage of State Legislative Seats Won by GOP in the Lower House)]/4.

## *Chapter 6*

## % GOP Registrants

The percentage of Republican registrants was measured as follows:
Republican Registrants/Total Parish or County Registrants

## % Black

For each parish or county in the analysis, % Black was calculated as follows:
Black Population/Total Population
It was necessary to interpolate estimates of black populations using the two actual sets of figures available. Using a technique very similar to one developed by Combs, Hibbing, and Welch (1984), we took the percent of the state population labeled as black for each decade, subtracted the figure for the preceding decade, and then divided by ten (years). The aforementioned calculation allowed us to fill in the gaps (1960–1970; 1970–1980; 1980–1990; 1990–2000; 2000–2008) using a linear growth pattern.[5]

## Black Electoral Strength

For each state in the analysis, this variable was calculated at the parish or county level as follows:
Number of Blacks Registered to Vote/Total Number of Registered Voters

## In-Migration

In-migration was calculated for each state in our analysis as follows:
Number of White Residents Born outside the Southern Region[6]/
Total Parish or County Population

A straight-line linear interpolation/extrapolation method was used to create annual estimates.

## Median Household Income

Median Household Income is the median value of:

Total Income by Household by Parish or County

A straight-line linear interpolation/extrapolation method was used to create annual estimates, and these estimates were adjusted to account for inflation using the Bureau of Labor Statistics' Consumer Price Index calculations (2008 = 1).[7]

## Catholic

This variable was calculated at the parish level in Louisiana as:

Number of Catholic Adherents/Total Parish Population

Membership figures for Catholic adherents were gathered from national surveys conducted by the Glenmary Research Center. Because these surveys were not conducted annually, we used a linear interpolation technique (described above) to create annual estimates of Catholic membership.

## Evangelical Protestant

This variable was calculated using the following formula:

Number of Evangelical Protestant Adherents/Total Parish or County Population

The scheme used to classify Protestant denominations as *evangelical* is found in Green et al. 1996, 188–89. Membership figures for evangelical denominations were gathered from national surveys conducted by the Glenmary Research Center. Because these surveys were not conducted annually, we used a linear interpolation technique (described above) to create annual estimates of Evangelical Protestant membership.

## % Urban

For each parish or county, this variable was calculated as:

Population Count Living in Urban Areas/Total Parish or County Population

A straight-line linear interpolation/extrapolation method was used to create annual estimates.

## % Military

For counties in North Carolina, this indicator was calculated as:

Active Military Personnel/Total County Population

A straight-line linear interpolation/extrapolation method was used to create annual estimates.

## Chapter 7

### Black Registration

This is a parish/county-level contextual variable added to available survey data. Specifically, this variable was calculated at the parish or county level as follows:

Number of Blacks Registered to Vote/Total Number of Registered Voters
Note: The coding of the variables from the survey data utilized is described in the text
and endnotes of chapter 7.

## Chapter 8

### State-Level Models

### Republican Strength

For a given year, this index was calculated as follows:

(% Republican Vote [Senate Election] + % Republican Vote [Gubernatorial Election] +
% Republican Vote [Average Republican Congressional Vote])/3.[1]

### Black Mobilization

For each state in the analysis, this variable was calculated as follows:
Number of Blacks Registered to Vote/Total Black Voting-Age Population

### % Black

For each state in the analysis, % Black was calculated as follows:
Black Population/Total Population

### Black Median Household Income

Black median household income is the median value of:
Total Income of Households Headed by Black Householder by County/Parish

A straight-line linear interpolation/extrapolation method was used to create annual
estimates and these estimates were adjusted to account for inflation using the
Bureau of Labor Statistics' Consumer Price Index calculations (2008 = 1).[7]

### County-Level Models

### Republican Strength

The percentage of Republican registrants was measured as:
Republican Registrants/Total Parish or County Registrants

### Black Mobilization

For each county/parish in the analysis, this variable was calculated as follows:
Number of Blacks Registered to Vote/Total Black Voting-Age Population

% Black

For each county/parish in the analysis, % Black was calculated as follows:
Black Population/Total Population

Black Median Household Income

Black median household income is the median value of:
Total Income of Households Headed by Black Householder by County/Parish
A straight-line linear interpolation/extrapolation method was used to create annual
  estimates, and these estimates were adjusted to account for inflation using the
  Bureau of Labor Statistics' Consumer Price Index calculations (2008 = 1).[7]

# APPENDIX C | Ancillary Statistical Models

TABLE C.5.1 Explaining State-Level GOP Party Growth in the South, 1962–2008

| | MODEL 1 | MODEL 2 |
|---|---|---|
| *Political:* | | |
| Republican Strength$_{t-1}$ | .7469** (.0336) | .7628** (.0358) |
| Sub-State Party Competition$_{t-1}$ | .1129** (.0161) | .0822** (.0182) |
| Presidential Vote | .0002 (.0001) | — |
| Black Electoral Strength | .1431** (.0374) | .1468** (.0353) |
| % Black | .2814 (.2069) | .2174 (.2082) |
| Goldwater 1964 | — | −.0217 (.0145) |
| Nixon 1968 | — | −.0103 (.0105) |
| Nixon 1972 | — | -.0054 (.0103) |
| Ford 1976 | — | -.0196* (.0087) |
| Reagan 1980 | — | -.0060 (.0062) |
| Reagan 1984 | — | — |
| Bush 1988 | — | .0061 (.0065) |
| Bush 1992 | — | .0001 (.0084) |
| Dole 1996 | — | .0185 (.0095) |
| Bush 2000 | — | .0418** (.0130) |
| Bush 2004 | — | .0447** (.0159) |
| Bush 2008 | — | .0370 (.0196) |
| Demographic: | | |
| In-Migration | -.0055 (.0450) | −.1180* (.0511) |
| Evangelical Protestants | .4728** (.1383) | .3565** (.1354) |
| Economic: | | |
| Per Capita Income ($1,000) | .0001 (.0004) | −.0012 (.0008) |
| Agricultural Sector Employment | −.1906 (.1128) | −.1595 (.0945) |
| $R^2$ | .973 | .977 |
| $N$ | 253 | 253 |

NOTES: GMM-IV Coefficients with fixed effects and robust standard errors in parentheses. In Model 2, the 1984 presidential election is used as the excluded category.

$^*p < .05$ (two-tailed test); $^{**}p < .01$ (two-tailed test)

TABLE C.6.1 Panel Unit-Root Tests for GOP Registrants, North Carolina

| TEST | TEST STATISTICS |
|---|---|
| Proportion: | |
| Levin, Lin, and Chu | −4.870*** |
| Im, Pesaran, and Shin | .097 |
| Logged: | |
| Levin, Lin, and Chu | −11.086*** |
| Im, Pesaran, and Shin | −14.809*** |

NOTES: For both tests, a significant test statistic allows for the rejection of the null hypothesis that the series is nonstationary.

*$p < .10$; **$p < .05$; ***$p < .01$

TABLE C.6.2 Panel Unit-Root Tests for GOP Registrants, Louisiana

| TEST | TEST STATISTICS |
|---|---|
| Proportion: | |
| Levin, Lin, and Chu | 22.182 |
| Im, Pesaran, and Shin | 14.023 |
| Logged: | |
| Levin, Lin, and Chu | −15.451*** |
| Im, Pesaran, and Shin | −5.405*** |

NOTES: For both tests, a significant test statistic allows for the rejection of the null hypothesis that the series is nonstationary.

*$p < .10$; **$p < .05$; ***$p < .01$

TABLE C.6.3  TSCS Granger Tests, North Carolina

| Black Mobilization Granger-causes GOP Registrants | $F_1$ |
|---|---|
| Lags (Years) | |
| t–1 | $3.404^{**}$ |
| t–2 | $4.013^{**}$ |
| t–3 | $1.503^{**}$ |

| Black Mobilization Granger-causes GOP Registrants | $F_2$ |
|---|---|
| Lags (Years) | |
| t–1 | $3.378^{**}$ |
| t–2 | $3.905^{**}$ |
| t–3 | $1.510^{**}$ |

NOTES: Critical Values: $^*p < .05$; $^{**}p < .01$
GOP Registrants is logged.
A significant F1 test statistic indicates the presence of a causal relationship.
A significant F2 test statistic indicates the causal process is heterogeneous or does not occur across all counties, while an insignificant test statistic indicates the causal process is homogeneous or uniform across all counties.


TABLE C.6.4  TSCS Granger Tests, Louisiana

| Black Mobilization Granger-causes GOP Registrants | $F_1$ |
|---|---|
| Lags (Years) | |
| t–1 | $2.111^{**}$ |
| t–2 | $1.254^{*}$ |
| t–3 | $.910$ |

| Black Mobilization Granger-causes GOP Registrants | $F_2$ |
|---|---|
| Lags (Years) | |
| t-1 | $2.109^{**}$ |
| t-2 | $1.226^{*}$ |
| t-3 | $.872$ |

NOTES: Critical Values: $^*p < .05$; $^{**}p < .01$
GOP Registrants is logged.
A significant F1 test statistic indicates the presence of a causal relationship.
A significant F2 test statistic indicates the causal process is heterogeneous or does not occur across all parishes, while an insignificant test statistic indicates the causal process is homogeneous or uniform across all parishes.

TABLE c.6.5 Explaining County-Level GOP Registration in North Carolina, 1966–2008

| | MODEL |
|---|---|
| Log GOP Registrants$_{t-1}$ | .8613** (.0225) |
| Black Electoral Strength | .2385* (.0962) |
| Percent Black | −.8915** (.1454) |
| In-Migration | −.1426** (.0285) |
| Evangelical Protestants | −.0710* (.0477) |
| Percent Military | −.2364 (.2547) |
| Percent Urban | .1212** (.0252) |
| Median Household Income ($1,000) | .0017** (.0006) |
| $R^2$ | .93 |
| N | 4,100 |

NOTES: GMM-IV Coefficients with fixed effects and robust standard errors in parentheses. Dependent Variable (*GOP Registrants*) is logged.

*$p < .05$ (two-tailed test); **$p < .01$ (two-tailed test)

TABLE c.6.6 Explaining Parish-Level GOP Registration in Louisiana, 1966–2008

| | MODEL 1 | MODEL 2 |
|---|---|---|
| Log GOP Registrants$_{t-1}$ | .9504** (.0045) | .9500** (.0047) |
| Black Electoral Strength | .3553** (.1228) | .3286** (.1267) |
| Percent Black | −1.2867** (.2026) | −1.2422** (.2079) |
| In-Migration | .5662** (.0670) | .5716** (.0721) |
| Evangelical Protestants | — | .0951 (.1273) |
| Catholic | −.0790 (.0552) | — |
| Percent Urban | −.0689** (.0167) | −.0707** (.0167) |
| Median Household Income ($1,000) | −.0050** (.0008) | −.0048** (.0008) |
| $R^2$ | .99 | .99 |
| N | 2,624 | 2,624 |

NOTES: OLS GMM-IV Coefficients with fixed effects and robust standard errors in parentheses. Dependent Variable (*GOP Registrants*) is logged.

*$p < .05$ (two-tailed test); **$p < .01$ (two-tailed test)

TABLE C.8.1 TSCS Unit-Root Tests for Black Mobilization

PANEL A: DEEP SOUTH

| Test | Test statistics |
|---|---|
| Levin, Lin, and Chu | $-6.413^{***}$ |

NOTES: A significant test statistic allows for the rejection of the null hypothesis that the series is nonstationary.

$^*p < .10;\ ^{**}p < .05;\ ^{***}p < .01$

PANEL B: LOUISIANA

| Test | Test statistics |
|---|---|
| Levin, Lin, and Chu | $-18.071^{***}$ |

NOTES: A significant test statistic allows for the rejection of the null hypothesis that the series is nonstationary.

$^*p < .10;\ ^{**}p < .05;\ ^{***}\ p < .01$

PANEL C: NORTH CAROLINA

| Test | Test statistics |
|---|---|
| Levin, Lin, and Chu | $-30.052^{***}$ |

NOTES: A significant test statistic allows for the rejection of the null hypothesis that the series is nonstationary.

$^*p < .10;\ ^{**}p < .05;\ ^{***}\ p < .01$

TABLE C.8.2 Explaining County-Level Black Mobilization in Louisiana and North Carolina, 1966–2008

|  | LOUISIANA | NORTH CAROLINA |
|---|---|---|
| Republican Strength $_{t-1}$ | $.0474^*$ (.0209) | $.4118^{**}$ (.0452) |
| Black Mobilization $_{(t-1)}$ | $.8448^{**}$ (.0145) | $.7383^{**}$ (.0293) |
| % Black | $.2059^{**}$ (.0365) | $.0860^{**}$ (.0726) |
| Jackson 1984 | $.0155^{**}$ (.0033) | $.0913^{**}$ (.0075) |
| Presidential Election Year | $.0051^*$ (.0024) | $.0493^{**}$ (.0027) |
| Obama 2008 | $.0213^{**}$ (.0034) | $.0816^{**}$ (.0063) |
| Constant | $.0550^{**}$ (.0144) | .0315 (.0227) |
| Estimation Procedure | FE | FE |
| $R^2$ | .90 | .68 |
| N | 2,688 | 4,200 |

NOTES: OLS coefficients with fixed effects and robust standard errors in parentheses.

$^*p < .05$ (two-tailed test); $^{**}p < .01$ (two-tailed test)

# ENDNOTES

## Chapter 1

1. Following the 2010 elections, Republicans controlled nine of the eleven Southern governors' mansions, had unified control of seven of the eleven state legislatures in the South (and control of one chamber of the legislature in two other states), held sixteen of the twenty-two U.S. Senate seats in the region, and eighty-nine of 126 U.S. House seats.

2. See Hood and McKee (2010) for a more detailed discussion of in-migration and political change in the region. In addition, this study provides evidence that in-migrants into North Carolina are now more likely to register as unaffiliated but vote Democratic. This demographic in the Tar Heel State is also shown to have helped elect Democratic presidential candidate Barack Obama in 2008.

## Chapter 2

1. Although South Carolina has had a Republican U.S. senator since Strom Thurmond switched parties in 1964, the first Republican to win election in South Carolina (besides Thurmond) was Lindsey Graham, who won 54 percent of the vote against Alex Sanders in 2002 to take the seat held by Democrat Earnest Hollings since 1966.

2. Between 1950 and 1960, the Arkansas congressional delegation included six House seats. Prior to 1950, it was as large as seven.

3. The size of state legislatures varies greatly across the region and thus the scale for each figure is not the same.

4. Following the 2010 election cycle, Republicans held majorities in both legislative chambers in seven states (Alabama, Florida, Georgia, North Carolina, South Carolina, Tennessee, and Texas) and a majority in one chamber in an additional two states (Louisiana and Virginia).

5. ANES did not conduct studies in 1954 and 2006. We were able to fill the gap in 2006 with the CCES.

6. Interpolation was used to fill in the gaps between missing years for both the number of blacks who were registered to vote and for the total number of registered voters in each Southern state.

7. Louisiana has consistently recorded annual registration data on partisanship for over half a century. North Carolina has recorded annual registration data on partisanship since 1966. The Louisiana party registration data can also be delineated by race.

8. For example, if there are 1,000 whites in the Louisiana Democratic Party in 2006 and the frequency distribution for the time indicates that 5 percent fell into the *extremely conservative* category, then the number of white Democrats in 2006 who were *extremely conservative* would be fifty. If these fifty extremely conservative whites were contained within a Democratic Party with 1,500 total registrants, then this group would account for 3.3 percent of total Democratic identifiers in Louisiana in 2006.

9. The skewness statistic for these distributions is recorded in italics just under the mean values for Table 2.1. Skewness is a measure of the symmetry, with normal distributions registering a skewness value of 0. Positive skewness values indicate a longer left tail on a distribution, or in our case a liberal skew, while negative values represent a larger right tail, or a more conservative skew.

*Chapter 3*

1. Although a small number of African Americans were able to vote during this time period, the overwhelming majority were prevented from registering and subsequently voting.

2. For analyses of the impact of structural reforms of this type on turnout, see Fenster (1994), Oliver (1996), and Rhine (1995).

3. For example, in 1998 over 70 percent of the African American population was registered to vote in Alabama and Mississippi, while in Arkansas, Florida, and Virginia, just over 50 percent of the African American population was registered to vote.

4. According to Tate, "black participation appears to be firmly anchored to a number of individual-level demographic attributes, including socioeconomic status" (1991, 1172).

5. See Harris, Sinclair-Chapman, and McKenzie (2005) for a description of research on the effects of both these forces.

6. See Nadeau and Stanley (1993), Shafer and Johnston (2001), and Terrel (2000) for general overviews of this literature.

7. Although we recognize the difference between partisan identification and voting behavior, the two are very closely related in the South during this period of time.

8. Lipset and Rokkan (1967) also highlight the significance of the development of competitive local party organizations for long-term partisan growth.

*Chapter 4*

1. The other two states were North Carolina and Tennessee. Wilkinson (1968) notes that the Virginia Republican Party was historically the third strongest in the eleven states of the former Confederacy, behind Tennessee and North Carolina. Republican candidates in Virginia were consistently able to garner a third of the vote from the mid-1940s through the mid-1960s, until ultimately winning in 1969 with Linwood Holton.

2. "State GOP Nominates Dalton as Candidate for Governorship," *Richmond Times-Dispatch*, 21 June 1953.

3. "School Closing Scored by State Republicans," *Richmond Times-Dispatch*, 14 December 1958.

4. *The Richmond News Leader*, 10 March 1963.

5. "State GOP Plans for 1965; Differences Are Set Aside," *Richmond Times-Dispatch*, 22 November 1964.

6. "Clyde Pearson, 1925–2000: Judge led State's 'Republican Renaissance,'" *Roanoke Times*, 20 March, 2010.

7. Linwood Holton. In-person interview. 30 November 2007. Weems, VA.

8. Almond received 63.2 percent of the vote compared to Dalton's 36.4 percent.

9. Eisenberg (1972) notes that early efforts in the mid-1960s by the Democratic Party to court black voters confronted hostility from those voters toward the Byrd organization and what it had stood for in the past.

10. These data come from Bartley and Graham (1978). They utilize a technique that we would today refer to as homogeneous precinct analysis to estimate black voting patterns.

11. "The 1964 Presidential Election in Virginia: A Political Omen?" *The University of Virginia News Letter*, Vol. 41, No. 8, 15 April 1965.

12. "1969 Politics in Virginia: The General Election," *The University of Virginia News Letter*, Vol. 46, No. 9, 15 May 1970.

13. Small pockets of mountain Republicans did exist in the Appalachian region of northeast Georgia in counties like Fannin, Towns, and Union. These Republicans could trace their roots all the way back to the fight over secession.

14. The Talmadge imprint on state politics, like that of the Long family in Louisiana, was characterized by exceptional longevity. The faction was led by Eugene Talmadge beginning in 1926 and continued upon his death in 1946 with son Herman. Herman Talmadge served as a U.S. senator from Georgia until he was defeated in 1980 by Republican candidate Mack Mattingly.

15. Margaret Shannon, "Quality's the Ticket," *Atlanta Journal*, 24 November 1961.

16. George Goodwin, "Georgia GOPs Here to Pick Four Delegates," *Atlanta Journal*, 31 May 1952.

17. Margaret Shannon, "Quality's the Ticket," *Atlanta Journal*, 24 November 1961.

18. Wright Bryan, "Georgia Floor Fight Climaxed Long Day of Uncertainties," *Atlanta Journal*, 10 July 1952.

19. Numerous newspaper articles outline the intraparty fighting between the Taft and Eisenhower factions. See, for example, "Georgia GOP Plans Full Slate, Bar Told Group," *Atlanta Journal*, 18 April 1954; Charles Pou, "State Republican Differences Fanned Again on Press Gallery," *Atlanta Journal*, 11 March 1954; Pat Watters, "State GOP Feud Breaks Out Again," *Atlanta Journal*, 9 April 1954; and "Shartzer Demands Hill Quit GOP Job," *Atlanta Journal*, 10 April 1954.

20. Shartzer was reelected chair in 1956. Curtis Driskell, "Georgia Republicans Re-elect Shartzer, Pick 11 Officers," *Atlanta Constitution*, 20 May 1956.

21. While the Eisenhower faction certainly engaged in party-building activities to a far greater extent than their GOP predecessors, they were also criticized for not going far enough. One *Atlanta Journal* exposé stated "in the eight recent years when there was a Republican in the White House, the GOP in Georgia played patronage politics more than party-building politics." Margaret Shannon, "Plight: Never-Has-Been," *Atlanta Journal*, 19 November 1961.

22. The *Atlanta Journal* reports the GOP was organized in 135 of 159 Georgia counties in 1956. "State GOP's Call Parley to Organize," *Atlanta Journal*, 11 March 1956.

23. "GOP Fails to Sustain Appeal to Dixie Voters," *Atlanta Constitution*, 14 October 1954.

24. "Georgia GOP Striding Ahead," *Atlanta Constitution*, 22 May 1956.

25. James Saxon Childers, "Mild Miss Twiggs Holds Rights Fort," *Atlanta Journal*, 21 August 1956.

26. James Saxon Childers, "Force No Part of Plank, Delegate Leaders Report," *Atlanta Journal*, 21 August 1956. "GOP Shifts on Civil Rights," *Atlanta Constitution*, 21 August 1956.

27. "Georgia GOP to Give View of Little Rock," *Atlanta Journal*, 3 October 1957. "GOP Erases Gains in South," *Atlanta Journal*, 6 October 1957.

28. Robert Joiner, "Bid to Censure Ike Rejected by State GOP Strategists," *Atlanta Journal*, 4 October 1957.

29. "Political Leaders Score Mix Decision," *Atlanta Journal*, 13 September 1958.

30. Charles Pou, "GOP Plank Feared Worse than Demo," *Atlanta Journal*, 23 July 1960. "Dixie GOP's Worried Over Rights," *Atlanta Journal*, 24 July 1960.

31. Charles Pou, "Nixon-Rocky Plank on Rights Adopted," *Atlanta Journal*, 27 July 1960.

32. Curtis Driskell and Fred Powledge, "GOP's Shartzer Quits; Dorsey Takes Over," *Atlanta Journal*, 22 January 1961.

33. Margaret Shannon, "Quality's the Ticket," *Atlanta Journal*, 24 November 1961.

34. Ralph McGill, "GOP and the Scrooch Owl," *Atlanta Journal*, 7 January 1962.

35. Margaret Shannon, "Happy GOP Opens Smith Campaign," *Atlanta Journal*, 1 April 1962.

36. Gordon Roberts, "GOP's Smith Killed in Highway Collision," *Atlanta Journal*, 5 June 1962.

37. Charles Pou, "State GOP Votes Rights Hands-Off," *Atlanta Journal*, 7 July 1963.

38. Sally Rugaber, "Fulton GOP Votes to Back Goldwater," *Atlanta Journal*, 23 July 1964. Charlotte Johns, "DeKalb GOPs Tiff, Back Goldwater," *Atlanta Journal*, 23 July 1964. Ann Warshall, "Chatham GOP Delegates go to Goldwater," *Atlanta Journal*, 23 July 1964.

39. Charles Pou, "9 Districts Give Delegates to Barry," *Atlanta Journal*, 22 March 1964.

40. Charles Pou, "Atlanta Battered in GOP Test Vote," *Atlanta Journal*, 2 May 1964.

41. Charles Pou, "Tribble, Pickett Get Top GOP Jobs," *Atlanta Journal*, 3 May 1964.

42. Charles Pou, "Atlanta GOP Continues Battle Against Party 'Coup,'" *Atlanta Journal*, 5 May 1964.

43. "Goldwater Can Survive Loss of Negro Votes, Tribble Says," *Atlanta Constitution*, 4 May 1964.

44. Marvin Wall, "New Directions for Georgia Republicans," *Atlanta Constitution*, 5 May 1964.

45. Walter Rugaber, "GOP Says Negroes Will Return to Fold," *Atlanta Journal*, 4 November 1964.

46. Charles Pou, "GOP Platform 'Pleases' South," *Atlanta Journal*, 13 July 1964.

47. Richard M. Scammon, ed. 1968. *America Votes, 7.* Washington, DC: CQ Press.

48. Margaret Shannon, "Democrats Lose One Congressional Race," *Atlanta Journal,* 4 November 1964. Reg Murphy, "State Republicans Argue on 'Changes,'" *Atlanta Journal,* 8 November 1964.

49. "Sanders Sees Challenge in GOP, But No Menace," *Atlanta Journal,* 17 June 1965.

50. Reg Murphy, "Georgia GOP May Triple House Strength This Year," *Atlanta Journal,* 25 April 1965.

51. It is notable that in his tenure as party chair, Jones opposes all efforts to expel Georgia Republicans who may belong to right-wing organizations like the John Birch Society. "State GOP Elects Jones Chairman," *Atlanta Journal,* 20 June 1965. Charles Pou, "State GOP Chief Denies He's Bircher," *Atlanta Journal,* 7 October 1965.

52. William O. Smith, "Election Slate Sets A Record," *Atlanta Journal,* 18 September 1966.

53. Callaway's father had served on the board of directors for U.S. Steel (personal interview); "Rights Fight is Planned by Callaway," *Augusta Chronicle,* 5 November 1964.

54. Howard "Bo" Callaway. In-person interview. 10 August 2007. Pine Mountain, GA.

55. Howard "Bo" Callaway. In-person interview. 10 August 2007. Pine Mountain, GA.

56. "Rights Fight is Planned by Callaway," *Augusta Chronicle,* 5 November 1964.

57. Howard "Bo" Callaway. In-person interview. 10 August 2007. Pine Mountain, GA.

58. Margaret Shannon, "Callaway Rights Rider May Help in State Race," *Atlanta Journal,* 10 August 1966.

59. ADA or Americans for Democratic Action is a liberal interest group that rates members of Congress on their voting records. A score of one hundred indicates perfect agreement with the ADA's positions and a zero indicates perfect disagreement. By definition, one can infer that a member with a score of zero is extremely conservative. Interestingly, none of the nine Democratic congressmen from Georgia during this time were given scores of zero by the ADA.

60. Howard "Bo" Callaway. In-person interview. 10 August 2007. Pine Mountain, GA.

61. After defeating Ellis Arnall in the Democratic primary run-off, Maddox was quoted as saying, "If anyone asks me about the Negro problem, and it is a problem . . . those views are the same as those of Governor George Wallace of Alabama." Sam Hopkins, "A Smashing Upset for Segregationists," *Atlanta Constitution,* 29 September 1966.

62. "Rights Fight is Planned by Callaway," *Augusta Chronicle,* 5 November 1964.

63. In a 2007 in-person interview, Callaway said that he was motivated to oppose the 1964 Civil Rights Act and the 1965 Voting Rights Act out of conservative principles and not racism. Joe Brown, "Racist Charges Baffle Callaway," *Atlanta Constitution,* 4 November 1966; Dick Hebert and Joe Brown, "Callaway Sees Tough Fight Against 'Same Old Crowd,'" *Atlanta Constitution,* 5 October 1966. Tom Greene, "Callaway Predicts State, U.S. Crisis," *Atlanta Journal,* 14 October 1966. William O. Smith, "Maddox and Callaway Clash over Race, Aid," *Atlanta Journal,* 17 October 1966.

64. Bill Shipp, "3 Negro Leaders Reunite for Arnall," *Atlanta Constitution*, 5 November 1966.

65. Bacote Collection (1956–1964).

66. Howard "Bo" Callaway. In-person interview. 10 August 2007. Pine Mountain, GA.

67. Richard M. Scammon, ed. 1968. *America Votes, 7*. Washington, DC: CQ Press.

68. *Journal of the House of Representatives of the State of Georgia*, 1967, p. 58.

69. Estimates produced using the EI (Ecological Inference) technique (King 1997). (Results available from authors by request.)

70. William O. Smith, "GOP Fails on Breakthrough, Loses 5 Seats in Assembly," *Atlanta Journal*, 13 November 1966.

71. Even after his defeat, Callaway continued to be an integral player in the Georgia Republican Party, being elected to national committeeman in 1968 and serving in this position until appointed by President Nixon to be secretary of the Army in May of 1973. Milo Dakin, "Old Feud Boils in State GOP," *Atlanta Constitution*, 4 May 1973.

72. These data come from two primary sources: Bartley and Graham (1978) and the Bacote Collection (n.d.). Both sources utilize a technique that we would refer to today as homogeneous precinct analysis to estimate black voting patterns. In the Fulton County elections where there is an overlap between these two sources, there is a remarkable degree of congruity between these two estimates, all of which are within a percentage point or less of one another.

73. Following the abolition of the white primary and poll tax, black registration was occurring prior to implementation of the VRA in urban areas, especially Atlanta. The power structure in the Democratic Party relied on malapportionment schemes in the state legislature and in Democratic primary elections (county-unit system) to ensure that black urban votes were extremely diluted (see Key [1949] for a description of the county-unit system). Certainly, the VRA helped to aid in the continuation of black registration and participation in urban areas. Sources for registration data include the Georgia Secretary of State, the Clarence Bacote Papers (1960–1980), and the *Report of the U.S. Commission on Civil Rights, 1959*.

74. The historical findings pertaining to Virginia and Georgia, along with the empirical work presented in the next four chapters, aptly dispel the falsehood that the Southern region was monolithic in political terms.

*Chapter 5*

1. Although we recognize the difference between partisan identification and voting behavior, the two are very closely related in the South during this period of time.

2. Lipset and Rokkan (1967) also highlight the significance of the development of competitive local party organizations for long-term partisan growth.

3. Estimates from 1960 through 1970 are obtained from David's work, while estimates for the remaining years are calculated by the authors.

4. Comparisons between our measure of Republican Party strength and actual party registration data from Louisiana from 1960 through 2008 and North Carolina from 1966 to 2008 indicate a high level of congruity ($r = .949$ for LA and $.950$ for NC). (Data available from the authors upon request.)

5. Also note that the character of *Republican Strength*—a ratio with, obviously, an explicit upper limit—prevents it from satisfying the formal requirements for a nonstationary variable. However, the unit-root test results provide additional support for our contention that the variable is stationary (rather than nonstationary, or even near nonstationary).

6. These presidential vote percentages were duplicated for time points containing off-year elections (i.e., 1962, 1966).

7. It should be noted that, while we can gauge interparty competition directly, there is no equivalent way to measure the relative strength of party organizations in the region during the time period under study. The most comprehensive study of party organization to date is the Cotter et al. (1984) Party Transformation Study. This study measures Party Organizational Strength (or POS) by administering a detailed questionnaire to a multipart sample of party officials at both the state and county levels. In this manner, Cotter et al. were able to create a composite measure of POS using responses from a variety of items dealing with such issues as budget, staff, and candidate recruitment activities. While the Cotter et al. measure is a proven and highly reliable indicator of party organizational strength at the subnational level, a number of issues prevented its use in this analysis. To begin, the POS measures were only calculated at the state level from 1960 through 1984, and within this time frame, only every five years. In addition, some state parties are missing from their analysis. In conducting a model over time with panel data, the use of the Cotter et al. POS measure would produce unacceptable gaps over time and across states.

8. Given that our dependent variable is a composite index derived from vote percentages, we do not include a legislative vote component, in contrast to Aistrup (1996), in our index of substate party competition.

9. While, undoubtedly, some blacks are included in this measure, most of the denominations that collectively yield the total number of evangelical Protestants have very few black adherents.

10. The time series cross-sectional framework, although relatively uncommon in studies of Southern politics, is becoming an increasingly important and prominent analytical tool within the literature (see, for example, Hood et al. 1999).

11. Only even years are included in the analysis (i.e., 1960, 1962, . . . 2008).

12. Multicollinearity was not detected as an issue for the models presented in this chapter. All variance inflation factors were below 4.

13. As we noted earlier, where it is possible to compare the index with actual party registration figures, the correlations are quite high (r = .95).

14. Models in Table 1 were produced using the xtreg procedure in Stata 11. Tests using the xtserial procedure revealed evidence of residual autocorrelation in these model estimates—even with the inclusion of a lagged dependent variable. To assess the robustness of our results in the face of this issue, we estimated a GMM fixed-effects instrumental variable model with standard errors that are robust to both autocorrelation and heteroskedasticity (xtivreg2 procedure in Stata). These results are reported in Table C.5.1 in Appendix C. You will note that the effects of the primary substantive variables—*Black Electoral Strength* and *Substate Party Competition*—are still highly significant and signed in the proper direction. With the exception of the *Presidential Vote* (and presidential dummy variables) and the *Evangelical* variables, the results are statistically and substantively comparable for all of the remaining variables

as well. Given the comparability of the results, the more straightforward interpretation of the OLS results, and the fact that the GMM-IV results are based on an abbreviated time frame, we focus our interpretation on the OLS results. We do, however, note the distinctiveness of the *Evangelical* results in our discussion of the effects of that variable.

15. The functional form presented in Figures 5.3 and 5.4 is an impulse-response function, where the effect of the variable in question is calculated as both a direct and an indirect effect. The value for each time period is composed of the direct effect for that year plus an exponentially decreasing effect experienced through the lagged dependent variable. This indirect effect was calculated carried out to five time periods (ten years). See Hamilton (1994) for a more detailed discussion of impulse-response functions.

16. Remember, the value of substate competitiveness that is included in the model is lagged. So, as the theory of relative advantage suggests, the demonstration of increased competitiveness on the part of Republican candidates during election period t leads to an additional increase in Republican support in election period t + 1.

*Chapter 6*

1. Louisiana contains sixty-four parishes, and North Carolina has one hundred counties.

2. Although registrants do indicate a political party preference, North Carolina changed to a modified-open primary in 1987, which allowed nonpartisans (*unaffiliateds*) to vote in the Republican primary (since 1987) and the Democratic primary (since 1995). Louisiana congressional elections have changed from closed (prior to 1978), to a nonpartisan blanket (1978–2007), back to closed (2008–2010), and then back to the nonpartisan blanket format (beginning in 2012). State and local elections have utilized the nonpartisan blanket primary since 1978. Presidential primaries have always been closed. The other states that collect additional registration data are Florida (party and race), Georgia (race), and South Carolina (race).

3. Charles Jonas was even elected as a Republican U.S. House member from a western district in 1952.

4. This coalition elected Governor Daniel Lindsay Russell in 1896.

5. There is a great deal of debate among scholars regarding just how progressive North Carolina was politically, especially on the question of race. There is little doubt though that North Carolina, like other states in the region, used Jim Crow laws and voter disenfranchisement techniques to maintain the racial caste system. See Fleer (1994) for more discussion on this issue.

6. For a short period of time, 1994–1996, the GOP held majority control of the state House of Representatives.

7. Following the 2010 election, Republicans controlled forty-nine county boards, the Democrats fifty, with the one remainder evenly split. Chris Cooper and Gibbs Knotts, "County Seats: The GOP's Rise to Parity," *The News and Observer*, 8 December 2010.

8. Source: "North Carolina Poll." 1 November 2011 (www.publicpolicypolling.com).

9. Because there is no representative annual survey data of partisan affiliation that covers all parishes in Louisiana and all counties in North Carolina, we would argue that party registration data is certainly an able substitute. Although we would

agree that partisan affiliation and party registration are not identical measures, they are certainly highly correlated.

10. See Hood and McKee (2010) for a detailed discussion of in-migration and political change in the South.

11. Source: Department of Defense Military Personnel Statistics for FY 2008 (http://siadapp.dmdc.osd.mil/).

12. Models in Tables 6.1 and 6.2 were produced using the xtreg procedure in Stata 11. Tests using the xtserial procedure revealed the presence of residual autocorrelation in the model estimates. To assess the robustness of our results, we estimated the alternative GMM fixed-effect instrumental variables models (xtivreg2). These models should be robust in the presence of both autocorrelation and heteroskedasticity. Looking at Tables C.6.5 and C.6.6 in Appendix C, we note the high degree of congruity between the OLS and GMM-IV models. Of particular interest, the coefficient for *Black Electoral Strength* for both the Louisiana and North Carolina models is positive and statistically significant.

13. In order to test for the possibility of a unit root, we utilized two procedures: the Levin, Lin, and Chu test and the Im, Pearsan, and Shin test. The results of these unit-root tests both before and after transformation are located in Tables C.6.1 (NC) and C.6.2 (LA) in Appendix C.

14. See Hood, Kidd, and Morris (2008) for the technical specifications related to these tests. We should also note that these panel Granger tests do not rule out the possibility of a contemporaneous relationship between black mobilization and Republican registration.

15. The results of our panel Granger tests are located in Tables C.6.3 (NC) and C.6.4 (LA) in Appendix C. Evidence of *heterogeneous causality* exists out to three lag periods (t-3) for North Carolina and two (t-2) for Louisiana.

16. Several alternative models were also specified for North Carolina. We also included a lagged version of *Black Electoral Strength* at one time period (t-1). In this case, the coefficient was signed in the hypothesized direction, but failed to reach statistical significance. As the evidence from Table C.6.1 concerning the presence of a unit root is mixed, we also reran the model with the original dependent variable series (proportion of Republican registrants). The results for these models are very similar to those reported in Table 6.1. In particular, *Black Electoral Strength* is signed in a positive direction and statistically significant in the case of both the contemporaneous (t) and lagged effect (t-1).

17. In another model variant, we included a version of *Black Electoral Strength* lagged one time period (t-1). The coefficient for this variable of interest was again statistically significant and signed in the hypothesized direction.

18. The indirect effect is calculated out to five years. See endnote 15 of chapter 5 for more information on this process.

*Chapter 7*

1. In chapter 5, we showed that black mobilization had an impact on GOP growth in both the Rim South and the Deep South. However, the magnitude of the effect is a function of the size of the African American percentage of registered voters, a variable that was by the mid-to-late 1970s primarily a function of the relative size of the African American population. Thus, we would expect a greater effect in the Deep South.

2. 1991: 1 = grade school; 2 = high school; 3 = some college; 4 = college degree; 5 = graduate or professional degree. 2001: 1 = high school or less; 2 = some college; 3 = college degree; 4 = graduate or professional degree.

3. Income measure for 1991: 1 = less than $10,000; 2 = $10–19,999; 3 = $20–29,999; 4 = $30–39,999; 5 = $40–49,999; 6 = $50–59,999; 7 = $60–69,999; 7 = $70,000 or above.

Income measure for 2001: 1 = less than $25,000; 2 = $25–49,999; 3 = $50–74,999; 4 = $75–99,999; 5 = $100–150,000; 6 = $150,000 or above.

4. Imputations were performed using Stata's mi impute pmm procedure. See Appendix A for sources of black registration data.

5. Probabilities were simulated in Clarify 2.1 using the imputed datasets from the analysis.

6. The standard question probing respondent ideology, a key control variable in these analyses, was not asked by the ANES until 1972.

7. Again, although we see a state-level effect in the Rim South and the Deep South, it is possible that the relatively smaller mobilized black population—and the relatively smaller samples—obscure individual-level effects in the South.

8. *Party Identification*: 1 = Strong Democrat; 2 = Weak Democrat; 3 = Independent-Democrat; 4 = Independent; 5 = Independent-Republican; 6 = Weak Republican; 7 = Strong Republican.

9. For the SFP models, education is measured as 1: less than 9th grade; 2: 9th to 11th grade; 3: high school or equivalent; 4: some college; 5: BS or higher. For the analyses using the ANES, education is measured as a dichotomy where 0: less than BS; 1: BS or higher.

10. For the SFP, the income variable is coded as 1: $0–19,999; 2: $20,000–29,000; 3: $30,000–39,999; 4: $40,000–49,999; 5: $50,000–59,999; 6: $60,000 or more. Family income from the ANES time series cumulative file is coded 1: 0–16th percentile; 2: 17 to 33rd percentile; 3: 34th to 67th percentile; 4: 68th to 95th percentile; 5: 96th to 100th percentile. The income variable is missing for respondents from the 2002 survey year.

11. Religious indicators from the ANES data are not congruent across study years and are therefore not included in the analyses presented.

12. Analyses using the ANES data are weighted as instructed in the codebook.

13. Probabilities were simulated in Clarify 2.1 using the imputed datasets from the analyses presented. The remaining variables in the models were set to their mean or modal values.

## Chapter 8

1. Even those who develop participation models that go well beyond SES (see Brady, Verba, and Schlozman 1995 and Verba, Scholzman, and Brady 1995) admit that socioeconomics cannot be ignored.

2. This is based on 2008 data for income for African American households.

3. Black household income is certainly not a perfect indicator of the full set of SES measures, nor is it a perfect indicator of community poverty levels or the level of economic inequality among African Americans. Still, the literature does not prepare us for an inverse relationship between income and mobilization.

4. See Hood, Kidd, and Morris (2008) for details of the analysis and results.

5. This distinction between the likely effects of GOP growth on black mobilization is also borne out—or nearly so, except for the understandable case of North Carolina—in earlier research (Hood, Kidd, and Morris 2008).

6. According to Tate, "black participation appears to be firmly anchored to a number of individual-level demographic attributes, including socioeconomic status" (1991, 1172).

7. We also assessed the impact of the Jackson candidacy in 1988 on black registration, but found no evidence of an effect.

8. Note that results are similar if we use black median household income.

9. Only even years are included in the analysis (i.e., 1966, 1968, . . . 2008).

10. Fixed-effect models in Tables 8.1 and 8.2 were produced using the xtreg procedure in Stata. GMM fixed-effect instrumental variables models were estimated using the xtivreg2 procedure. Tests conducted do not reveal the presence of a unit root for any of the dependent variable series utilized for either the state or substate models. See Table C.8.1 in Appendix C for the results of these tests.

11. In order for the Census Bureau to impute a value for black median family income, a county/parish had to have a certain level of black residents. Counties/parishes that failed to meet this threshold level did not, therefore, have a value for this income measure and are consequently missing from the models that include an income measure.

12. See chapter 5 for more discussion of these models.

13. The $p$-value for the Wooldridge test for autocorrelation provided by Stata is barely significant at the .05 level ($p = .0467$).

14. See footnote 15, chapter 5 for more information on the calculations used to produce these estimates. The indirect effect is calculated out to five years.

15. However, there is significantly greater evidence of autocorrelation in the FE results for both Louisiana and North Carolina, so we only report the IV-FE results. The $p$-value for the Wooldridge test for autocorrelation for the Louisiana data is significant at the .001 level ($p = .0000$). The $p$-value for the Wooldridge test for autocorrelation for the North Carolina data is also significant at the .001 level ($p = .0000$). Note that the baseline FE results—which are reported in Table C.8.2 in Appendix C—are substantively and statistically consistent with the IV-FE results presented here for both states.

16. Figures 8.3 and 8.6 are based on the coefficient estimates from models that included the measure of black income.

17. Wake County includes the Raleigh area, and Shreveport is in Caddo Parish.

*Chapter 9*

1. Sabrina Tavernise and Robert Gebeloff, "Many U.S. Blacks Moving to South, Reversing Trend," *The New York Times*, 24 March 2011.

2. Source: Decennial U.S. Census data on population.

3. "Lone Star Rising, A Special Report on Texas," *The Economist*, 11–17 July 2009.

4. Source: *America Votes 2004*.

5. Information on 2008 registration and voting rates by race/ethnicity and state is from U.S. Department of Commerce, Bureau of the Census, 2008, "Table 4.B: Reported Voting and Registration of the Voting-Age Population, by sex, race and

Hispanic origin, for States: November 2008" (http://www.census.gov/hhes/www/socdemo/voting/publications/p20/2008/tables.html).

6. Source: Georgia Secretary of State.

*Appendix A*

1. For more information on this variable, see Aubrey W. Jewett, 1997. *Partisan Change in Southern State Legislatures*. Ph.D. dissertation. Florida State University.

*Appendix B*

1. Special transformations had to be made for Louisiana for each election following the 1978 institution of an open primary system. We used the following method to calculate our index of GOP party strength for 1978 through 2008:

> (1.) If there was only one election (open primary): GOP = Percent of Total Republican Vote (including votes won by other Republican Candidates in the Primary)
>
> (2.) If there was both a primary and a general election and:
>> a. The general election contained both a Republican and a Democrat: GOP = Percent of Total Vote Won by Republican Candidate
>> b. The general election contained two Democratic candidates: GOP = 0 percent
>> c. The general election contained two Republican candidates: GOP = 100 percent

2. For example, in 1960 the black population in Georgia was 28.4 percent. In 1970, blacks comprised 25.8 percent of the state's population. The growth rate for blacks in Georgia during this time period was therefore 25.8–28.4/10 = -.26.

3. Interpolation was used to fill in the gaps between missing years for both the number of blacks who were registered to vote and the total number of registered voters in each Southern state.

4. The Census Bureau defines the Southern region as the eleven original states of the Confederacy plus five border states: Delaware, Kentucky, Maryland, Oklahoma, and West Virginia.

5. For example, in 1960 the black population in Georgia was 28.4 percent. In 1970, blacks comprised 25.8 percent of the state's population. The growth rate for blacks in Georgia during this time period was therefore: 25.8–28.4/10 = -.26.

6. The Census Bureau defines the Southern region as the eleven original states of the Confederacy plus five border states: Delaware, Kentucky, Maryland, Oklahoma, and West Virginia.

7. Source: U.S. Department of Labor, Bureau of Labor Statistics, Historical Consumer Price Index Table, 1913–2010 (www.bls.gov/cpi/).

# WORKS CITED

Abramowitz, Alan I. 2011. *The Disappearing Center: Engaged Citizens, Polarization, and American Democracy.* New Haven, CT: Yale University Press.

Aistrup, Joseph A. 1996. *The Southern Strategy Revisited: Republican Top-Down Advancement in the South.* Lexington, KY: University of Kentucky Press.

Aldrich, John H. 1993. "Rational Choice and Turnout." *American Journal of Political Science.* 37(1):246–78.

Aldrich, John H. 2000. "Presidential Address: Southern Parties in State and Nation." *Journal of Politics.* 62(3):643–70.

Aldrich, John H., and John D. Griffin. 2000. Ambition in the South: The Emergence of Republican Electoral Support, 1948–1998. Paper presented at the Twelfth Biennial Symposium on Southern Politics, March 2–3, 2000, The Citadel, Charleston, SC.

American National Election Studies (www.electionstudies.org). *Time Series Cumulative Data File [dataset].* Stanford University and the University of Michigan [producers and distributors]. 2010.

Anderson, R. Bruce. 1997. "Electoral Competition and Southern State Legislatures: The Dynamics of Change." In *Southern Parties and Elections,* Robert P. Steed, Laurence W. Moreland, and Tod A. Baker, eds. Tuscaloosa, AL: University of Alabama Press.

Atkinson, Frank B. 1992. *The Dynamic Dominion, Realignment and the Rise of Virginia's Republican Party Since 1945.* Fairfax, VA: George Mason University Press.

Bacote Collection. Robert W. Woodruff Archives Library. Atlanta, GA.

Banducci, Susan A., Todd Donovan, and Jeffrey A. Karp. 2004. "Minority Representation, Empowerment, and Participation." *Journal of Politics.* 66(2):534–56.

Bartels, Larry M. 2008. *Unequal Democracy: The Political Economy of the New Gilded Age.* Princeton, NJ: Princeton University Press.

Bartley, Numan V. 1970. *From Thurmond to Wallace.* Baltimore, MD: The Johns Hopkins Press.

Bartley, Numan V., and High D. Graham. 1978. *Southern Elections, County and Precinct Data, 1950–1972.* Baton Rouge, LA: Louisiana State University Press.

Bass, Jack, and Walter De Vries. 1976. *The Transformation of the Southern Electorate.* New York: Basic Books.

Beck, Nathaniel, and Jonathan N. Katz. 1995. "What to Do (And Not to Do) With Time-Series Cross-Section Data." *American Political Science Review.* 89(3):634–47.

Beck, Nathaniel, and Jonathan N. Katz. 1996. "Nuisance vs. Substance: Specifying and Estimating Time-Series-Cross-Section Models." *Political Analysis.* 6(1):1–36.

Beck, Paul Allen. 1977. "Partisan Dealignment in the Postwar South." *American Political Science Review.* 71(2):477–98.

Bennett, Stephen Earl, and Linda L. M. Bennett. 1986. "Political Participation: Meaning and Measurement." In *Annual Review of Political Science,* Samuel Long, ed. Norwood, NJ: Ablex Publishing.

Black, Earl. 1976. *Southern Governors and Civil Rights.* Cambridge, MA: Harvard University Press.

Black, Earl, and Merle Black. 1987. *Politics and Society in the South.* Cambridge, MA: Harvard University Press.

Black, Earl, and Merle Black. 1992. *The Vital South.* Cambridge, MA: Harvard University Press.

Black, Earl, and Merle Black. 2002. *The Rise of Southern Republicans.* Cambridge, MA: Harvard University Press.

Black, Merle. 1978. "Racial Composition of Congressional Districts and Support for Federal Voting Rights in the American South." *Social Science Quarterly.* 59(3):435–50.

Bobo, Lawrence, and Franklin D. Gilliam. 1990. "Race, Sociopolitical Participation, and Black Political Empowerment." *American Political Science Review.* 84(2):377–97.

Brady, Henry E., Sidney Verba, and Kay Lehman Schlozman. 1995. "Beyond SES: A Resource Model of Political Participation." *American Political Science Review.* 89(2):271–94.

Browning, Rufus P., Dale Rogers Marshall, and David H. Tabb. 1984. *Protest is Not Enough: The Struggle of Blacks and Hispanics for Equality in Urban Politics.* Los Angeles: University of California Press.

Bullock III, Charles S. 1985. "Congressional Roll Call Voting in a Two-Party South." *Social Science Quarterly.* 66(4):789–804.

Bullock III, Charles S., and David J. Shafer. 1997. "Party Targeting and Electoral Success." *Legislative Studies Quarterly.* 22(4):573–84.

Bullock III, Charles S., and M. V. Hood III. 2006. "A Mile-Wide Gap: The Evolution of Hispanic Political Emergence in the Deep South." *Social Science Quarterly,* 87(5):1117–35.

Campbell, Angus, Philip E. Converse, Warren E. Miller, and Donald E. Stokes. 1960. *The American Voter.* New York: Wiley.

Campbell, Bruce A. 1977. "Change in the Southern Electorate." *American Journal of Political Science.* 21(1):37–64.

Campbell, Bruce A. 1977. "Patterns of Change in the Partisan Loyalties of Native Southerners: 1952–1972." *Journal of Politics.* 39(3):283–316.

Carlson, James M. 1980. "Political Context and Black Participation in the South." In *Party Politics in the South.* Robert P. Steed, Laurence W. Moreland, and Tod A. Baker, eds. New York: Praeger.

Carmines, Edward G. 1991. "The Logic of Party Alignments." *Journal of Theoretical Politics.* 3(1):65–80.

Carmines, Edward G., and Harold W. Stanley. 1990. "Ideological Realignment in the Contemporary South: Where Have All The Conservatives Gone?" In *The Disappearing South? Studies in Regional Change and Continuity.* Robert P. Steed, Laurence W. Moreland, and Tod A. Baker, eds. Tuscaloosa, AL: University of Alabama Press.

Carmines, Edward G., and James A. Stimson. 1980. "The Two Faces of Issue Voting." *American Political Science Review.* 74(1):78–91.

Carmines, Edward G., and James A. Stimson. 1989. *Issue Evolution, Race and the Transformation of American Politics.* Princeton, NJ: Princeton University Press.

Carmines, Edward G., and James Woods. 2002. "The Role of Party Activists in the Evolution of the Abortion Issue." *Political Behavior.* 24(4):361–77.

Clark, John A., and Brad Lockerbie. 1998. "Split-Partisan Identification." In *Party Activists in Southern Politics: Mirrors and Makers of Change.* Charles D. Hadley and Lewis Bowman, eds. Knoxville, TN: University of Tennessee Press.

Clark, John A., and Charles Prysby. Southern Grassroots Party Activists Project. 2001 [Computer file]. ICPSR04266-v1. Greensboro, NC: John A. Clark and Charles Prysby [producers]. 2005. Ann Arbor, MI: Inter-university Consortium for Political and Social Research [distributor]. 2006-03-17. doi:10.3886/ICPSR04266

Cobb, James C. 1999. *Redefining Southern Culture: Mind and Identity in the Modern South.* Athens, GA: University of Georgia Press.

Cohen, Cathy J., and Michael C. Dawson. 1993. "Neighborhood Poverty and African American Politics." *American Political Science Review.* 87(2):286–302.

Colby, David C. 1986. "The Voting Rights Act and Black Registration in Mississippi." *Publius: The Journal of Federalism.* 16(4):123–37.

Conway, M. Margaret. 2000. *Political Participation in the United States.* Washington, DC: CQ Press.

Coombs, Michael W., John R. Hibbing, and Susan Welch. 1984. "Black Constituents and Congressional Roll Call Votes." *Western Political Quarterly.* 37(3):424–34.

Cotter, Cornelius P., James L. Gibson, John F. Bibby, and Robert J. Huckshorn. 1984. *Party Organizations in American Politics.* New York: Praeger.

Dabney, Virginius. 1971. *Virginia, The New Dominion.* Garden City, NY: Doubleday & Co.

David, Paul T. 1972. *Party Strength in the United States, 1872–1970.* Charlottesville, VA: University of Virginia Press.

Dawson, Michael C. 1994. *Behind the Mule: Race and Class in African-American Politics.* Princeton, NJ: Princeton University Press.

Downs, Anthony. 1957. *An Economic Theory of Democracy.* New York: Harper and Row.

Eamon, Thomas F. 2008. "The Seeds of Modern North Carolina Politics." In *The New Politics of North Carolina.* Christopher A. Cooper and H. Gibbs Knotts, eds. Chapel Hill, NC: University of North Carolina Press.

Eisenberg, Ralph. 1972. "Virginia, The Emergence of Two-Party Politics." In *The Changing Politics of the South.* William C. Harvard, ed. Baton Rouge, LA: Louisiana State University Press.

Fenster, Mark J. 1994. "The Impact of Allowing Day of Registration Voting on Turnout in U.S. Elections from 1960 to 1992." *American Politics Quarterly.* 22(1):74–87.

Fiorina, Morris P, Samuel J. Abrams, and Jeremy C. Pope. 2010. *Culture War: The Myth of a Polarized America*. 3rd ed. New York: Longman.

Fleer, Jack D. 1994. *North Carolina Government and Politics*. Lincoln, NE: University of Nebraska Press.

Gay, Claudine. 2001. "The Effect of Black Congressional Representation on Political Participation." *American Political Science Review*. 95(3):589–602.

Giles, Micheal W. 1977. "Percent Black and Racial Hostility: An Old Assumption Revisited." *Social Science Quarterly*. 58(3):412–17.

Giles, Micheal W., and Arthur Evans. 1986. "The Power Approach to Intergroup Hostility." *Journal of Conflict Resolution*. 30(3):460–85.

Giles, Micheal W., and Kaenan Hertz. 1994. "Racial Threat and Partisan Identification." *American Political Science Review*. 88(2):317–26.

Giles, Micheal W., and Melanie A. Buckner. 1993. "David Duke and Black Threat: An Old Hypothesis Revisited." *Journal of Politics*. 55(3):702–13.

Giles, Micheal W., and Melanie A. Buckner. 1996. "Comment." *Journal of Politics*. 58(4):1171–80.

Glaser, James M. 1994. "Back to the Black Belt: Racial Environment and White Racial Attitudes in the South." *Journal of Politics*. 56(1): 21–41.

Green, John C., James L. Guth, Corwin E. Smidt, and Lyman A. Kellstedt. 1996. *Religion and the Culture Wars*. New York: Rowman & Littlefield.

Green, John C., Lyman A. Kellstedt, Corwin E. Smith, and James L. Guth. 1998. "The Soul of the South: Religion and the New Electoral Order." In *The New Politics of the Old South*. Charles S. Bullock III and Mark J. Rozell, eds. New York: Rowman & Littlefield.

Green, John C., Lyman A. Kellstedt, Corwin E. Smith, and James L. Guth. 2002. "The Soul of the South: Religion and Southern Politics in the New Millennium." In *The New Politics of the Old South*. 2nd ed. Charles S. Bullock III and Mark J. Rozell, eds. New York: Rowman & Littlefield.

Green, John C., Lyman A. Kellstedt, Corwin E. Smith, and James L. Guth. 2010. "The Soul of the South: Religion and Southern Politics in the New Millennium." In *The New Politics of the Old South*. 4th ed. Charles S. Bullock III and Mark J. Rozell, eds. New York: Rowman & Littlefield.

Green, John C., Mark J. Rozell, and Clyde Wilcox. 2003. *The Christian Right in American Politics: Marching to the Millennium*. Washington, DC: Georgetown University Press.

Green, William H. 2000. *Econometric Analysis*. 4th ed. New York: Prentice Hall.

Griffin, John D., and Michael Keane. 2006. "Descriptive Representation and the Composition of African American Turnout." *American Journal of Political Science*. 50(4):998–1012.

Grofman, Bernard, Robert Griffin, and Amihai Glazer. 1992. "The Effect of Black Population on Electing Democrats and Liberals to the House of Representatives." *Legislative Studies Quarterly*. 17(3):365–79.

Grosser, Paul. 1982. "Political Parties." In *Louisiana Politics, Festival in a Labyrinth*. James Bolner, ed. Baton Rouge, LA: Louisiana State University Press, 255–83.

Gujarati, Damodar N. 1988. *Basic Econometrics*. 2nd ed. New York: McGraw-Hill.

Hadley, Charles D., and Lewis Bowman. Southern Grassroots Party Activists Project, 1991–1992: [Computer file]. 2nd ICPSR version. New Orleans, LA: Charles D. Hadley and Lewis Bowman [producers]. 1993. Ann Arbor, MI: Inter-university

Consortium for Political and Social Research [distributor]. 1997. doi:10.3886/ICPSR06307

Hamilton, James D. 1994. *Time Series Analysis*. Princeton, NJ: Princeton University Press.

Harris, Frederick C. 1999. *Something Within: Religion in African-American Political Activism*. New York: Oxford University Press.

Harris, Frederick C., Valeria Sinclair-Chapman, and Brian D. McKenzie. 2005. "Macrodynamics of Black Political Participation in the Post-Civil Rights Era." *Journal of Politics*. 67(4):1143–63.

Heard, Alexander. *A Two Party South?* Chapel Hill, NC: University of North Carolina Press.

Heinemann, Ronald L. 1996. *Harry Byrd of Virginia*. Charlottesville, VA: University of Virginia Press.

Hood III, M. V. 2005. "Race and the Ideological Transformation of the Democratic Party: Evidence from the Bayou State." *American Review of Politics*. 25:67–78.

Hood III, M. V., and Irwin L. Morris. 1998. "Boll Weevils and Roll-Call Voting: A Study in Time and Space." *Legislative Studies Quarterly*. 23(2):245–69.

Hood III, M. V., and Seth C. McKee. 2010. "What Made Carolina Blue? In-migration and the 2008 North Carolina Presidential Vote." *American Politics Research*. 38(2):266–302.

Hood III, M. V., Quentin Kidd, and Irwin Morris. 1999. "Of Byrd[s] and Bumpers: Using Democratic Senators to Analyze Political Change in the South, 1960–1995." *American Journal of Political Science*. 43(2):465–87.

Hood III, M. V., Quentin Kidd, and Irwin L. Morris. 2001. "The *Key* Issue: Constituency Effects and Southern Senators' Roll-Call Voting on Civil Rights." *Legislative Studies Quarterly* 26(4): 599–621.

Hood III, M. V., Quentin Kidd, and Irwin L. Morris. 2004. "A Report on the Reintroduction of the Elephas maximus in the Southern United States: Explaining the Rise of Republican State Parties, 1960–2000." *American Politics Research*. 32(1):68–101.

Hood III, M. V., Quentin Kidd, and Irwin L. Morris. 2008. "Two Sides of the Same Coin?: Employing Granger Causality Tests in a Time Series Cross-Section Framework." *Political Analysis*. 16(3):324–44.

Hood III, M. V., Quentin Kidd, and Irwin L. Morris. "The Reintroduction of the *Elephas maximus* to the Southern United States: The Rise of Republican State Parties, 1960–2000." 2010. In *Controversies in Voting Behavior*, 5th ed., David Kimball, Richard G. Niemi, and Herbert F. Weisberg, editors. Washington, DC: CQ Press.

Jackman, Robert W. 1993. "Rationality and Political Participation." *American Journal of Political Science*. 37(1):279–90.

Jang, Seung-Jin. 2009. "Get Out on Behalf of Your Group: Electoral Participation of Latinos and Asian Americans." *Political Behavior*. 31(4):511–35.

Jelen, Ted G., and Marthe A. Chandler. 2000. "Culture Wars in the Trenches: Short-Term Forces in Presidential Elections, 1968–1996." *American Review of Politics*. 21(1):69–87.

Katz, Richard S. 2001. "Are Cleavages Frozen in the English-Speaking Democracies?" In *Party Systems and Voter Alignments Revisited*. Lauri Karvonen and Stein Kuhnle, eds. New York: Routledge.

Keech, William R. 1968. *The Impact of Negro Voting*. Chicago: Rand McNally.

Keele, Luke, and Ismail White. 2011. "African American Turnout in Majority-Minority Districts." Unpublished manuscript.

Kellstedt, Lyman A. 1989. "Evangelicals and Political Realignment." In *Contemporary Evangelical Political Involvement*. Corwin E. Smidt, ed. New York: University Press of America.

Key, Jr., V. O. 1949. *Southern Politics in State and Nation*. New York: Knopf.

King, Gary. 1997. *A Solution to the Ecological Inference Problem: Reconstructing Individual Behavior from Aggregate Data*. Princeton, NJ: Princeton University Press.

Knack, Stephen. 1995. "Does 'Motor Voter' Work? Evidence from State-Level Data." *Journal of Politics*. 57(3):796–811.

Kruse, Kevin M. 2005. *White Flight, Atlanta and the Making of Modern Conservatism*. Princeton, NJ: Princeton University Press.

Ladd, Everett Carll, and Charles D. Hadley. 1978. *Transformations of the American Party System*. New York: W. W. Norton.

Lamis, Alexander P. 1988. *The Two-Party South*. Oxford, UK: Oxford University Press.

Lamis, Alexander P. 1990. *The Two-Party South*. 2nd ed. Oxford, UK: Oxford University Press.

Lamis, Alexander P. 1999. *Southern Politics in the 1990s*. Baton Rouge, LA: Louisiana State University Press.

Landry, David M., and Joseph B. Parker. 1982. "The Louisiana Political Culture." In *Louisiana Politics, Festival in a Labyrinth*. James Bolner, ed. Baton Rouge, LA: Louisiana State University Press.

Lassiter, Matthew D. 2006. *The Silent Majority*. Princeton, NJ: Princeton University Press.

Latimer, James. 1961. *Virginia Politics, 1950–1960*. Unpublished manuscript in the James H. Latimer Papers, Library of Virginia, Richmond.

Leighley, Jan E. 2001. *Strength in Numbers? The Political Mobilization of Racial and Ethnic Minorities*. Princeton, NJ: Princeton University Press.

Leighley, Jan E., and Arnold Vedlitz. 1999. "Race, Ethnicity, and Political Participation: Competing Models and Contrasting Explanations." *Journal of Politics*. 61(4):1092–114.

Levendusky, Matthew. 2009. *The Partisan Sort: How Liberals Became Democrats and Conservatives Became Republicans*. Chicago: University of Chicago Press.

Levin, Andrew, Chien-Fu Lin, and Chia-Shang James Chu. 2001. "Unit Root Tests in Panel Data: Asymptotic and Finite-Sample Properties." *Journal of Econometrics*. 108(1):1–24.

Lipset, Seymour M., and Stein Rokkan. 1967. *Party Systems and Voter Alignments*. New York: The Free Press.

Lublin, David. 2004. *The Republican South: Democratization and Partisan Change*. Princeton, NJ: Princeton University Press.

Luebke, Paul. 1998. *Tar Heel Politics, 2000*. Chapel Hill, NC: University of North Carolina Press.

Maggiotto, Michael A., and Gary D. Wekkin. 2000. *Partisan Linkages in Southern Politics*. Knoxville, TN: University of Tennessee Press.

Matsubayashi, Tetsuya. 2009. "Racial Environment and Political Participation." *American Politics Research*. 38(3):471–501.

Matthews, Donald R., and James W. Prothro. 1966. *Negroes and the New Southern Politics*. New York: Harcourt, Brace, & World.

McKee, Seth C. 2009. *Republican Ascendancy in Southern U.S. House Elections*. Boulder, CO: Westview.

McKee, Seth C., M. V. Hood III, and David Hill. 2012. "Achieving Validation: Barack Obama and Black Turnout in 2008." *State Politics and Policy Quarterly*. 12(1):3–22.

Nadeau, Richard, and Harold W. Stanley. 1993. "Class Polarization in Partisanship among Native Southern Whites, 1952–90." *American Journal of Political Science*. 37(3):900–19.

Nye, Mary Alice, and Charles S. Bullock III. 1993. "Civil Rights Support: A Comparison of Southern and Border State Representatives." *Legislative Studies Quarterly*. 17(1): 81–94.

Oliver, J. Eric. 1996. "The Effects of Eligibility Restrictions and Party Activity on Absentee Voting and Overall Turnout." *American Journal of Political Science*. 40(2):498–513.

Ostrom Jr., Charles W. 1978. *Time Series Analysis: Regression Techniques*. Sage Paper series on Quantitative Applications in the Social Sciences, 07-001. Beverly Hills, CA: Sage.

Owens, Chris T. 2005. "Black Substantive Representation in State Legislatures from 1971–1994." *Social Science Quarterly*. 86(4):779–91.

Parent, Wayne. 2004. *Inside the Carnival: Unmasking Louisiana Politics*. Baton Rouge, LA: Louisiana State University Press.

Parent, Wayne, and Huey Perry. 2010. "Louisiana: African Americans, Republicans, and Party Competition." In *The New Politics of the Old South*, 4th ed. Charles S. Bullock III and Mark J. Rozell, eds. New York: Rowman & Littlefield.

Peirce, Neal R. 1975. *The Border South States*. New York: W. W. Norton.

Petrocik, John R. 1987. "Realignment: New Party Coalitions and the Nationalization of the South." *Journal of Politics*. 49(2):347–75.

Platt, Matthew. 2008. "Participation for What? A Policy-Motivated Approach to Political Activism." *Political Behavior*. 30(3):391–413.

Poole, Keith T., and Howard Rosenthal. 2007. *Ideology and Congress*. Piscataway, NJ: Transaction Press.

Preuhs, Robert R. 2006. "The Conditional Effects of Minority Descriptive Representation: Black Legislators and Policy Influence in the American States." *Journal of Politics*. 68(3):585–99.

Primo, David M., Matthew L. Jacobsmeier, and Jeffrey Milo. 2007. "Estimating the Impact of State Policies and Institutions with Mixed-Level Data." *State Politics and Policy Quarterly*. 7(4):446–59.

Prysby, Charles. 2010. "North Carolina: Tar Heel Politics in the Twenty-first Century." In *The New Politics of the Old South*, 4th ed. Charles S. Bullock III and Mark J. Rozell, eds. New York: Rowman & Littlefield, 155–80.

Rhine, Staci. 1995. "Registration Reform and Turnout Change in the American States." *American Politics Quarterly*. 23(4):409–26.

Rhodes, Terrel L. 2000. *Republicans in the South: Voting for the State House, Voting for the White House*. Westport, CT: Praeger.

Riker, William H., and Peter C. Ordeshook. 1968. "A Theory of the Calculus of Voting." *American Political Science Review*. 62(1):25–43.

Rocha, Rene R., Caroline J. Tolbert, Daniel C. Bowen, and Christopher J. Clark. 2010. "Race and Turnout: Does Descriptive Representation in State Legislatures Increase Minority Voting?" *Political Research Quarterly.* 63(4):890–907.

Rosenstone, Steven, and John Mark Hansen. 1993. *Mobilization, Participation, and Democracy in America.* New York: Macmillan.

Scher, Richard K. 1997. *Politics in the New South: Republicanism, Race and Leadership in the Twentieth Century.* 2nd ed. Armonk, NY: M. E. Sharpe.

Segura, Gary M., and Shaun Bowler, eds. 2005. *Diversity in Democracy: Minority Representation in the United States.* Charlottesville, VA: University of Virginia Press.

Shafer, Byron E., and R. G. C. Johnston. 2001. "The Transformation of Southern Politics Revisited: The House of Representatives as a Window." *British Journal of Political Science.* 31(October):601–25.

Shafer, Byron E., and R. G. C. Johnston. 2006. *The End of Southern Exceptionalism: Class, Race, and Partisan Change in the Postwar South.* Cambridge, MA: Harvard University Press.

Skowronek, Stephen. 1993. *The Politics Presidents Make: Leadership from John Adams to George Bush.* Cambridge, MA: Belknap Press.

Skowronek, Stephen. 2008. *Presidential Leadership in Political Time: Reprise and Reappraisal.* Lawrence, KS: University of Kansas Press.

Sosna, Morton. 1987. "More Important than the Civil War? The Impact of World War II on the South." In *Perspectives on the American South: An Annual Review of Society, Politics, and Culture,* Vol. 4. James C. Cobb and Charles R. Wilson, eds. New York: Gordon and Breach.

Southern Focus Poll (www.http://www.irss.unc.edu) 1992–2001 data files [dataset]. Odum Institute, University of North Carolina [distributor], 2011.

Stanley, Harold W. 1987. *Voter Mobilization and the Politics of Race: The South and Universal Suffrage, 1952–1984.* New York: Praeger.

Stanley, Harold W., and David S. Castle. 1988. "Partisan Changes in the South: Making Sense of Scholarly Dissonance," In *The South's New Politics: Realignment and Dealignment.* Robert Swansbrough and David Brodsky, eds. Columbia, SC: University of South Carolina Press.

Stanley, Harold W. 2008. "Hispanics in the South." Keynote address at the biennial meeting of the Citadel Symposium on Southern Politics. Charleston, SC.

Stern, Mark. 1987. "Black Voter Registration in the South: Hypotheses and Occurrences." In *Black in Southern Politics.* Laurence W. Moreland, Robert P. Steed, and Tod A. Baker, eds. New York: Praeger.

Strong, Donald S. 1955. "The Presidential Election in the South, 1952." *Journal of Politics.* 17(3):343–89.

Strong, Donald S. 1960. *Urban Republicanism in the South.* Tuscaloosa, AL: University of Alabama, Bureau of Public Administration.

Sundquist, James L. 1983. *Dynamics of the Party System: Alignment and Realignment of Political Parties in the United States.* Washington, DC: Brookings Institution Press.

Swain, Carol M. 1993. *Black Faces, Black Interests: The Representation of African Americans in Congress.* Cambridge, UK: Cambridge University Press.

Tate, Katherine. 1991. "Black Political Participation in the 1984 and 1988 Presidential Elections." *American Political Science Review.* 85(4):1159–76.

Tate, Katherine. 1993. *From Protest to Politics: The New Black Voters in American Elections.* Cambridge, MA: Harvard University Press.

Tate, Katherine. 2003. *Black Faces in the Mirror: African Americans and their Representatives in the U.S. Congress.* Princeton, NJ: Princeton University Press.

Teixeira, Ruy A. 1992. *The Disappearing American Voter.* Washington, DC: Brookings Institution Press.

Timpone, Richard J. 1995. "Mass Mobilization or Government Intervention: The Growth of Black Registration in the South." *Journal of Politics.* 57(2):425–42.

Timpone, Richard J. 1998. "Structure, Behavior, and Voter Turnout in the United States." *American Political Science Review.* 92(1):145–58.

Tindall, George Brown. 1972. *The Disruption of the Solid South.* Athens, GA: University of Georgia Press.

U.S. Census Bureau. Current Population Survey. Table 4b. Reported Voting and Registration of the Voting-Age Population, by Sex, Race and Hispanic Origin, for States: November 2008. Internet.

U.S. Census Bureau. Statistical Abstract of the United States: various years and editions, 1954 to 2010. Washington, DC (http://www.census.gov/statab/www/).

U.S. Census Bureau. Table 3: Annual Estimates of the Resident Population by Sex, Race, and Hispanic Origin: April 1, 2000 to July 1, 2008 (SC-EST2008-03-01).

Verba, Sidney, and Norman H. Nie. 1972. *Participation in America: Political Democracy and Social Equality.* Chicago: University of Chicago Press.

Verba, Sidney, Kay Lehman Schlozman, and Henry E. Brady. 1995. *Voice and Equality: Civic Voluntarism in American Politics.* Cambridge, MA: Harvard University Press.

Vogt, George L. 1978. *The Development of Virginia's Republican Party.* Charlottesville, VA: University of Virginia dissertation.

Voss, D. Stephen. 1996. "Beyond Racial Threat: Failure of an Old Hypothesis in the New South." *Journal of Politics.* 58(4):1156–70.

Voter Registration for Fulton County. 1960–1980. Clarence Bacote Collection. Robert W. Woodruff Archives Library. Atlanta, GA.

Voter Registration. 1956–1964. Clarence Bacote Collection. Robert W. Woodruff Archives Library. Atlanta, GA.

Walton Jr., Hanes. 1997. *African-American Power and Politics: The Political Context Variable.* New York: Columbia University Press.

Washington, Ebonya. 2006. "How Black Candidates Affect Voter Turnout." *Quarterly Journal of Economics.* 121(3):973–98.

Watson, Stanley J. 1996. "Race and Realignment Reconsidered: Issue Evolution in the South Since 1972." *American Review of Politics.* 17 (Summer):145–70.

Wawro, Gregory. 2002. "Estimating Dynamic Panel Models in Political Science." *Political Analysis.* 10(1):25–48.

Whitby, Kenny J. 1985. "Effects of the Interaction Between Race and Urbanization on Votes of Southern Congressmen." *Legislative Studies Quarterly.* 10(4):505–17.

Wilcox, Clyde. 2000. *Onward Christian Soldiers.* 2nd ed. Boulder, CO: Westview Press.

Wilkinson III, J. Harvie. 1968. *Harry Byrd and the Changing Face of Virginia Politics 1945–1966*. Charlottesville, VA: University of Virginia Press.

Wilson, Sven E. and Daniel M. Butler. 2007. "A Lot More to Do: The Sensitivity of Time-Series Cross-Section Analyses to Simple Alternative Specifications." *Political Analysis*. 15(2): 101–123.

Wolfinger, Raymond E., and Robert B. Arseneau. 1978. "Partisan Change in the South, 1952–1976." In *Political Parties: Development and Decay*. Louis Maisel and Joseph Cooper, eds. Beverly Hills, CA: Sage.

Wolfinger, Raymond E., and Steven J. Rosenstone. 1980. *Who Votes?* New Haven, CT: Yale University Press.

Wooldridge, Jeffrey M. 2000. *Introductory Econometrics: A Modern Approach*. Boston: South-Western College Publishing.

Wright, Gerald C. 1977. "Contextual Models of Electoral Behavior: The Southern Wallace Vote." *American Political Science Review*. 71(2):497–508.

# INDEX

Bass, Jack, 6, 56, 102, 121–23, 126, 137

Bealer, Alex, 87

Beck, Nathaniel, 106, 141, 167

Bennett, Linda L. M., 62

Bennett, Stephen Earl, 62, 165

Black, Earl, 7, 17, 46, 54, 59, 61, 64, 67, 101, 111, 140–41

Black, Merle, 7, 17, 46, 54, 59, 61, 64, 67, 101, 111, 140–41, 163

"black-belt hypothesis," 7, 63–64, 67, 102, 121–22, 141, 163, 175

black-context effect, 8

*Black Electoral Strength* variable, 103, 109, 111–13, 131, 133–36, 155, 167, 180–81

*Black Income* variable, 167–68, 170, 174

black mobilization, 3–4, 9–13, 14, 38–46, 52, 55–56, 60–63, 66–70, 95, 101–2, 107–11, 113–17, 121, 133, 137, 139, 143, 148–49, 153, 159–75, 180, 182

    county-level, *See* county-level black mobilization

    from 1966–2008, 170

    explaining Southern, 160–67

    and GOP growth, 171, 174

    and GOP growth feedback loop, 163

    half-century of growth in, 38–46

    and relative advantage, 68–70

    understanding, 60–63

    and voter registration, *See* voter registration

*black political empowerment*, 9, 62–63, 161–62, 180

black population by state (1960–2010), 164

black registration rates, 38–39, 45, 93, 102, 113, 123, 136, 144–54, 160–62, 165–68, 171–72, 204–5, 218n73, 222n4, 223n7

    and black voting age population, 167–68

    and boxplots, 160, 172

    county-level, 123

    effect of on Republican growth in south, 113

    from 1950 through 2008, 38–39

    from 1976 through 2008, 102

    and Jessie Jackson, 223n7

    and "political context" effect, 169

*Black Registration* variable, 144–54

black voting age population, 167–68

Bobo, Lawrence, 62, 161–62

*Born Again* variable, 144, 147

*bottom up* theory, 56, 100–101, 110–13

Bowman, Lewis, 143

Brady, Henry E., 62, 165, 222n1

*Brown v. Board of Education* (1954), 75, 93

Browning, Rufus P., 62, 161–62

Broyhill, Joel, 77

Buckner, Melanie A., 7, 59, 141

Bullock III, Charles S., 7–8, 60, 67, 101, 104, 184

Byrd, Garland, 89

Byrd, Sr., Harry F., 72–83, 215n9

    and "massive resistance," 75

Callaway, Howard "Bo," 72, 89–91, 217n53

Campbell, Bruce A., 141

Carmines, Edward G., 64, 94, 140, 142

Carter, Jimmy, 7, 124

Castle, David S., 6, 55–57, 102, 121

*catalyst*, 11, 65, 99–100, 115

Catholicism, 15–16, 127, 131–32, 134–35, 137, 194, 204, 210

Chandler, Marthe A., 141

*Church Attendance* variable, 144, 147, 149–51

Civil Rights Act (1964), 4, 89–90, 217n63

"civic skills," 62, 165

Clark, John A., 143

class, 5–6, 57–58, 111, 113, 115, 126–27, 140, 181–82, 187–89

    as engine of American politics, 187–89

    transformation hypothesis, 111

    *See* middle class; upper-middle class; upper class; working class

*class transformation hypothesis*, 111

Clement, Frank, 17

Clinton, William Jefferson, 18

Cobb, James C., 5, 57, 102, 121–22